ISLAM AND DEVELOPMENT

The study of Islam since the advent of 9/11 has made a significant resurgence. However, much of the work produced since then has tended to focus on the movements that not only provide aid to their fellow Muslims, but also have political and at times violent agendas. This tendency has led to a dearth of research on the wider Muslim aid and development scene.

Focusing on the role and impact of Islam and Islamic FBOs, an arena that has come to be regarded by some as the 'invisible aid economy', *Islam and Development* considers Islamic theology and its application to development and how Islamic teaching is actualized in case studies of Muslim FBOs. It brings together contributions from the disciplines of theology, sociology, politics and economics, aiming both to raise awareness and to function as a corrective step within the development studies literature.

...with its compilation of nine thematic as well as case-based chapters, this book offers an in-depth examination of mainly non-governmental sources and structures of Islamic faith-based, or at least faith-inspired, aid and charity. Although much of it is never reflected in the donor statistics, it is nonetheless often embedded in the fabric of 'real society' or sectors thereof. The work documents an interaction and intertwining between aid, charity and religion that, throughout history, has been more the rule than exception. As such, the practical relevance of this book goes well beyond academia, and also targets aid professionals, policy makers and development journalists.

Bruno De Cordier, Ghent University, Belgium

Islam and Development
Exploring the Invisible Aid Economy

Edited by

MATTHEW CLARKE
Deakin University, Australia

DAVID TITTENSOR
Deakin University, Australia

ASHGATE

Published by
Ashgate Publishing Limited
Wey Court East
Union Road
Farnham
Surrey, GU9 7PT
England

Ashgate Publishing Company
110 Cherry Street
Suite 3-1
Burlington, VT 05401-3818
USA

www.ashgate.com

British Library Cataloguing in Publication Data
A catalogue record for this book is available from the British Library

The Library of Congress has cataloged the printed edition as follows:
Islam and development : exploring the invisible aid economy / edited by Matthew Clarke and David Tittensor.
pages cm
Includes index.
ISBN 978-1-4094-7080-9 (hardcover) 1. Economic development—Religious aspects—Islam. 2. Economic development—Islamic countries. 3. Non-governmental organizations—Islamic countries. 4. Charities—Islamic countries. 5. Economics—Religious aspects—Islam. 6. Islamic fundamentalism. I. Clarke, Matthew, 1969- II. Tittensor, David.
BP173.75.I7663 2014
361.7'5—dc23

2013045822

ISBN 9781409470809 (hbk)
ISBN 9781409470816 (ebk – PDF)
ISBN 9781409470823 (ebk – ePUB)

Printed in the United Kingdom by Henry Ling Limited,
at the Dorset Press, Dorchester, DT1 1HD

Contents

List of Figures and Tables

Figures

Tables

Notes on Contributors

Dr Ameer Ali is a Lecturer in Economics at the Murdoch University Business School. His research interests are in the economic and socio-economic development of Islamic societies, in contemporary relationships between Islam and politics, and in the Muslim diasporas in Australia and the West.

Dr Jan A. Ali is a Sociologist of Religion (Islam). He is a Senior Lecturer in Islam and Modernity in the School of Humanities and Communication Arts and simultaneously holds a title as the Community and Research Analyst in the Religion and Society Research Centre at the University of Western Sydney.

Misita Anwar is a PhD candidate in The Centre for Community Networking Research, in the Faculty of Information Technology, Monash University. She has been working as a lecturer at Makassar State University, Indonesia since 2000. Her interests include ICT for Development, particularly mobile phones for development, wireless technology, digital capacity building and literacy, as well as information management systems.

Professor Matthew Clarke is the Head of the School of Humanities and Social Sciences, Deakin University (Australia). He is the author of six books, including *Religion and Development: Theology and Practice* published in 2011.

Associate Professor Ismet Fanany is coordinator of Indonesian language and culture studies in the School of Humanities and Social Sciences, Faculty of Arts and Education, Deakin University. His research interests include contemporary Indonesian language and society; Islamic communities, especially in Indonesia and the Malay world; and post-disaster management and reconstruction.

Dr Rebecca Fanany is a Senior Lecturer in Indonesian at Deakin University. Her research interests include Language, culture and health; Cultural consonance; Conceptualizations of health.

Dr Gerhard Hoffstaedter is a Lecturer in Anthropology at the University of Queensland. His research interests are Southeast Asia (especially Malaysia); anthropology of Islam; religion in international development; refugee politics; religious pluralism in Southeast Asia.

Associate Professor Graeme Johanson is both an adjunct in the Faculty of Information Technology and Director of The Centre for Community Networking Research at Monash University.

Dr Peter Riddell is Vice Principal (Academic) at the Melbourne School of Theology. His research interests are Islam in Southeast Asia, Theology and Development, and Christian–Muslim Relations.

Mohammad Musfequs Salehin is a PhD candidate at the University of Sydney and his thesis is entitled 'Development, State and Religious Non-Governmental Organizations in Bangladesh'. His areas of research include development, FBOs, Islam and gender issues.

Dr David Tittensor is a Research Fellow at the Centre for Citizenship and Globalisation at Deakin University (Australia). His research interests include the study of Muslim movements, Turkish politics and society, religion and development, and the Middle East.

Aimatul Yumna is a PhD candidate in the School of Humanities and Social Sciences, Deakin University Australia. She has been a lecturer at Padang State University Indonesia and the University of Indonesia for seven years in economic and finance related subjects. Her research interests are corporate finance, Islamic finance, and microfinance practices.

Introduction
The Invisible Aid Sector

David Tittensor and Matthew Clarke

Introduction

This volume addresses the nexus between Islam and the global humanitarian sector. It considers the role that faith plays in guiding Muslims with regard to charitable giving and how development projects are implemented on the ground from an Islamic ethical perspective. The impetus for such a volume derives from the fact that Islam is the world's fastest growing religion, has a burgeoning aid sector, and continues to remain relatively misunderstood, particularly in the West. Thus, the aim of this volume is to provide a more balanced and nuanced account of Islamic humanitarian activities, by exploring the theology, growth of the sector, and the uses to which Islamic aid is put. This volume is important therefore as it renders more visible the Muslim aid sector. Islam is often regarded as a violent religion that sees the world in an 'us versus the rest' binary, and in more recent times Islamic charities have been implicated as pivotal actors in this struggle through funding acts of terror. Such perceptions constrain proper analysis and certainly entrench the invisibility of Muslim aid.

In other words, this volume seeks to provide a positive account that tells the often untold story that takes place on the margins of the mainstream aid sector, and in doing so, make Islamic aid practices more relatable. This is not to suggest that the contributions in this volume are without criticism, quite the contrary. Rather, the hope is to show the potential for Islam to be a constructive addition to the aid arena and highlight the role that faith can play more broadly in the fight against poverty and inequality. For, in the aid sector, the role of religion has been a point of contention that is only beginning to be explored; a fact that perhaps places Islam at a double disadvantage.

The Current State of Play

An interest in the role of religion in development began to manifest within both the sector and academia during the 1990s with Jim Wolfensohn, the President of the World Bank from 1995 to 2005, seeking to introduce faith back into the development arena. He brought together civil society, business and cultural institutions in a series of high-level meetings in 1998, 1999, 2002 and 2005 in an attempt to build links with communities of faith. This move culminated in country-level pilots to develop a joint approach to deal with issues such as HIV and AIDS. An additional outgrowth from the 1999 meeting was the World Faiths Development Dialogue (WFDD), a small autonomous institution, which seeks to encourage dialogue about issues of poverty, diversity and equity, and has since conducted inter-faith interventions in Ethiopia, Guatemala, and Tanzania.[1]

This activism on the part of the World Bank and the WFDD has led both government agencies and academics to also examine the role that faith can play in development. In 2005 a consortium, funded by the Department for International Development (DFID), was formed between academic institutions in the UK, India, Pakistan, Nigeria and Tanzania, non-academic and non-government bodies, including Islamic Relief, to further explore the relationship between faith and development. As part of the research programme, the consortium sought to map the Muslim NGO sector in the UK.[2] However, the mapping exercise proved a difficult one. It was found that obtaining information about the 56 organizations identified was not at all a formality, but on the contrary was time consuming and led to the endeavour being overtaken by other initiatives. In particular, the paper noted the following barriers to achieving a cohesive picture of the Muslim NGO sector in the UK:

- The field is fluid and many organizations do not see that the contribution they make to relief and development places them within the sector.
- Their work is underpinned by a different discourse to mainstream development which can preclude the majority of them from partnering with secular agencies and or public sector agencies;
- Many Muslim NGOs, on account of their diasporic nature, see themselves as 'mainstream' in their country of origin as opposed to being part of the UK community; and
- There is limited interaction between Muslim NGOs themselves due to competition and some actors being seen as having political inclinations.[3]

Basically, it was found that the Muslim NGO sector in the UK operates almost entirely on the margins of the mainstream development arena and is internally fragmented, and as a result, tends to go largely unnoticed.

---

[1] Katherine Marshall, 'Faith and Development: Rethinking Development Debates', *Devlopment Dialogue on Values and Ethics* (2005), http://web.worldbank.org/WBSITE/EXTERNAL/EXTABOUTUS/PARTNERS/EXTDEVDIALOGUE/0,contentMDK:20478626~menuPK:64192472~pagePK:64192523~piPK:64192458~theSitePK:537298,00.html. (accessed 28 July 2013).

[2] M. Kroessin, 'Mapping UK Muslim Development NGOs '*Religions and Development Working Paper 30* (International Development Department: University of Birmingham, 2009).

[3] Ibid.

These findings are not unusual. Indeed, these issues are widespread and affect the sector as a whole. A more recent report by IRIN also found that there is a distinct lack of co-ordination amongst Muslim NGOs, and that they are wary of working with Western agencies, such as the UN, because they see them as being politically motivated. As one senior aid worker put it: 'We try to coordinate with – and not be coordinated by – the UN because of neutrality issues', because '[t]he UN is not considered to be a neutral organization, especially in a conflict set-up'.[4]

This lack of co-ordination and trust was partly caused by pre-existing misapprehension of Muslim charitable work within the West which was exacerbated by the advent of and fallout from 9/11. In a report by the CIA in 1996 it was asserted that one third of all Islamic charities and non-governmental organizations (NGOs) were directly or indirectly linked to terrorism,[5] and in 2001, in the wake of 9/11 and the subsequent 'war on terror', Islamic charities came under even greater scrutiny. Organizations that had largely remained unnoticed up until then were suddenly heavily scrutinized and subjected to incredible public pressure from government policies that became wide-reaching and increasingly repressive. For example, in 2003 the US Congress called for a ban on a number of charities across the globe which saw the offices of the Saudi-based charity al-Haramain shut its doors in Bosnia, Somalia and Chad.[6] Others, such as the al-Aqsa Foundation also had a chain of its offices closed across Europe because of suspected links with Hamas, while major Western Islamic charities Interpal and Islamic Relief had to defend themselves against allegations of supporting terrorism.[7] By 2009 the list of Islamic charities under suspicion had grown to 500.[8]

---

[4] IRIN, 'Analysis: Arab and Muslim aid and the West – "Two China Elephants"', (2011), http://www.irinnews.org/report/94010/analysis-arab-and-muslim-aid-and-the-west-two-china-elephants. (accessed 15 August 2013).

[5] J.B. Alterman and Karin von Hippel, 'Preface', in *Understanding Islamic Charities*, ed. J.B. Alterman and Karin von Hippel (Washington: Center for Strategic and International Studies 2007), vi.

[6] Mayke Kaag, 'Aid, *Umma*, and Politics: Transnational Islamic NGOs in Chad', in *Islam and Muslim Politics in Africa*, ed. Benjamin Soares and René Otayek (UK: Palgrave Macmillan, 2008). BBC News, 'UK and US freeze Islamic charity', *BBC News* (2003), http://news.bbc.co.uk/2/hi/business/2950314.stm. (accessed 30 August 2010); Jeremy Scott-Joynt, 'Charities in terror fund spotlight', *BBC News* (2003), http://news.bbc.co.uk/2/hi/business/3186840.stm; BBC News, 'RBS fined £5.6m for anti-terror failings', *BBC News* (2010), http://www.bbc.co.uk/news/business-10850093 (accessed 30 August 2010).

[7] J. Millard Burr and Robert O. Collins, *Alms for Jihad: Charity and Terrorism in the Islamic World* (New York Cambridge University Press, 2006); Dominic Casciani, 'Islamic charity cleared of Hamas link', *BBC News* (2003), http://news.bbc.co.uk/2/hi/uk_news/3135392.stm. (accessed 30 August 2010); Chris McGreal, 'Israel accuses British-funded Islamic charity of being front for terrorists', *The Guardian*, 31 May 2006.

[8] BBC News, 'RBS fined £5.6m for anti-terror failings'.

Essentially the 1990s and the early 2000s had been a period of increasing hostility for Muslim charities and NGOs. Whilst there may be a case to be made with regard to some Islamic NGOs supporting terrorist organizations, it has rarely been proven, with only one such conviction as of 2012, and as such, there is a dire need for increased understanding.[9] Fortunately, this has begun to take place, but it remains a fledgling movement.

All this has led to Muslim agencies and donors looking to create their own parallel systems to the one's led by the Organization for Economic Cooperation and Development (OECD) Development Assistance Committee (DAC) and the UN's Office for the Coordination of the Humanitarian Assistance (OCHA). This endeavour is being led by the Organization of Islamic Cooperation (OIC), which set up its own humanitarian affairs department in 2008.[10] The rationale behind establishing a separate system is on account of a fundamentally different approach to aid that Western agencies simply do not wish to take the time to learn about. There is limited understanding in the West of the basic drivers behind Islamic aid in *zakat* (alms) and *sadaqa* (voluntary charity), or Muslim cultural values more broadly. For example, one Arab aid worker lamented the Western centric code of ethics that accompanies the UN's aid endeavours, citing hijab-wearing and the issue of women's empowerment. He explained: 'How we understand it is not how the UN understands it' and added that there is a fear that for the UN women's empowerment means 'removing the hijab [covering a woman's hair], destroying the family institution and throwing religion out the window'.[11]

This current seeming incompatibility between Muslim donor countries and agencies with the mainstream aid sector is presenting a challenge to the hegemony of the Western aid fraternity, and is having a transformative effect on the development landscape. Muslim countries, such as Saudi Arabia, notwithstanding an already long history of providing humanitarian assistance, have become increasingly active in recent years. Yet, despite this activity, little is known about how much many Muslim countries give and what it is used for as they prefer to use direct government to government transfers, or to provide their funds directly through the Red Cross/Red Crescent Societies, rather than utilizing multilateral

---

[9] See Marie Juul Petersen, 'Islamizing Aid: Transnational Muslim NGOs after 9.11.', *VOLUNTAS: International Journal of Voluntary and Nonprofit Organizations* 23, no. 1 (2012): 126–55.

[10] Andrea Binder, Claudia Meier, and Julia Steets, 'Humanitarian Assistance: Truly Universal? A Mapping Study of Non-Western Donors', *GPPi Research Paper No. 12* (Berlin: Global Public Policy Institute 2010). It is important to note that this is not confined to the Muslim world. Other non-Muslim donor countries, such as Brazil, Russia and India, are also forming their own alliances and do not necessarily wish to join the OECD's Development Assistance Committee. IRIN, 'Aid Policy: The rise of the "new" donors', (2011), http://www.irinnews.org/indepthmain.aspx?indepthid=91&reportid=94003. (accessed 17 August 2013).

[11] 'Analysis: Arab and Muslim aid and the West – "Two China Elephants"'.

agencies.[12] As of 2006, the UAE was one of only three non-Western donors to sign up to the UN's OCHA Donor Support Group,[13] and at the time of writing remains the sole Islamic member. As a result of this tendency to eschew Western multilateralism, it is routinely reported that the figures provided by Muslim countries for humanitarian assistance are under-representative.[14] In 2004, for example, it was stated that the proportion of assistance from non-DAC donors in three Gulf countries channelled through the UN only constituted around 5 per-cent of all their aid recorded by the Financial Tracking System (FTS) run by the UN.[15] Yet, when certain countries are isolated it becomes clear that they make significant financial contributions that outrank those of some of their western counterparts. Saudi Arabia, for instance, with the provision of US$1.3 billion in aid over a five year period up to 2010 has contributed more than many established DAC donors, and was placed between Germany and Switzerland on the FTS rankings.[16] Similarly, both Kuwait and Qatar were reported to have outstripped some of their Western DAC counterparts in 2003.[17]

This evolution of the Muslim aid sector on the periphery of the mainstream international development scene becomes even more apparent when one considers, based on the figures available, where the money goes from Muslim donor countries. Perhaps, not surprisingly, it is almost exclusively given to fellow Muslim states. In 2010 the vast majority of funds from Saudi Arabia and Turkey were provided to Pakistan, while the UAE provided the majority of its aid to both Pakistan and Yemen. Indeed, during the period from 2000 to 2010 the main recipients of funding from non-DAC donors have regularly been Pakistan (four times in the top three), and the West Bank and Gaza Strip (five times in the top three), results which caused Global Humanitarian Assistance's (GHA) Kerry Smith to question whether the reporting to the FTS simply reflects the dominance

---

12 Adele Harmer and Lin Cotterrell, 'Diversity in donorship: The changing landscape of official humanitarian aid', *HPG Research Report* (London: Overseas Development Institute, 2005); E. Villanger, 'Arab Foreign Aid: Disbursement Patterns, Aid Policies and Motives', *CMI Report No.2* (Bergen: Chr Michelsen Institute, 2007).

13 Andrea Binder, Claudia Meier, and Julia Steets, 'Humanitarian Assistance: Truly Universal? A Mapping Study of Non-Western Donors'.

14 See Global Humanitarian Assistance, 'Non-DAC donors: Arab donors' humanitarian aid contributions', (2011), http://www.globalhumanitarianassistance.org/wp-content/uploads/2011/07/Arab-donors-humanitarian-aid.pdf. (accessed 17 August 2013); E. Villanger, 'Arab Foreign Aid: Disbursement Patterns, Aid Policies and Motives'; Debra Shushan and Christopher Marcoux, 'The Rise (and Decline?) of Arab aid: Generosity and Allocation in the Oil Era', *World Development* 39, no. 11 (2011): 1969–80.

15 Adele Harmer and Lin Cotterrell, 'Diversity in donorship: The changing landscape of official humanitarian aid'.

16 Binder, Meier, and Steets, 'Humanitarian Assistance: Truly Universal? A Mapping Study of Non-Western Donors'.

17 Harmer and Cotterrell, 'Diversity in donorship: The changing landscape of official humanitarian aid'.

of two donors in Saudi Arabia and the UAE.[18] A more recent report appears to confirm this suspicion, detailing that 35 per cent of all humanitarian assistance from the Gulf States between 2003 and 2012 went to just the West Bank and Gaza, Pakistan and Sudan.[19]

The situation is also much the same for Islamic NGOs, including those based in the West. The vast majority of Muslim charities focus almost exclusively on Muslim countries and those with substantial Muslim minority populations. For example, the list of development projects of Islamic Relief Worldwide's 'Where We Work' webpage lists only Lebanon, Afghanistan, Indonesia and Chechnya with regard to past projects,[20] and the same applies to Human Appeal International Australia, with only a few priority countries, Fiji, Kenya and Sri Lanka, having small Muslim minority populations, with 6.3, 11.1 and 7.6 per cent respectively.[21]

This single-mindedness of both Muslim donor countries and Islamic charities that are based in the West goes against the fundamental principles of normative aid practice, which argues for neutrality and universality with regard to both ethnicity and faith when providing humanitarian assistance. Despite the efforts by groups such as the WFDD, religion is still a hotly contested matter with regard to development. This is particularly true in the US. Even though the Bush administration sought to bring Faith Based Organizations (FBOs) into the aid sector in 2004 by overturning the longstanding ruling that USAID should not provide funding to religious organizations, the new rule explicitly stated that 'inherently religious activities' such as worship, religious instruction, and proselytization must be separated 'by time or space' from humanitarian activities.[22] Similarly, the Red Cross' code of conduct makes the point about separation of religion and aid practice even more explicitly in points two and three:

2. Aid is given regardless of the race, creed or nationality of the recipients and without adverse distinction of any kind. Aid priorities are calculated on the basis of need alone.

---

[18] Kerry Smith, 'Non-DAC Donors and Humanitarian Aid: Shifting Structures, Changing Trends', *Briefing Paper* (Global Humanitarian Assistance, 2011).

[19] GHA, 'Global Humanitarian Assistance Report'. (2013) http://www.globalhumanitarianassistance.org/wp-content/uploads/2013/07/GHA-Report-2013.pdf (accessed 15 August 2013).

[20] Islamic Relief Worldwide, 'Where we work', http://www.islamic-relief.com/wherewework/Default.aspx?depID=4. (accessed 19 August 2013).

[21] Humanitarian Appeal International Australia, 'Countries of Operation', https://www.humanappeal.org.au/about-us/countries-of-operation. (accessed 19 August 2013); See CIA World Fact Book https://www.cia.gov/library/publications/the-world-factbook/ (accessed 7 March 2014).

[22] Gerard Clarke, 'Agents of transformation? Donors, Faith-Based Organisations and International Development', *Third World Quarterly* 28, no. 1 (2007), 82.

3. Aid will not be used to further a particular political or religious standpoint.[23]

In essence, in the West, religion can be a guiding, or inspirational driver to provide aid, but must not shape or direct the kind of interventions provided, or be a determining factor with regard to who receives aid and who does not. Thus, this obvious bias of Muslim donor countries and charities combined with a lack of transparency around funding, along with the formation of their own development systems, means that Islamic aid routinely lacks visibility in the West, a fact which leads to misunderstanding. This is particularly the case when the dominant trope is that Islamic aid is simply a vehicle for terrorism.

Yet, when one begins to consider this further, such bias begins to become less problematic. For example, as Holenstein points out, the separation of religion and state and the subsequent extension to development is an entirely Western European experience that transpired over centuries of conflicts between Popes and States, and is an anathema to other cultures[24] – the Muslim world being no exception. Indeed, Islam is seen as a complete system that governs all aspects of life. Moreover, one of the five pillars that all Muslims are obligated to follow is to provide 2.5 per cent of their income to charity for the poor in the form of *zakat*, and as *zakat* is part of the faith, and is regarded as a form of *ibadah* (worship), it is only to be undertaken by Muslims. Therefore, for some, non-Muslims are excluded, in that they are not expected to give or meant to be the target recipients.[25] In other words, there is a distinct need to better understand the context in which different cultural/religious groups operate, and again this is precisely the endeavour of this volume. Moreover, this need is particularly pressing as a largely independent Islamic aid bloc begins to emerge and establish its own agenda. The following contributions therefore deal with this issue of bias, or exclusivity, amongst the others flagged above, such as compatibility, collaboration, the role of *zakat*, religious ethics and practice, aid flows and women's rights/empowerment, with a view to rendering the Muslim aid sector that presently resides in the periphery more visible and relatable.

Structure of the Book

In doing so, the volume approaches these issues in two parts. Part I, entitled *Islam in Development*, provides five chapters that explore Islam's relationship to

[23] International Federation of Red Cross and Red Crescent Societies, 'Code of Conduct', http://www.ifrc.org/en/publications-and-reports/code-of-conduct/. (accessed 21 August 2013).

[24] A. Holenstein, 'Governmental Donor Agencies and Faith-Based Organizations', *International Review – Red Cross* 87, no. 858 (2005): 367–73.

[25] Sayed Afzal Peerzade, 'The Definition and Measurement of Poverty: An Integrated Islamic Approach', *The Pakistan Development Review* (1997): 87–97.

development from a theological and textual viewpoint. Part II, entitled *Islam in Practice*, contains four chapters that draw on case studies from Indonesia, Aceh and Bangladesh and give real insight into how Islamic aid and development play out on the ground.

Chapter 1 by Jan Ali begins with a historical review of the practice of *zakat*, and interrogates whether or not this pillar of worship has been and can be an effective means of poverty alleviation. Shifting gears, David Tittensor, in Chapter 2, argues for the role of faith in development to be reconsidered in relation to the issue of bias in the provision of aid. In doing so, he draws on the works of Amartya Sen and Martha Nussbaum that seek to expand conventional understandings of aid to include well-being, and cites the cases of both Tablighi Jamaat and the Gülen Movement – from India and Turkey respectively – and how their religious interventions are at times precisely what Muslims are looking for. Staying on the issue of bias, Matthew Clarke in Chapter 3 provides a comparative analysis of both Western and Islamic international aid flows and the drivers behind the aid given, and raises the question as to whether such bias is not in fact a universal condition within the sector as a whole. Chapter 4 by Peter Riddell examines the prospect of collaboration with Muslim agencies from a Christian perspective, and suggests that such co-operation could be mutually beneficial with regard to access and successful interventions. Lastly, rounding off Part I, Chapter 5 by Ameer Ali charts the growth of the Islamic Banking and Finance sector and details its less than harmonious relationship with international aid contributions.

Part II picks up from where Ameer Ali leaves off. Aimatul Yumna, in Chapter 6, provides a detailed case study of the application of Islamic banking and finance principles by local NGOs in Indonesia to microfinance, and how this is being utilized as a culturally appropriate means of poverty alleviation. Chapter 7 by Misita Anwar and Graeme Johanson tells a similar story, with another case study from Indonesia of how the introduction of ICTs coupled with Islamic ethics is helping female entrepreneurs successfully run their business without compromising their faith. In doing so, both Anwar and Johanson bring to the fore the viewpoint that religion is a more pressing concern than material advancement and that it needs to be factored into the development puzzle. Chapter 8 moves to Aceh, where Ismet Fanany and Rebecca Fanany explore the response of the locals to the 2004 tsunami and interrogate how their religious convictions not only define how they view such natural disasters, but also govern how they should respond, and that Western agencies need to be more culturally aware when providing humanitarian assistance. Lastly, in Chapter 9, Mohammad Salehin tackles the always controversial issue of women's empowerment through microfinance. Drawing on interviews with both workers and recipients of Islamic NGOs providing microfinance in Bangladesh, he problematizes the Western notions of women's empowerment by showing that women choose to frequent Islamic NGOs that subject them to Islamic gender norms, yet still feel empowered.

Conclusion

The aim of this volume is to increase the visibility of Muslim aid. It is important to note that this is not meant to be a comprehensive account. Rather, it is designed to provide a broad introduction to the subject through a variety of contributions that engage with both the theology behind charitable giving and aid in Islam and provide insight into the lived reality through a number of empirical case studies. Greater understanding will benefit a range of stakeholders, and increasing the visibility of Muslim aid will enhance opportunities for co-operation between Muslim donors and Muslim charities and with their non-Muslim counterparts. Also, increasing religious literacy around Islam is vital for both secular and non-Muslim faith-based organizations to be more effective. Greater understanding will also reduce misperceptions of Muslim aid, particularly those held in the West.

Moreover, while this volume purposely takes an appreciative approach to understanding Muslim aid, this approach is not simply another mask behind which Muslim aid can remain hidden. Throughout this volume there is a critical view of Muslim aid and charities and a focus on how such aid can be improved. This is important because, just as with non-Muslim aid, the focus on all these endeavours remains to improve the lives of the world's poor. Finally, it is hoped that this book will not only render Muslim aid more visible, but also function as a catalyst for future research on what is an emergent and important part of the wider global humanitarian sector.

References

Alterman, J.B., and Karin von Hippel. 'Preface'. In *Understanding Islamic Charities*, edited by J.B. Alterman and Karin von Hippel. Washington: Center for Strategic and International Studies, 2007.

BBC News. 'RBS Fined £5.6m for Anti-Terror Failings'. *BBC News* (2010). Published electronically 3 August http://www.bbc.co.uk/news/business-10850093.

———. 'UK and US Freeze Islamic Charity'. *BBC News* (2003). Published electronically 30 May http://news.bbc.co.uk/2/hi/business/2950314.stm.

Binder, Andrea, Claudia Meier, and Julia Steets. 'Humanitarian Assistance: Truly Universal? A Mapping Study of Non-Western Donors'. *GPPi Research Paper No. 12*. Berlin: Global Public Policy Institute, 2010.

Burr, J. Millard, and Robert O. Collins. *Alms for Jihad: Charity and Terrorism in the Islamic World.* New York: Cambridge University Press, 2006.

Casciani, Dominic. 'Islamic Charity Cleared of Hamas Link'. *BBC News* (2003). Published electronically 24 September. http://news.bbc.co.uk/2/hi/uk_news/3135392.stm.

Clarke, Gerard. 'Agents of Transformation? Donors, Faith-Based Organisations and International Development'. *Third World Quarterly* 28, no. 1 (2007): 77–96.

GHA. 'Global Humanitarian Assistance Report', 2013. http://www.globalhumanitarianassistance.org/wp-content/uploads/2013/07/GHA-Report-2013.pdf.

Global Humanitarian Assistance. 'Non-DAC Donors: Arab Donors' Humanitarian Aid Contributions'. (2011). http://www.globalhumanitarianassistance.org/wp-content/uploads/2011/07/Arab-donors-humanitarian-aid.pdf.

Harmer, Adele, and Lin Cotterrell. 'Diversity in Donorship: The Changing Landscape of Official Humanitarian Aid'. *HPG Research Report*. London: Overseas Development Institute, 2005.

Holenstein, A. 'Governmental Donor Agencies and Faith-Based Organizations'. *International Review – Red Cross* 87, no. 858 (2005): 367–73.

Humanitarian Appeal International Australia. 'Countries of Operation'. https://www.humanappeal.org.au/about-us/countries-of-operation.

International Federation of Red Cross and Red Crescent Societies. 'Code of Conduct'. http://www.ifrc.org/en/publications-and-reports/code-of-conduct/.

IRIN. 'Aid Policy: The Rise of the "New" Donors'. (2011). Published electronically 19 October. http://www.irinnews.org/indepthmain.aspx?indepthid=91&reportid=94003.

———. 'Analysis: Arab and Muslim Aid and the West – "Two China Elephants"'. (2011). Published electronically 19 October. http://www.irinnews.org/report/94010/analysis-arab-and-muslim-aid-and-the-west-two-china-elephants.

Islamic Relief Worldwide. 'Where We Work'. http://www.islamic-relief.com/wherewework/Default.aspx?depID=4.

Kaag, Mayke. 'Aid, *Umma*, and Politics: Transnational Islamic NGOs in Chad'. In *Islam and Muslim Politics in Africa*, edited by Benjamin Soares and René Otayek. UK: Palgrave Macmillan, 2008.

Kroessin, M. 'Mapping UK Muslim Development NGOs'. *Religions and Development Working Paper 30*. International Development Department: University of Birmingham, 2009.

Marshall, Katherine 'Faith and Development: Rethinking Development Debates'. *Development Dialogue on Values and Ethics* (2005). http://web.worldbank.org/WBSITE/EXTERNAL/EXTABOUTUS/PARTNERS/EXTDEVDIALOGUE/0,contentMDK:20478626~menuPK:64192472~pagePK:64192523~piPK:64192458~theSitePK:537298,00.html.

McGreal, Chris 'Israel Accuses British-Funded Islamic Charity of Being Front for Terrorists'. *The Guardian*, 31 May 2006.

Peerzade, Sayed Afzal. 'The Definition and Measurement of Poverty: An Integrated Islamic Approach'. *The Pakistan Development Review* (1997): 87–97.

Petersen, Marie Juul. 'Islamizing Aid: Transnational Muslim NGOs after 9.11'. *VOLUNTAS: International Journal of Voluntary and Nonprofit Organizations* 23, no. 1 (2012): 126–55.

Scott-Joynt, Jeremy 'Charities in Terror Fund Spotlight'. *BBC News* (2003). Published electronically 15 October. http://news.bbc.co.uk/2/hi/business/3186840.stm.

Shushan, Debra, and Christopher Marcoux. 'The Rise (and Decline?) of Arab Aid: Generosity and Allocation in the Oil Era'. *World Development* 39, no. 11 (2011): 1969–80.

Smith, Kerry. 'Non-DAC Donors and Humanitarian Aid: Shifting Structures, Changing Trends'. *Briefing Paper*: Global Humanitarian Assistance, 2011.

Villanger, E. 'Arab Foreign Aid: Disbursement Patterns, Aid Policies and Motives'. *CMI Report No.2*. Bergen: Chr Michelsen Institute, 2007.

PART I
Islam in Development

Chapter 1
Zakat and Poverty in Islam

Jan A. Ali

Introduction

In Islam, Muslims are expected to assist each other and pay particular attention to the poor and needy in society. Very early in Islamic history, political and legal institutions emerged in which some of these responsibilities assumed a legal status whilst others were practised as social obligations or ethico-moral necessities. Among the responsibilities that became mandatory and implementable by the Islamic state were the annual disbursement of *zakat* (obligatory alms) and assistance to beneficiaries known as *al mustahiqqin* and the maintenance of dependents called *nafaqa*.

Islam is built upon five pillars: faith, prayer, alms, fasting, and pilgrimage and is therefore considered more than just a spiritual system. Among these pillars *zakat* comes in third position. It reveals Islam's acknowledgement of the existence of poverty in society and therefore highlights an obvious relationship between charity and poverty. This is a dialectic relationship in which charity is seen to lead to the alleviation or eradication of poverty and poverty in turn leads to charity.

Zakat as a means of support and relief for the poor and needy is a divine commandment. It reflects Islam's strong focus on social and economic justice and serves to provide, through the enforcement of social obligation, fiscal measures, and legal responsibility, a fair and equitable redistribution of wealth. Its fundamental function as a social justice practice is, through an equitable growth for all members, to alleviate affliction and maintain harmony and stability in society. *Zakat* is an annual financial obligation prescribed to all financially capable Muslims and is a basic institution that seeks to fulfil the needs of the poor and needy in the form of an established socio-economic security system. Of course *zakat* is not the only institution in Islam for the purpose of alleviating or even eradicating poverty, as other institutions such as *waqf* (religious endowment) and *infaq* (charity to please God without asking for any favour) also exist. However, it is worth noting that *zakat*, which is clearly prescribed in the Qur'an and sunna (tradition of Prophet Muhammad), is the most important and prominent institution of social justice and charity in Islam expressly designed as a tool for addressing poverty and fulfilling the needs of the poor and needy and, therefore, the central focus of this chapter.

Zakat clearly highlights the fact that the Islamic religion is against inequality, injustice, discrimination, exploitation, deprivation, and suffering, though its very existence also suggests that Islam acknowledges, at the same time, that poverty itself is a common social characteristic of all societies. Even historically, Muslims have demonstrated great success using *zakat* in addressing poverty in society, however, the successful effects of the institution of *zakat* has been felt only in some limited periods, otherwise poverty has widely featured in the Muslim world under all Muslim empires throughout history. A systematic and strategic approach to alleviating or eradicating poverty has rarely been undertaken and poverty alleviation has definitely failed to feature as an integral part of a universal campaign.

In the 2005 United Nation Millennium Development Goals people who were seen to be poor were those 'individuals living in households with command over no more than $1 per day per person valued at international prices'.[1] Whilst many countries have their own measuring devices and absolute poverty lines, this is an example of the universal absolute poverty line. According to Ayub Mehar the Muslim world is the largest part of the Third World and a large part of its population is living in poverty.[2] The Muslim world constitutes 20 per cent of the world's total population and 23 per cent of its surface area, yet its share of World Domestic Product is only 4.5 per cent. Also, despite the fact that Muslim countries combined have a 7.5 per cent share of global trade the rate of poverty in the Muslim World is increasing quickly. Currently there are around 1.6 billion Muslims in the world[3] and 1.2 billion of them are living in Muslim countries and out of these, 650 million Muslims are living below the poverty line.[4]

Muslim countries are far worse than the rest of the world when it comes to the experiences of poverty and policies and strategies linked to poverty alleviation. The Human Development Report confirms this when it found that 21 Muslim countries out of the 57 members of the Organization of the Islamic Conference (now the Organization of Islamic Cooperation) were amongst the 36 least developed nations in the world, mainly in sub-Saharan Africa and South Asia.[5] The Muslim world is vast, stretching from Senegal to the Philippines, covering six regions: North Africa, Sub-Saharan Africa, the Middle East, Central Asia, South Asia, and Southeast Asia. Apart from a very few countries in Southeast Asia, such as Malaysia, and the Middle East, such as Saudi Arabia, there are elevated and increasing poverty rates in both urban and rural areas of a vast majority of Muslim countries. Levels of poverty have also been linked with increasing inequality alongside declining education, employment, and productivity. In Indonesia alone, for instance, which is home to the largest Muslim population in the world, over

---

1 United Nations, 'The UN Millennium Development Goals', (2005), http://www.un.org/millenniumgoals/ (accessed 23 Novermber, 2011).

2 Ayub Mehar, 'Pluralism in Muslim Societies: Its Effects on Development Process' (paper presented at the 1st Global Conference, Inter-Disciplinary.Net: A Global Network for Dynamic Research and Publishing, Oxfordshire, 19–21 September, 2003).

3 Pew Forum on Religion & Public Life, 'The Future of the Global Muslim Population', (Washington DC: Pew Research Center, 2011).

4 Mehar, 'Pluralism in Muslim Societies: Its Effects on Development Process'.

5 UNDP, 'Human Development Report', (New York: Oxford University Press, 2002), 151–2.

half of the national population – approximately 129 million people – are poor or susceptible to poverty with incomes of less than US$2 per day. Bangladesh and Pakistan number 122 million each, followed by India, at around 100 million Muslims living below the poverty line.[6] It is estimated that almost a third of Muslim countries' populations are currently living on incomes of less than US$2 per day, accounting for more than 660 million people of the world's poor.[7]

As such, this chapter examines the concept of *zakat*. It acknowledges that the concept and the institution of *zakat* is indeed complex, and equally complex is the relationship between poverty and *zakat*. It seeks to make a modest contribution to the debate surrounding poverty in Islam and *zakat*. The chapter highlights that poverty is a pervasive socio-economic problem in almost all Muslim societies today and recognizes that there are numerous causes of it, but opts to concentrate on economic causes of poverty only.

The chapter argues that *zakat* as a divine commandment and a tool for addressing poverty has failed to make its impact felt on society and bring about permanent removal of poverty among *zakat* recipients because *zakat* collections are insufficient to provide income support to all the poor in any given country. The *zakat* collection policies and strategies are inefficient and any attempt at alleviation of poverty through *zakat* disbursement needs to put a specific and strong focus on capacity building or increase the productive capacity of the poor.

The Concept of Zakat

Zakat is an Arabic term which means 'growth', 'increase', 'that which purifies' or 'alms'. One will find that the reference to *zakat* is made over two dozen times in the Qur'an. At three places in the Qur'an God issues specific commands on the payment of *zakat* whilst twenty-seven times *zakat* and prayer are mentioned together. In one place in particular *zakat* is mentioned with prayers in the same sequence of verses, 'those who humble themselves in their prayers' (Qur'an 23: 2) and 'who are active indeed in charity' (Qur'an 23: 4).[8] These two fundamental religious practices are clear indicators of the significance of the vertical relationship between Muslims and God founded on prayer and charity on the one hand, and the horizontal relationship between Muslims through dispensing part of one's wealth to another, particularly to one in need, on the other. Paying *zakat*, therefore, on the

---

[6] Muhammed Obaidullah, 'Fighting Against Poverty in Islamic Societies', *Muslim Economy* (2007), http://islamicvoice.com/December2007/MuslimEconomy/ (accessed 15 February, 2012).

[7] Siddig Salih, 'The Challenges of Poverty Alleviation in IDB Member Countries', *Occasional Papers* (Jeddah: Islamic Development Bank, 1999).

[8] For this chapter I used the following edition of the Qur'an: Abdullah Yusuf Ali, *Roman Transliteration of the Holy Quran with Full Arabic Text* (Lahore: Sh. Muhammad Ashraf, 1938).

part of Muslims is an act of worship and obedience to God. It is for this reason the horizontal relationship is considered by Muslims to be worship, albeit in a lower form, because it shows one's concern for others, both at an individual level as well as at the level of the umma (community of believers). *Zakat* is an obligatory or legal almsgiving and is seen by Muslims as part of their service to God. God commands believers to give charity regularly and freely with a particular emphasis on concern for the poor, the needy, and the wayfarer. It is clear that *zakat* is an Islamic welfare and social system and one of the five pillars of Islam under which Islamic social and economic justice practices operate.

The significance of the institution of *zakat* can not only can be derived from the Qur'an but also from the *sunna* (tradition of the Prophet Muhammad), which places great emphasis on the importance and mandatoriness of *zakat*. In one hadith it is recorded that Prophet Muhammad instructed the governor of Yemen at the time, Mu'ādh b. Jabal (d.18/639), 'Tell them that Allah has decreed upon them alms on their wealth, to be taken from their rich and to be given to their poor'.[9]

In the Qur'an *zakat* is often called '*sadaqah*'. These are two names for the same thing. In the Qur'an God says, 'of their wealth take *sadaqah* that so thou mightest purify and sanctify them' (Qur'an 9: 103) and '*sadaqat* are for the poor and the needy' (Qur'an 9: 60).

In Islam there are two types of *zakat*: *zakat al-fitr* which is a flat 'fee' levied on each Muslim (except the destitute) and is due before the prayer of *Eid al-Fitr* (end of Ramadan celebration) and *zakat al-mal* which could be described as a 'wealth tax'. It is the latter type of *zakat* which this chapter is concerned with and the following discussion will revolve around it.

Zakat in Islamic Law

First and foremost it is critical to bear in mind that a variety of legal views on *zakat* exist in Muslim communities and societies. In Sunni Islam there are four famous jurisprudential schools of thought and beyond this there are views expressed by great figures in Islamic history such as Ibn al Musayyib, 'Umar bin Abd al 'Aziz, Maymun bin Mahran, Abu 'Ubaid, al Tabari, and Dawud al Zahiri. All these views represent a valuable scientific heritage. Also important to remember is the fact that shari'a injunction in each matter regarding *zakat* may not always be sufficient and further explanation and virtues of the rulings may be required. This is an approach no different from that of the Qur'an which not only seeks to provide rulings, but also their rationale, objectives, and benefits to humanity both at individual as well as collective levels. Having said this, all Muslim jurists agree that the shari'a (Islamic law) refers to *zakat* as a determined share of wealth prescribed by God to be given out to the poor and needy and 'that the welfare of the people and relief of

[9] Al-Tayib Zein Al-Abdin, 'The Disbursement of Zakāh', *Islamic Studies* 42, no. 1 (2003): 127.

their hardships is the basic objective of the Shariah'.[10] The shari'a concedes that the wealth remaining with the owner after the *zakat* has been paid is purified and he or she is then at liberty to use it freely. Payment of *zakat*, therefore, is an act of wealth purification which is an act of worship in itself. Apart from this, *zakat* payment is associated with the idea of 'return' in which wealth is taken away from the rich and 'returned' to the poor and is never taken from the rich to the rich. This idea of return can be seen in the Qur'anic text:

> That which God has returned to His Messenger from the [conquered] people of the towns is for God and the Messenger and those close [to the messenger] and for the orphan and the pauper and the traveller, so that it does not become something which circulates among the rich among you (Qur'an 59: 7).

The return of wealth from the rich to the poor in a never-ending cycle of return has an economic function too. When *zakat* is paid on a regular basis by the rich to the poor, the wealth eventually finds its way into the economic system and allows the economy to flow smoothly. If *zakat* is withheld, however, during the year in which it is due, then the wealth in the owner's possession is considered to be held against shari'a and is 'impure'. This wealth fails to regenerate further wealth because hoarded goods cannot move. Hoarding and greed are imprudent economic exercises that potentially lead to the fracturing of social and political structures in society.

Zakat, therefore, is considered to be an essential act of worship and constitutes the third most important pillar of Islam. It is discussed as a pillar in the Qur'an as well as in *sunna*. *Zakat* is a practice introduced by Prophet Muhammad under God's direct instruction and is viewed by Muslims as a religious duty for all practising faithfuls. In fact in the Qur'an God instructs Prophet Muhammad and every head of Islamic state after him that 'out of their wealth take *sadaqah*, so thou mightest purify and sanctify them. And pray on their behalf, verily thy prayers are a source of security for them, and God is one who hears and knows' (Qur'an 9: 71). As such, *zakat* has played a crucial part throughout Islamic history and continues to be pivotal religious practice for many Muslims. It was Abu Bakr, the first Caliph of Islam, who first established a statutory *zakat* system, however, the practice of state-managed *zakat* ended after the reign of Umar bin Abdul Aziz, who was the Caliph from 717 to 720AD.[11] Abu Bakr, upon assuming leadership after the death of Prophet Muhammad, declared war on those who refused to pay *zakat*.[12]

---

[10] M. Chapra, 'Monetary Policy in an Islamic Economy', in *Money and Banking in Islam*, ed. Ziauddin Ahmed, Munawar Iqbal, and M Fahim Khan (Islamabad: Institute of Policy Studies, 1983), 35.

[11] Anita M. Weiss, *Islamic Reassertion in Pakistan: The Application of Islamic Laws in a Modern State*, 1st ed., Contemporary issues in the Middle East (Syracuse, N.Y.: Syracuse University Press, 1986).

[12] Elias Shoufani, *Al-Riddah and the Muslim Conquest of Arabia* (Toronto: University of Toronto Press, 1973).

It is defined in *fiqh* (Islamic jurisprudence) as 'a due right on specific items of assets/properties, in specific percentages with consideration of the passage of a year and satisfaction of the condition of nisab'.[13] A number of schools of Islamic jurisprudence assert that *zakat* is an obligation on 'all adult (who reach maturity) sane Muslims, female or male, who own properties that fulfill certain conditions'.[14] An important point to note is that *tamlik* (ownership) is a crucial part of *zakat*. It denotes that *zakat* must be dispensed to the poor or the needy, making the recipient an authorized owner of the disbursement who then has the right to utilize *zakat* freely for him/herself.

The items that are subject to *zakat* are determined in the texts of the Qur'an and hadiths (narrations and practice of Prophet Muhammad). These include gold and silver, cattle, agricultural goods, and goods produced for sale. Islamic jurists locate '*zakat*able' items into two categories: bare and non-bare assets. The bare assets called *amwal zahirah* are those items that are visibly identified, such as property, livestock and agricultural goods. The non-bare assets and merchandise known as *amwal batinah* are those items such as cash and sellable goods that are not readily observable, particularly by outsiders.

The *nisab* (excess savings or capital upon which *zakat* becomes obligatory and is calculated, taking into account the *zakat* payer's own and family basic needs as well as their financial obligations and payable debts) of *zakat* refers to the minimum level of *zakat*able assets upon which payment of *zakat* becomes compulsory. When an asset reaches the *nisab*, *zakat* becomes payable on it. The *zakat* is calculated on the full amount of the asset including the amount of *nisab*. *Zakat* becomes due on some items after the completion of one lunar year whilst some items are exempted from this condition. In the case of the former some of the items include cash, gold, silver, livestock, and sellable goods. In the case of the latter, items such as agricultural goods, *zakat* becomes obligatory at harvest time.

Zakat involves giving a fixed portion of one's wealth to the poor and needy, and according to Sunni majority Muslim scholars there are four rates of *zakat* that depend on the type of assets one possesses. The most common is a fixed rate of 2.5 per cent on capital income (cash, gold, silver, sellable goods, and receivable debts). On land crops that are produced from rain or spring water or water extracted from the river the rate of 10 per cent *zakat* applies and the rate depletes to 5 per cent when the crops are produced from animal powered irrigated water.[15] For resources existing underground, the hadith is unclear, but the scholars

---

[13] The Fiqhi Encyclopedia quoted in Habib Ahmed, 'Role of Zakah and Awaqaf in Poverty Alleviation ' *Occasional Paper 8* (Jeddah: Islamic Development Bank and Islamic Research and Training Institute, 2004), 26.

[14] Yusuf Al-Qaradawi, *Fiqh al Zakah*, 2nd ed. (Beirut: Mu'assasat al Risalah Publishers, 1973), 95.

[15] Ahmed, 'Role of Zakah and Awqaf in Poverty Alleviation'.

of Islam consent to 20 per cent *zakat* on hidden 'treasures' and 5 per cent on extracted minerals.[16]

In contemporary times there are numerous new items of income and wealth that determine the financial position of individuals and institutions that are not covered in the classic *fiqh*. Contemporary scholars of Islam such as Fazlur Rahman,[17] Munawar Iqbal,[18] and Yusuf Al-Qaradawi[19] have explored some of these concerns and suggested that many assets and sources of income should have *zakat* levied on them. However, there is no consensus as to which of these new items should be considered for *zakat* levy. One such item which many Muslims do not consider should attract *zakat* is wages or salaries. Al-Qaradawi believes that Muslims should pay 2.5 per cent *zakat* on wages and salaries once the yearly income, after deducting normal expenses, reaches *nisab*. Income from rental properties such as real estate and revenues from factories, and other similar manufacturing establishments including agriculture and livestock industries, should attract 10 per cent *zakat* on net returns.[20] More recently it has been suggested that *zakat* should be applied on the net worth of a business, including fixed assets appearing at the end of the financial year. The basis for this suggestion is that fixed assets of business are properties that are de facto used to generate profit in the same way as profit is generated from the sale of goods. This suggestion covers factories, rental properties, and businesses for profit.[21]

The recipients of *zakat* are determined by God Himself in the Qur'an. In the Qur'an God says:

> Sadaqat [here it means *zakat*] are only for the fuqara (poor), and miskin (the needy), and those employed to collect (the funds), and to attract the hearts of those who have been inclined (towards Islam), and to free the captives, and for those in debt, and for Allah's cause, and the wayfarer. A duty imposed by Allah: and Allah is All-knower, All-Wise (Qur'an 9: 60).

This verse identifies eight categories of those who qualify to receive *zakat* funds. These are:

i. *Al-Fuqara* (those living in absolute poverty)
ii. *Al-Masakin* (those who are unable to meet their basic needs)

---

16 Muhammad Akram Khan, 'Some Accounting Issues Relating to Zakāh', *Islamic Studies* 39, no. 1 (2000): 103 20.

17 Fazlur Rahman, *Economic Doctrines of Islam*, 1st ed., vol. 1 (Lahore: Islamic Publication, 1974).

18 Munawar Iqbal, 'Introduction', in *Islamic Economic Institutions and the Elimination of Poverty*, ed. Munawar Iqbal (Leicester: Islamic Foundation, 2002).

19 Al-Qaradawi, *Fiqh al Zakah*.

20 Ibid.

21 Monzer Kahf, 'Zakat: Unresolved Issues in the Contemporary Fiqh', *Journal of Islamic Economics* 2, no. 1 (1989): 1–22.

iii. *Al-Amilina Alaiha* (the collectors and administrators of *zakat*)
iv. *Al-Muallafatu Qulubuhum* (non-Muslims who show attraction or inclination towards Islam)
v. *Fir-Riqab* (people attempting to free slaves)
vi. *Al-Gharimin* (people consumed by overwhelming debt who need to meet their basic needs)
vii. *Fi Sabilillah* (those engaged in the cause of Allah), and
viii. *Ibnus-Sabil* (wayfarers).

There are other Qur'anic verses (Qur'an 76: 8; Qur'an 51: 19; and Qur'an 70: 24–25) and the sunna of Prophet Muhammad that identify orphans, the destitute, and prisoners of war as people who also qualify to receive *zakat*. As a process of wealth redistribution, the collection and redistribution of *zakat* is a substantial exercise in alleviating poverty.

Poverty in Islam and the Institution of Zakat

Islam locates poverty (*faqr*) in the broader socio-cultural, economic, and political context. Poverty is a serious concern in Islam, so much so that Prophet Muhammad encouraged Muslims to seek refuge from it in the same way as one is to take refuge from *kufr* (disbelief).[22] It is abundantly clear in the pages of Muslim history that during the early years of Islam and during Muhammad's prophetic career that poverty was a considerable concern and focus. Bonner notes, 'Poverty was clearly of considerable, even central, importance for early Islam itself'.[23] In this period Muslim history reveals that it was mainly the poor, weak and disadvantaged sections of the Meccan society who answered Prophet Muhammad's call to Islam. The Qur'an consistently reminds believers of their important responsibility for the poor, weak, disadvantaged, and needy.

> Not only did the Qur'an provide guidance for dealing with the poor; it also dominated much of the thought and behavior concerned with economic activity. Indeed, poverty and economic activity were closely tied in early Islam. A kind of 'economy of poverty' prevailed in Islamic theory and practice.[24]

Islam being a complete way of life and a religion of balance places equal emphasis on spiritual as well as temporal affairs so that socio-economic ills such as poverty should be addressed quickly and effectively, so harmony and order

---

[22] Mohammad Farooq, 'The Challenge of Poverty and the Poverty of Islamic Economics', *Journal of Islamic Economics, Banking and Finance* 4, no. 2 (2008): 35–58.

[23] Michael Bonner, 'Poverty and Economics in the Qur'an', *Journal of Interdisciplinary History* 35, no. 3 (2005): 392.

[24] Ibid.

can be maintained in society. In Islam the dichotomy between rich and poor or between wealth and poverty cannot be understood only in terms of whether one possesses or does not possess material wealth, but also whether one is in possession or not of spiritual wealth.[25] Having said this, the economic concept of poverty and its alleviation and eradication inevitably and indirectly address the poverty of spirituality. This is clearly argued by Rahman who claims that in Islam, Muslims can elevate their spiritual lives by improving their material life through eradicating material deprivation in society for their own benefit as well as for the benefit of others by giving *zakat*.[26]

Alleviation and eradication of poverty is not an impossible task, as Muslims believe that God has created enough provisions for everyone. This is evident in the following verse: 'And surely, We gave you authority on the earth and appointed you therein provisions (for your life). Little thanks do you give' (Qur'an 7: 10). However, Muslims are encouraged to strive towards decent living and to meet their needs. In the Qur'an God commands 'And when the prayer is finished, then disperse in the land and seek Allah's bounty (Qur'an 62: 10). If there are material deficiencies then they are obviously due to social and economic disequilibrium, not because there are insufficient provisions.

It is a common Muslim belief that life on earth is temporary and a test. All human actions will be judged completely and justly by God on the Day of Judgment. The 'life test', among other trials, aims to assess the way Muslims deal with income disparity and wealth at their disposal. In this regard, it is expected of all individuals – rich and poor – to perform their responsibilities diligently and in light of established Islamic principles.[27]

Since Islam encourages balanced living, strong warning is given against extreme income inequality and poverty and immediate remedial action is recommended in order to maintain harmony and order in society. Every individual is encouraged and expected to invest complete effort in meeting his or her needs as can be understood from the following narration by Anas ibn Malik:

> A man of the Anssar came to the Prophet (P.B.U.H) and begged from him. He (the Prophet) asked: Have you nothing in your house? He replied: Yes, a piece of cloth, a part of which we wear and a part of which we spread (on the ground), and a wooden bowl from which we drink water.
>
> He said: Bring them to me. He then brought these articles to him and he (the Prophet) took them in his hands and asked: Who will buy these? A man said: I shall buy them for one dirham. He said twice or thrice: Who will offer more than one dirham? A man said: I shall buy them for two dirhams.

---

[25] M. Mannan, 'The Economics of Poverty in Islam with Special Reference to Muslim Countries', in *Distributive Justice and Need Fulfilment in an Islamic Economy*, ed. Munawar Iqbal (Leicester: The Islamic Foundation, 1988).

[26] Rahman, *Economic Doctrines of Islam*, 1.

[27] Iqbal, 'Introduction'.

> He gave these to him and took the two dirhams and, giving them to the Ansari, he said: Buy food with one of them and hand it to your family, and buy an axe and bring it to me. He then brought it to him. The Apostle of Allah (P.B.U.H) fixed a handle on it with his own hands and said: Go, gather firewood and sell it, and do not let me see you for a fortnight. The man went away and gathered firewood and sold it. When he had earned ten dirhams, he came to him and bought a garment with some of them and food with the others.
>
> The Apostle of Allah (P.B.U.H) then said: This is better for you than that begging should come as a spot on your face on the Day of Judgment. Begging is right only for three people: one who is in grinding poverty, one who is seriously in debt, or one who is responsible for compensation and finds it difficult to pay.[28]

However, Islam acknowledges the existence of situations and circumstances in some instances which may be beyond one's control and meeting basic needs may not be possible. It is for these extreme scenarios that Islam has instituted social and economic relief systems so that people with basic needs or in poverty can be given support. The Qur'an states, 'And those in whose wealth there is recognised right, For the beggar who asks, and for the unlucky who has lost his wealth' (Qur'an 70: 24–25).

The responsibility of the wealthy for the poor has been established in a variety of ways in Islam. These responsibilities can be seen to be expressed in the institution of *zakat* and different charitable acts and institutions such as *waqf* (religious endowment). As seen in the Qur'anic quote above, *zakat* imposed on the wealth of the rich is declared as a right of the poor. There is a range of other charitable acts such as *awqaf* (voluntary act of charity) strongly encouraged by Islam in order to ensure the basic needs of people are fulfilled.

The period of *Khulafa-i Rashidun* (Rightly Guided Caliphs) reveals that all four Caliphs recognized the importance of meeting the needs of the poor and needy and that this was for them both an individual as well as a state responsibility. The classical scholars of Islam identified meeting the basic needs of the members of Islamic society as *fard kifayah* (a collective responsibility).[29] They considered fulfilling these needs as one of the central objectives of the shari'a. Since shari'a prescribes the protection of religion, life, progeny, dignity, and property, religion and life especially can be safeguarded by fulfilling the basic needs including, among other things, food, shelter, and clothing. In this way alleviation or eradication of poverty through the provision of the basic needs of every member of society is the responsibility of every Muslim and this responsibility is discharged through the proper payment of *zakat*.

Muslims have a responsibility for themselves as well as for society; something of a dual individual and social responsibility. *Zakat* payment is one such practice

---

[28] Anas ibn Malik, 'Sunan Abu Dawood, Kitab al-Zakah, Book 9, Number 1637'.

[29] M. Siddiqi, 'The Guarantee of a Muslim Level of Living in an Islamic State', in *Distributive Justice and Need Fulfilment in an Islamic Economy*, ed. Munawar Iqbal (Leicester: The Islamic Foundation, 1988).

in Islam that enables a Muslim to be responsible for him or herself as well as for their peers. Islam has created *zakat* as a great social pillar enabling individuals to make efforts towards a common goal of social justice and equity. The doctrine of *zakat* introduced the first formal wealth transfer system or a system of social security around 622 when Prophet Muhammad emigrated to Medina and established the first Caliphate (Islamic state). This was the case and continues to be the case in Islam because the Qur'an itself exhorts believers to give *zakat* – charity. The Qur'an provides specific guidelines about charity in numerous verses. These verses give clear-cut illustrations of the significance of charity in the Islamic doctrine of faith and the relationship between the faithful and God, implying that the security of God's mercy and protection is not only in prayer but also in giving charity (Qur'an 98: 4–6). Two key reasons, one regarding purification of earnings already discussed above and the other, which states that giving charity is a show of gratitude to God, are clearly mentioned in the Qur'an (Qur'an 4: 36–7). Muslims are encouraged to be seriously involved in philanthropy, using wisdom and intellect to establish needs in society and address them through charity rather than relying on the needy to come forward with their requests. Implicit in this is the idea that Muslims must be proactive in the welfare of their society generally and identify its needs and fulfil them immediately. The poor part of society is a problem for all, not just for the poor, and the Qur'an urges believers capable of charity to reflect on the needs of the poor and provide compassionate and generous charity (Qur'an 2: 273). In this regard we can infer that charity in Islam has a function and purpose and, therefore, is something that requires serious attention and commitment from believers.

If we turn our attention to modern capitalism, consumers are not constrained by anything other than their financial abilities. In Islam however, the social relationship is based first on the idea of sacrifice, where Muslims must part with a certain amount of their income or wealth to charity to acquire virtue and felicity, and then they must develop a community-consciousness as responsible members of society to avoid conspicuous consumption of items such as luxury goods, through self-restraint informed by rationalism.[30] The producers of goods and services, as integral individual members of the Islamic community, are similarly instructed to produce commodities suitable for the community and to steer away from profiteering and various unfair trade practices.[31]

Poverty, whether in Islam or any other socio-religious context, is an important sociological issue facing societies. Poverty is defined as an inability to meet one's basic needs of food, shelter, and clothing, but it could also include having a living standard which is below the level of mainstream society because of a particularly

---

30 Samiul Hasan, 'Muslim Philanthropy and Social Security: Prospects, Practices, and Pitfalls' (paper presented at the 6th ISTR Biennial Conference, Bangkok, 9–12 July 2006).

31 Ozay Mehmet, 'Al-Ghazali on Social Justice: Guidelines for a New World Order from an Early Medieval Scholar', *International Journal of Social Economics* 24, no. 11 (1997): 1206.

substandard level of household income. Obviously then, there is a clear correlation between poverty and household income. But what exactly are the causes of poverty? This is sociologically a pressing question. Research on poverty informs us that the causes of poverty are numerous and complex.[32] Without going into too deep a discussion about the causes of poverty, let us briefly look at what exactly is behind this noxious phenomenon. When we talk about poverty we are obviously concerned with it in the context of Muslim societies, but of course the causes of poverty are not unique to this context.

There is no doubt that poverty, in general, is the result of poor and inefficient organization of social, economic, and political structures in society.[33] These structures operate in a very complex manner with processes constantly interacting with each other, in the end producing deprivation among a group of people who then become known as 'the poor'.[34] The poor are often weak and susceptible to adverse conditions and situations beyond their control. Basu notes that one of the most potent characteristics of poverty is its propensity to continue in a vicious cycle of reoccurrence.[35] Generally speaking, the concept of poverty extends from material needs, education, and health to wider notions of susceptibility, being prone to risk, non-representation, and helplessness.

Wilson argues that we don't know much about the causes of poverty because research often focuses on facts and definitions of poverty and not enough attention is paid to its causes and alleviation strategies.[36] For us to have any meaningful discernment of poverty and to develop alleviatory policies and strategies, it is absolutely critical to understand the underlying causes of poverty.

In the modern world poor economic structure is the most obvious and potent cause of poverty. This chapter concerns itself with the study of poverty in Islam and Muslim societies by focusing on economic factors but at the same time acknowledges that other socio-cultural and political factors or causes of poverty are necessary considerations in a substantive and sociological analysis of poverty. Habib Ahmed posits that 'The growth rates in output and population and the distribution of resultant incomes are important determinants of the extent of poverty in any society'.[37] Bourguignon explores the complexities of poverty in a microeconomic context by concentrating on the 'Poverty-Growth-Inequality Triangle'. In his view, the level of poverty depends on growth, distribution, and changes in the distribution

---

32 Francis Wilson, 'Drawing Together Some Regional Perspectives on Poverty', in *Poverty: A Global Review*, ed. Else Øyen, S.M. Miller, and Syed Abdus Samad (Oslo; Cambridge, MA: Scandinavian University Press, 1996).

33 Ahmed, 'Role of Zakah and Awqaf in Poverty Alleviation'.

34 World Bank *World Development Report 2000/2001: Attacking Poverty* (New York: Oxford University Press, 2001).

35 Kaushik Basu, *The Less Developed Economy: A Critique of Contemporary Theory* (Oxford Oxfordshire; New York, NY, USA: Basil Blackwell, 1984).

36 Wilson, 'Drawing Together Some Regional Perspectives on Poverty', 20.

37 Ahmed, 'Role of Zakah and Awqaf in Poverty Alleviation', 55.

of incomes over a period of time. The overall expansion in the economy can lead to a reduction in poverty, but if the income distribution is vexed, poverty can loom large.[38] Salih notes in the context of Islamic Bank Development member countries that 'Inadequate access to employment opportunities, to markets for the poor to sell goods and services and to physical assets (such as capital, land and credit)' account for the 'main causes of poverty'.[39] Income, as we can see, is an important economic factor. Changes in its distribution have a direct bearing on the growth effect and the distribution effect.[40] Growth in economy occurs when the distribution of income takes effect based on the increase in income and how this income increases is through the changes in the relative income across the general population. From this we are able to infer that there is a clear interaction between income level and growth, income distribution, human capital and poverty.

This is obviously a dynamic interaction and to gain a more refined understanding it is necessary to identify the factors responsible for household income and wealth in particular, because the entitlement of a household, according to Sen, is determined by the ownership relationship as well as the institutional arrangements.[41] Ahmed says that there are a number of entitlements which in a market economy affect income levels of households. These are:

i. Trade-based entitlement
ii. Production-based entitlement
iii. Own-labour entitlement
iv. Wealth/income transfer entitlement, and
v. Non-entitlement transfer.[42]

What resources people own and the opportunities to sell them at a profit is what ultimately determine the total household income. Thus, the factors affecting the household income include the capacity to sell one's labour and commodities, the price of these, and the purchase costs of sellable commodities and level of personal consumption.

In many Muslim countries many household incomes are apparently at very low levels. Of course there is a wide variation in how individual countries perform and compare with each other. Whilst there are some countries who have a high-to-reasonable GDP per capita with a low percentage of the population living in or

---

38 Francois Bourguignon, 'The Poverty-Growth-Inequality Triangle' (paper presented at the Indian Council for Research on International Economic Relations, New Delhi, February 4, 2004).

39 Salih, 'The Challenges of Poverty Alleviation in IDB Member Countries', 39.

40 Nanak Kakwani, 'Poverty and Economic Growth with Application to Côte D'Ivoire', *Review of Income and Wealth* 39, no. 2 (1993): 121–39.

41 Amartya Sen, *Poverty and Famines: An Essay on Entitlement and Deprivation* (Oxford: Clarendon Press 1981).

42 Ahmed, 'Role of Zakah and Awqaf in Poverty Alleviation', 58–9.

under poverty, such as Turkey and Tunisia, there are other countries with a very poor GDP per capita performance with a high percentage of the population living in or under poverty, such as Niger, which in 2003 had a US$208 per capita income and 61.4 per cent of the population was living under US$1 per day.[43] For Muslim countries which fall into the latter category (high percentage of population living in or under poverty) 'the income from zakah … is not sufficient to provide all the poor people with their basic needs for the rest of their lives or even for one year'.[44] The reason why *zakat* fails to make a major difference in many poor Muslim societies is because these societies do not have long-term *zakat* disbursement strategies. Some oil-rich Muslim countries such as Kuwait, Saudi Arabia, and United Arab Emirates have established agencies responsible for the distribution of part of the *zakat* to poor overseas Muslim countries in Africa and Asia. Their efforts, though commendable, did not remove poverty in the *zakat*-receiving countries.[45] The Central Zakat Council of Pakistan and Nasir Bank in Egypt make *zakat* funds available as a subsistence allowance on a monthly basis to the poor but it has failed to remove poverty permanently. Al-Abdin notes that:

> These examples illustrate that the contemporary *zakāh* institutions have accepted the opinion that the poor should be provided with what will remove their poverty permanently but their funds – which are scanty – do not enable them to implement this policy in case of all needy persons or families capable of work.[46]

Similarly, Habib Ahmed observes in his own research that:

> We have seen that for countries with low per capita income and higher concentration of poverty, the *zakah* collections may not be enough to provide income support to all the poor in the country. This calls for a strategy to use *zakah* in an efficient way. … Instead of giving out income support in the form of handouts, the focus should be to use funds to increase the productive capacity of the poor. This approach will effect [sic] poverty alleviation scheme[s] positively in the long run. Being productive and capable to generate income, the household will not only get rid of poverty, but will eventually be able to pay *zakah*. This will, on the one hand, release *zakah* funds that can be used on other households, and on the other hand, increase the *zakah* revenue pool so that a larger percentage of the poor can be included in subsequent years.[47]

---

43 Ibid., 68.

44 Al-Abdin, 'The Disbursement of Zakāh', 133.

45 Ibid.

46 Ibid., 133.

47 Ahmed, 'Role of Zakah and Awqaf in Poverty Alleviation', 72.

To gauge the actual potential and scope of *zakat* in reducing poverty is a major research undertaking and a complex task. Our understanding of the causes of poverty and the effects of *zakat* in alleviating poverty is limited. This seems to be due to a paucity of poverty-related studies in general but particularly in the Muslim context where:

> Islamic works in general and Islamic economics-oriented literature in particular have not taken up poverty as a challenge that requires a systematic and direct attention. … Muslim scholars have not even attempted to understand the phenomenon of poverty in a problem-solving manner. Indeed, that understanding of any problem is a prerequisite to identifying its solution is not a common-sense precept that has been recognized and appreciated by our scholars and intellectuals, as reflected in the paucity of poverty-focused works. … Thus, we do not have any account of why poverty exists, or how widespread is poverty, or what alleviates or exacerbates poverty.[48]

For the little data that exists we are assured that 'the potential *zakah* collections to alleviate poverty do not appear to be very promising, the actual collection figures of *zakah* are even discouraging'.[49] In other words, *zakat* is not making the difference needed on the ground in Muslim societies. Indeed, in countries with low per capita income and higher levels of poverty, *zakat* may not be sufficient to provide income support to all the poor in society. However, this doesn't mean that the *zakat* should be abandoned as a poverty alleviation tool. Perhaps new and efficient strategies are required and responsible government and non-government initiatives are needed.

Conclusion

Although the Muslim discourse of *zakat* recognizes the importance of this institution and its relationship with poverty, at empirical and sociological levels the appreciation of this relationship is grossly lacking. *Zakat* as an institution is dealt with by both individuals and governments in a peripheral, marginal and superficial way and not with a long-term permanent poverty alleviation objective.

Even though from the earliest days of the Prophet Muhammad the pursuit of justice and strong empathy toward the poor and the disadvantaged have been a hallmark principle (even if financed primarily through the booties of conquests), and the early history shows an exemplary commitment and effort to help the poor through redistribution programmes, policies and strategies, gradually poverty alleviation became a peripheral issue. No systematic poverty alleviation

[48] Farooq, 'The Challenge of Poverty and the Poverty of Islamic Economics', 45,47.

[49] Ahmed, 'Role of Zakah and Awqaf in Poverty Alleviation', 71.

programme evolved in Muslim history after the end of *Khulafa-i Rashidun* and this trend seems to have permeated into the contemporary period.

Islam generally and the Qur'an more specifically place great emphasis on and commitment to addressing injustices and inequality in society and empowering the weak and the disadvantaged. For Muslims to maintain Islam's and the Qur'an's relevance to the modern world, they need to focus on confronting poverty head on, intellectually and practically, with a long term *zakat* disbursement programme aiming to remove poverty among the poor permanently. This would require studying the problem of poverty in the Muslim world and beyond in terms of its nature, extent and causes. Having poverty as a focus and being equipped with a meaningful and dynamic understanding of it, Muslims can deploy the institution of *zakat* to much more effective use both within and outside their societies. This will be one way of demonstrating the relevance and importance of Islam in the modern world and harnessing global support for an Islamically developed poverty alleviation programme.

Zakat needs to be distributed to enrich its recipients. Many Muslim jurists agree that *zakat* to an individual or a household must be paid to pull them out of poverty and therefore suggest that smaller acts of charity do not have a long-term effect on either the recipient or society. From the Islamic doctrine of faith and prophetic tradition it is clear that the emphasis is on strategic philanthropy. In the contemporary world, where many governments and communities are struggling to remove poverty, giving out *zakat* to 'enrich the recipients' seems to be the best and perhaps the most effective approach.

References

Ahmed, Habib. 'Role of Zakah and Awaqaf in Poverty Alleviation'. *Occasional Paper 8*. Jeddah: Islamic Development Bank and Islamic Research and Training Institute, 2004.

Al-Abdin, Al-Tayib Zein 'The Disbursement of Zakāh'. *Islamic Studies* 42, no. 1 (2003): 127–36.

Al-Qaradawi, Yusuf. *Fiqh Al Zakah*. 2nd ed. Beirut: Mu'assasat al Risalah Publishers, 1973.

Ali, Abdullah Yusuf. *Roman Transliteration of the Holy Quran with Full Arabic Text*. Lahore: Sh. Muhammad Ashraf, 1938.

Basu, Kaushik. *The Less Developed Economy: A Critique of Contemporary Theory*. Oxford Oxfordshire; New York, NY, USA: Basil Blackwell, 1984.

Bonner, Michael. 'Poverty and Economics in the Qur'an'. *Journal of Interdisciplinary History* 35, no. 3 (2005): 391–406.

Bourguignon, Francois. 'The Poverty-Growth-Inequality Triangle'. Paper presented at the Indian Council for Research on International Economic Relations, New Delhi, February 4, 2004.

Chapra, M. 'Monetary Policy in an Islamic Economy'. In *Money and Banking in Islam*, edited by Ziauddin Ahmed, Munawar Iqbal and M. Fahim Khan. Islamabad: Institute of Policy Studies, 1983.

Farooq, Mohammad. 'The Challenge of Poverty and the Poverty of Islamic Economics'. *Journal of Islamic Economics, Banking and Finance* 4, no. 2 (2008): 35–58.

Hasan, Samiul 'Muslim Philanthropy and Social Security: Prospects, Practices, and Pitfalls'. Paper presented at the 6th ISTR Biennial Conference, Bangkok, 9–12 July 2006.

Iqbal, Munawar. 'Introduction'. In *Islamic Economic Institutions and the Elimination of Poverty*, edited by Munawar Iqbal. Leicester: Islamic Foundation, 2002.

Kahf, Monzer. 'Zakat: Unresolved Issues in the Contemporary Fiqh'. *Journal of Islamic Economics* 2, no. 1 (1989): 1–22.

Kakwani, Nanak. 'Poverty and Economic Growth with Application to Côte D'Ivoire'. *Review of Income and Wealth* 39, no. 2 (1993): 121–39.

Khan, Muhammad Akram. 'Some Accounting Issues Relating to Zakāh'. *Islamic Studies* 39, no. 1 (2000): 103–20.

Malik, Anas ibn. 'Sunan Abu Dawood, Kitab Al-Zakah, Book 9, Number 1637'.

Mannan, M. 'The Economics of Poverty in Islam with Special Reference to Muslim Countries'. In *Distributive Justice and Need Fulfilment in an Islamic Economy*, edited by Munawar Iqbal. Leicester: The Islamic Foundation, 1988.

Mehar, Ayub 'Pluralism in Muslim Societies: Its Effects on Development Process'. Paper presented at the 1st Global Conference, Inter-Disciplinary.Net: A Global Network for Dynamic Research and Publishing, Oxfordshire, 19–21 September, 2003.

Mehmet, Ozay. 'Al-Ghazali on Social Justice: Guidelines for a New World Order from an Early Medieval Scholar'. *International Journal of Social Economics* 24, no. 11 (1997): 1203–18.

Obaidullah, Muhammed 'Fighting against Poverty in Islamic Societies'. *Muslim Economy* (2007). http://islamicvoice.com/December2007/MuslimEconomy/.

Pew Forum on Religion & Public Life. 'The Future of the Global Muslim Population'. Washington DC: Pew Research Center, 2011.

Rahman, Fazlur *Economic Doctrines of Islam*. 1st ed. Vol. 1, Lahore: Islamic Publication, 1974.

Salih, Siddig. 'The Challenges of Poverty Alleviation in IDB Member Countries'. *Occasional Papers*. Jeddah: Islamic Development Bank, 1999.

Sen, Amartya. *Poverty and Famines: An Essay on Entitlement and Deprivation*. Oxford: Clarendon Press 1981.

Shoufani, Elias. *Al-Riddah and the Muslim Conquest of Arabia*. Toronto: University of Toronto Press, 1973.

Siddiqi, M. 'The Guarantee of a Muslim Level of Living in an Islamic State'. In *Distributive Justice and Need Fulfilment in an Islamic Economy*, edited by Munawar Iqbal. Leicester: The Islamic Foundation, 1988.

UNDP. 'Human Development Report'. New York: Oxford University Press, 2002.

United Nations. 'The UN Millennium Development Goals'. (2005). http://www.un.org/millenniumgoals/.

Weiss, Anita M. *Islamic Reassertion in Pakistan: The Application of Islamic Laws in a Modern State*. Contemporary Issues in the Middle East. 1st ed. Syracuse, N.Y.: Syracuse University Press, 1986.

Wilson, Francis 'Drawing Together Some Regional Perspectives on Poverty'. In *Poverty: A Global Review*, edited by Else Øyen, S.M. Miller and Syed Abdus Samad. Oslo; Cambridge, MA: Scandinavian University Press, 1996.

World Bank. 'World Development Report 2000/2001 – Attacking Poverty: Overview'. Washington DC: Oxford University Press, 2000.

Chapter 2
The Changing Nature of Islamic Mission: The Cases of Tablighi Jama'at and the Gülen Movement

David Tittensor

Islam and development are concepts that are not often coupled together and when they are it is often negative. In the post 9/11 climate much of what has been written on the subject in the small but growing body of literature is couched in terms of the war on terrorism, with charities accused of funding *jihadis*.[1] Another prominent concern is that Islamic humanitarianism is just a cover for *da'wa* (preaching), wherein they are trying to convert all to the faith. Further, compounding the discomfort felt towards Islamic NGOs and charities is the fact that the predominant view within the development arena in the West is that religion in general should be divorced from the provision of aid as it leads to discrimination, and is potentially divisive. This is spelt out very clearly, for example, by the Australian Council for International Development (ACFID) which states: 'Funds and other resources designated for the purpose of aid and development will be used only for those purposes and will not be used to promote a particular religious adherence'.[2] Further, the code of conduct states that aid and development refers to 'activities undertaken in order to reduce poverty and address global justice issues … and includes community projects, emergency management, community education, advocacy, volunteer sending, provision of technical and professional services and resources, environmental protection and restoration, and promotion and

---

[1] J. Millard Burr and Robert O. Collins, *Alms for Jihad: Charity and Terrorism in the Islamic World* (New York, Cambridge University Press, 2006); Matthew Levitt, *Hamas: Politics, Charity, and Terrorism in the Service of Jihad* (New Haven: Yale University Press, 2006); Jon B. Alterman and Karin Von Hippel, *Understanding Islamic Charities* (Washington, D.C.: Center for Strategic and International Studies, 2007).

[2] ACFID, 'Code of Conduct', (2010), http://www.acfid.asn.au/code-of-conduct/files/code-of-conduct.(accessed 3 June 2013), 10. This is even more clear when coupled with the definition of religious activity in the code, which states that any kind of proselytism, be it towards people of other faiths or from within the same faith is an act of misconduct: 'Activities undertaken with the intention of converting individuals or groups from one faith and/or denominational affiliation to another', ibid., 41.

protection of human rights'.[3] There is, according to ACFID, no place for religion or spirituality in aid activities.

This material and technocratic approach to development has naturally affected Christian NGOs and led them to secularize their language and downplay the role of religion in their activities, and in recent times Islamic NGOs have begun to follow suit. Prominent examples of this are Islamic Relief and Muslim Aid. Both have sought to align themselves with this development aid culture run by institutional donors such as AusAid[4] and the Department for International Development (DFID). Typically the language has become universal in orientation and simply emphasizes helping the poor and sustainable development while religion just functions as an ethical reference point. Petersen has labelled this more recent approach as 'invisible Islam' and a 'desacralized' form of aid.[5] However, as Wiktoriwicz points out, this is not possible for all Muslim NGOs, particularly those that did not originate in the West, as they often operate at the level of culture and discourse and as such are inherently political, in so far that they seek, through their education and health provision activities, to challenge cultural codes and values.[6] Further to this, most Muslim aid organizations disproportionately favour providing aid to fellow Muslims. This is yet another reason why many are wary of Muslim NGOs, as they challenge the normative Western model of doing things and have in recent times encroached on territory that others historically regarded as theirs – namely the market share of donors (and in some cases the market for souls).

However, such misgivings I contend are misplaced. As Clarke notes in chapter 3 of this volume, it would be naïve to think that Christian Aid groups are not also political, in that they too have cultural agendas. Indeed, it has been fairly well documented that Christian aid groups have functioned as proxies for states[7] and continue to peddle their religious wares in spite of explicit codes of conduct that counsel against proselytism. In particular, it has been well documented that World Vision and others have and continue to distribute bibles[8] and that the former vies

---

[3] Ibid.

[4] AusAid has since been subsumed by the Australian Department of Foreign Affairs and Trade.

[5] Marie Juul Petersen, 'For humanity or for the Umma? Ideologies of Aid in Four Transnational Muslim NGOs' (Unpublished Doctoral Thesis, University of Copenhagen, 2011).

[6] Quintan Wiktorowicz and Suha Taji Farouki, 'Islamic NGOs and Muslim Politics: A Case from Jordan', *Third World Quarterly* 21, no. 4 (2000): 685–99.

[7] See Sara Diamond, *Spiritual Warfare: The Politics of the Christian Right* (Boston: South End Press, 1989); *Roads to Dominion: Right-Wing Movements and Political Power in the United States* (New York: The Guilford Press, 1995).

[8] See Abdel-Rahman Ghandour, "Humanitarianism, Islam and the West: Contest or Cooperation?," *Humanitarian Exchange Magazine*, no. 25 (2003), http://www. odihpn.org/humanitarian-exchange-magazine/issue-25/humanitarianism-islam-and-the-west-contest-or-cooperation.

for the souls of those that they are providing services for through what has been dubbed 'lifestyle evangelism' – the practice of living the Christian way and hoping that those that are interacted with will see and respond to the love of Jesus, which is reflected in their kindnesses.[9] Further, in 2004 George Bush overturned the ban on USAID providing funding to aid organizations that engage in both sectarian and missionary activities paving the way for Christian evangelical organizations.[10] This begs the question: is allowing for such activities wrong? The answer is a qualified no. Provided that there is no coercion involved and the organization in question is not 'actively' seeking to convert someone from a different faith, it should be allowed to have a role in development practice rather than being pushed to the periphery and bleached from the mainstream. Certainly Islam is a missionary religion that can be highly political and there are some groups that have operated and will continue to do so along these lines. This was most certainly the case during the course of the Afghan War in the 1980s and the conflict in Bosnia-Herzegovina during the 1990s, which saw Muslim organizations and NGOs such as the Muslim Brotherhood and the International Islamic Relief Organization (IIRO) from Saudi Arabia mobilize along political lines.[11] However, Islamic NGOs, charities and movements are not monolithic. Rather, as Petersen notes, they range across a continuum[12] and in recent years a number of Muslim organizations have emerged that do not see the world in the simple *dar al-Islam* (house of Islam) and *dar al-Harb* (house of war) dichotomy that simply rejects the West. Rather, their mission has shifted away from opposition to simply helping Muslims negotiate the impacts of modernity and globalization whilst maintaining an Islamic sensibility.

The added value of this kind of aid work is particularly apparent if we consider an expanded understanding of development, one that moves beyond the material to include human development and well-being as articulated by Amartya Sen and others that have sought to build on his pioneering work. Thus, the aim of this chapter is to illustrate that within a wider, more nuanced understanding of aid and development, mission activity, be it Christian, Muslim or otherwise is not the problem that it is often presented as, but rather can play a positive role. This will be done through providing an account of human development, which

---

9 Erica Bornstein, *The Spirit of Development: Protestant NGOs, Morality and Economics in Zimbabwe*, Religion in History, Society & Culture (London ; New York: Routledge, 2003).

10 Gerard Clarke, 'Faith-Based Organisations and International Development: An Overview', in *Development, Civil Society and Faith-Based Organisations*, ed. Gerard Clarke and Michael Jennings (New York Palgrave Macmillan, 2008).

11 Jerome Bellion-Jourdan, 'Islamic Relief Organizations: Between "Islamism" and "Humanitarianism"', *ISIM Newsletter* 5, no. 1 (2000): 15; Jonathan Benthall and Jerome Bellion-Jourdan, *The Charitable Crescent: The Politics of Aid in the Muslim World* (London: I.B. Taurus, 2003).

12 Marie Juul Petersen, 'Islamizing Aid: Transnational Muslim NGOs After 9.11', *VOLUNTAS: International Journal of Voluntary and Nonprofit Organizations* 23, no. 1 (2012): 126–55.

will then be followed by two examples of transnational Muslim missionary movements –Tablighi Jama'at and the Gülen Movement, from Turkey and India respectively – that do not actively seek to convert non-Muslims and look to provide nominal Muslims and believers with both traditional and non-traditional aid practices that are aimed at creating spiritually centred people who are actively engaged within their communities.

Human Development, Well-being and Religion

For a long time development and well-being was defined in terms of GNP, GDP and income, or in other words, economic terms. This approach tended to treat the recipients of aid as beneficiaries rather than active agents and focused only on the means and not the ends, which led to what has been dubbed as the as the 'missing person' in economic aid.[13] Reflective of this is the fact that improved GNP and GDP and levels of income did not necessarily lead to improved quality of life. Rather, fast growing GNP and GDP in developing countries failed to prevent or reduce widespread socio-economic deprivation. This led to a shift in thinking about the nature of development and what was required, and culminated in the UNDP's *Human Development Report* in 1990.[14] In this landmark report Amartya Sen, amongst others, sought to significantly broaden what constitutes development and reintroduces the individual to the equation.

This other side of the development equation is what Sen has called the 'capability approach', which includes functionings and capabilities, and the freedom to exercise them. Functionings refers to the state of the person with regard to things he/or she does with his/her life, and capabilities reflects the capacity of that individual to achieve valuable functionings from a collection of options of which they are free to choose a combination. Examples of basic functionings are being adequately nourished, being in good health and so on, but may also include much more complex values, such as having self-respect and being socially integrated. In short, the capability approach is all about the range of 'doings and beings' of people that lead to a quality of life, or lack thereof.[15]

Sen is at pains to stress that there is no one list of functionings that can be measured to indicate well-being. Rather, these vary from culture to culture and are part of what he refers to as the 'evaluative space'. That is, what is of value to one person or group of people may not be viewed in the same way elsewhere. The only qualification that Sen makes is that the evaluative space is not utilitarian, in that it includes 'acts and states' that are important in themselves as opposed to having

[13] Abbas Mirakhor and Hossein Askari, *Islam and the Path to Human and Economic Development*, 1st ed. (New York: Palgrave Macmillan, 2010), 31.

[14] UNDP, *Human Development Report* (New York: Oxford University Press, 1990).

[15] Amartya Sen, 'Capability and Wellbeing', in *The Quality of life*, ed. Martha Craven Nussbaum and Amartya Sen (New York: Oxford University Press, 1993).

some form of yield or utility value. As such, he excludes the means of living, such as real wealth, primary goods and resources, as these are derivative variables that only indirectly impact on those acts and states that are important to well-being.[16]

Naturally this early account of human development is somewhat vague and incredibly subjective, and has come under some criticism for this intentional evasiveness. For example, Sugden brought into question whether such an approach itself has any utility:

> Given the rich array of functionings that Sen takes to be relevant, given the extent of disagreement among reasonable people about the nature of the good life, and given the unresolved problem of how to value sets, it is natural to ask how far Sen's framework is operational. Is it a realistic alternative to the methods on which economists typically rely – measurements of real income, and the kind of practical cost-benefit analysis which is grounded in Marshallian consumer theory?[17]

However, while Sen has maintained his position, many others have sought to overcome this issue and create their own value sets to give some guidance as to what constitutes the key components to the human side of development. Particularly pertinent in this regard are the works of Deepa Narayan et al.[18] and Martha Nussbaum.[19]

Narayan et al. in their study for the World Bank entitled *Can anyone hear us?*, which examined the impoverished in 50 different developing countries, sought to uncover what values are important to those suffering poverty. From this, Sabina Alkire, also from the World Bank, has subsequently synthesized this expansive text down to a list of six dimensions: material well-being, bodily well-being, social well-being, security, freedom of choice and action, and psychological well-being.[20] The two dimensions that are pertinent here are psychological and social well-being. In the section on the former, Narayan et al. note that God is often invoked as a means of comfort and solace. For example, a poor Pakistani man explained 'As God gives food to a tiny insect living in the stones, He makes sure that we have enough food to live'.[21] Alongside this, their account of social well-being (originally a subsection of psychological well-being entitled 'Cultural and Social Norms') highlights that poor people place more value on social solidarity than material wealth and will divest themselves of material assets in order to participate

---

16 Ibid.

17 Robert Sugden, 'Welfare, Resources, and Capabilities: A Review [Inequality Reexamined]', *Journal of Economic Literature* 31, no. 4 (1993): 1953.

18 Deepa Narayan et al., *Can Anyone Hear Us? Voices of the Poor* (New York: Published by Oxford University Press for the World Bank, 2000).

19 Martha Craven Nussbaum, *Women and Human Development: The Capabilities Approach* (Cambridge; New York: Cambridge University Press, 2000).

20 Sabina Alkire, 'Dimensions of Human Development', *World Development* 30, no. 2 (2002): 181–205.

21 Narayan et al., *Can Anyone Hear Us?*, 38.

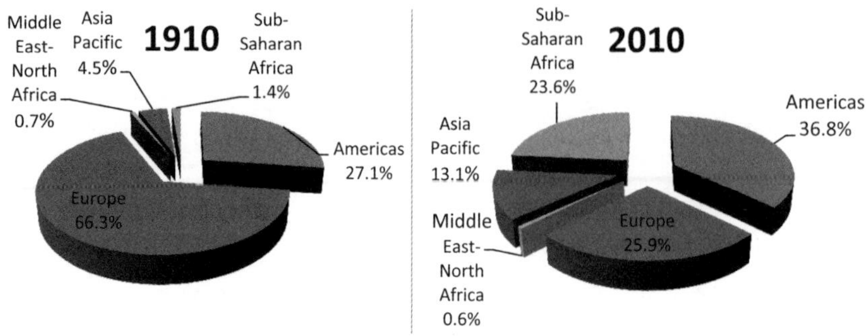

Figure 2.1 100 Years of Growth in Christianity

Source: Pew Forum on Religion & Public Life. 'Global Christianity: A Report on the Size and Distribution of the World's Christian Population'. Washington DC: Pew Research Center, 2011.

in rituals, celebrations and festivals. Thus, many people according to Narayan et al. are not simply interested in seeking the means to improve the quality of life on a material level, but are also interested in the end itself, which is feeling psychologically well and an important component of this is believing in God and being connected to their communities through shared rituals and celebrations.

Similarly, Nussbaum, although providing a longer list of categories for human well-being (10 dimensions), also identifies the importance of religion in two categories entitled, 'Senses, Imagination and Thought', and 'Affiliation' that accord well with those distilled from Narayan et al. by Alkire. Under 'Senses', Nussbaum argues that in order for one to feel 'truly human' one must have the freedom of religious exercise and search for meaning in life in one's own way. Additionally, with regard to affiliation, she notes that you need to protect those institutions that nourish the capability for association, and notes that religion is one such element, but rightly argues that it should not be grounds for discrimination.[22]

The fact that religion is routinely identified as an important element of the other side of human development is not surprising when you consider that religion is growing most rapidly in the Global South.[23] Both Christianity and Islam are on

[22] Nussbaum, *Women and Human Development: The Capabilities Approach*. Also, for an excellent account of the importance of religion and shared norms and ritual practice, with regard to development and psychological well-being, see chapter 8 by Fanany and Fanany in this volume.

[23] The expressions Global North and South refer to the divide between developed and developing countries. According to the Centre for the Global South at American University, the Global South comprises around 157 of 193 recognized states, predominantly from Asia (includes the Middle East), the Americas and Africa. See http://www.american.edu/sis/cgs (accessed 16 June, 2013).

the rise. Recent PEW reports indicate that Christianity has been overtaken in the Global North with regard to the number of adherents. Just over a century ago, as of 2010, approximately two thirds of the world's Christians lived in Europe. Today that number has dropped to around a quarter (25.9 per cent) with a plurality living in the Americas (36.8 per cent), sub-Saharan Africa (23.6 per cent), and Asia-Pacific (13.1 per cent), making Christianity a truly global religion (see Figure 1 above).[24] Similarly, Islam has grown exponentially and is the fastest growing population in the world today. From 1990 to 2010 the Muslim population has grown at an average rate of 2.2 per cent and is expected to continue at a reduced rate of 1.5 per cent – still well above average for replacement and double the birth rate for non-Muslims, which stands at 0.7 per cent – till 2030. Continued growth at the predicted rate will see the world's Muslim population rise from 1.6 billion in 2010 to 2.2 billion in 2030 (see Table 3.1); this would be one quarter of the world's projected 8.3 billion.[25] Further, this will place Islam only marginally behind Christianity, which is predicted to only rise from its current population of just under 2.2 billion as of 2010 to 2.6 billion by 2025.[26]

Table 2.1 Projection of World Muslim Population by 2030

	2010		**2030**	
	Estimated Muslim Population	Estimated Percentage of Global Muslim Population	Projected Muslim Population	Projected Percentage of Global Muslim Population
World	**1,619,314,000**	**100%**	**2,190,154,000**	**100%**
Asia-Pacific	1,005,507,000	62.1	1,295,625,000	59.2
Middle East-North Africa	321,869,000	19.9	439,453,000	20.1
Sub-Saharan Africa	242,544,000	15.0	385,939,000	17.6
Europe	44,138,000	2.7	58,209,000	2.7
Americas	5,256,000	0.3	10,927,000	0.5

Source: Pew Forum on Religion & Public Life. 'The Future of the Global Muslim Population: Projections for 2010–2030'. Washington DC: Pew Research Center, 2011.

24 Pew Forum on Religion & Public Life, 'Global Christianity: A Report on the Size and Distribution of the World's Christian Population', (Washington DC: Pew Research Center, 2011).

25 Pew Forum on Religion & Public Life, 'The Future of the Global Muslim Population: Projections for 2010–2030', (Washington DC: Pew Research Center, 2011).

26 Todd M. Johnson, 'Christianity in Global Context: Trends and Statistics', (n/d), http://www.pewforum.org/uploadedfiles/Topics/Issues/Politics_and_Elections/051805-global-christianity.pdf. (accessed 18 May 2013).

Thus, half of the world's population by around 2025 to 2030 will continue to be associated (nominal or otherwise) with two of the world's major religions. Add in other faith groups, such as Hinduism and Buddhism, which are reported to have around 1 billion and 500 million adherents respectively, and the percentage of the world's current population associated with a major religion jumps a further 22 per cent.[27] Therefore, given the prevalence of faith in the Global South and its likely continuance in the foreseeable future, it seems logical that faith-based organizations (FBOs) should have a role to play in not only nourishing people materially, but also spiritually. This is particularly so, when one considers that there are positive movements, like Tablighi Jama'at and the Gülen Movement, that have emerged, which are not interested in converting others, but are simply focused on providing holistic human development for their community of believers, and it is to these two prime examples that I now turn.

The Cases of Tablighi Jama'at and the Gülen Movement

Both Tablighi Jama'at and the Gülen Movement emerged in the early and mid-twentieth century respectively and have become two of the largest transnational Muslim movements in the world today. Tablighi Jama'at, which emerged in the 1920s in Mewat, North India, has expanded to have chapters in 165 countries around the world.[28] Similarly, the Gülen Movement, which emerged in the 1960s in Izmir, Turkey, as an outgrowth of Said Nursi's Nur movement,[29] has established over 1,000 schools and associated educational institutions in over 100 countries, and is estimated to have a gross value of $25 billion.[30]

The interesting common element between these two movements, which are quite different in their emphases (i.e. importance of secular education), is that they were both born out of persecution in their respective countries and have resolved

[27] Pew Forum on Religion & Public Life, 'The Global Religious Landscape: A Report on the Size and Distribution of the World's Major Religious Groups as of 2010', (Washington DC: Pew Research Center, 2012).

[28] Jan Ali, 'Islamic Revivalism: A Study of the Tablighi Jamaat in Sydney', unpublished PhD thesis, University of New South Wales, 2006. The development of Tablighi Jama'at has been well documented. For an account of its origins and global expansion see Marc Gaborieau, 'The Transformation of Tablighi Jama'at into a Transnational Movement', in *Travellers in Faith: Studies of the Tablighi Jama'at as a Transnational Islamic Movement for Faith Renewal*, ed. Muhammad Khalid Masud (Boston: Brill, 2000).

[29] For an account of Said Nursi's views and the subsequent development of the Gülen Movement see Bekim Agai, 'The Gülen Movement's Islamic Ethic of Education', in *Turkish Islam and the Secular State: The Gülen Movement*, ed. M. Hakan Yavuz and John L. Esposito (Syracuse, N.Y.: Syracuse University Press, 2003).

[30] Helen Rose Ebaugh, *The Gülen Movement: A Sociological Analysis of a Civic Movement Rooted in Moderate Islam* (New York: Springer, 2010).

not to counter-attack or blame the West for their plight. The Tablighis formed as a response to aggressive conversion drives by Hindu radicals in the 1920s that saw over 1 million Muslims converted,[31] while the Gülen Movement emerged as a response to radical Jacobin laicism in Turkey, borrowed from the French, that sought to bleach religion from the public sphere and replace it with positivism. Rather than act in a violent and oppositional manner, both movements adopted inward-looking self-reflective practices aimed at self-improvement, at being 'better' Muslims, and have set forth tenets to help their followers achieve this spiritual aim and take the message to their brethren. Further, as will be seen, an important element of this is shying away from formal politics, as the movements are more geared towards a personal piety that also plays down the importance of the material.

Tablighi Jama'at

> When you (Muslims) are not able to defend and maintain Allah's commands in your own individual being and in your life (for which you are sovereign and face no barriers), then how could the task of governing the affairs of the world be entrusted to you? Allah's purpose to hand over the affairs of state to the community of the faithful is to implement in the world the will and commands of Allah. When you are not practising it within your limited prerogative, then with what hope could the guardianship of the world be delegated to you?[32]

This was the response of the founder of the Tablighi Jama'at, Maulana Muhammad Ilyas Kandhalawi (d.1944), to the plight of Muslims in Mewat after the Shuddhi conversions. The answer to the wrongs meted out to the community lay not at the hands of their oppressors, but in their own conduct. In order for the situation to be rectified, Muslims needed to turn to their faith in earnest and become more observant. Thus, Maulana Ilyas set forth six fundamentals that need to be followed, designed to emulate the life of the Prophet:

1. *Kalimah* (the article of faith that states there is only one God and his messenger)
2. *Salaat* (ritual prayer to be conducted five times daily)

---

[31] Yoginder Sikand, 'Muslim Reactions to the Shuddhi Campaign in Early Twentieth Century North India', *The Milli Gazette*, January 15, 2001. It is important to note here that while it was Hindus that struck against their Muslim Indian counterparts, the rift between Hindus and Muslims was fermented by the British Raj which operated on the divide and rule principle. For a good example of this see Anil Baran Ray, 'Communal Attitudes to British Policy: The Case of the Partition of Bengal 1905', *Social Scientist* 6, no. 5 (1977): 34–46.

[32] Mohammad Talib, 'Tablighis in the Making of Muslim Identity', in *Islam, Communities and the Nation: Muslim Identities in South Asia and Beyond*, ed. Mushirul Hasan (New Delhi: Manohar Publishers & Distributors, 1998), 313–14.

3. *Ilm and Dhikr*[33] (knowledge and remembrance of Allah)
4. *Ikram-i-Muslim* (the treatment of fellow Muslims with honour and respect)
5. *Ikhlas-i-Niyat* (performing every act for the sake of Allah)
6. *Tafrigh-i-Waqt* (to spare time and undertake the work of Allah).[34]

The final principle of 'sparing time' is crucial to the work of Tablighi Jama'at and involves the practice of *khuruj* (tour). This is where a group of men (up to 10, depending on the size of the community)[35] travel from place to place entreating Muslims to join them and return to the fold of pristine Islam.[36] The length of time that one engages in *khuruj* depends on the individual's level of involvement with the Tablighis. The movement is extremely flexible, in that people can move in and out and take on as much as they choose, as there is no formal process of joining the movement or of maintaining membership. However, as Barbara Metcalf notes, a pattern has emerged in that initiates are asked to spend just one night a week, then one weekend a month and then 40 continuous days, and then at least once in their life to spend 120 days of a year engaged in the Tablighi mission of sharing the message.[37] Thus, essentially, anybody can become a lay preacher without having to undergo rigorous religious training, making joining the ranks easy. Indeed, by some accounts only three days is enough to become a Tablighi.[38]

Alongside this, when embarking on a tour movement members would don the traditional garb of white robes and skull caps and would divest themselves of any luxuries such as mattresses, would undertake their own cooking, and wash their own clothes. Further, the trip is funded by the participants themselves. The rationale behind this is to show that there is no difference between any men and to get them beyond what they regard as the overreliance on material resources, for wealth is seen as divisive.[39] Further, this form of elective sacrifice serves as a means of spiritual elevation, as only the Tablighi who has given over his trust to

33 The *dhikr* is the recitation of the 99 names of God. Depending of on the religious movement in question it is conducted either vocally or silently.

34 Jan Ali, 'Islamic Revivalism: The Case of the Tablighi Jamaat', *Journal of Muslim Minority Affairs* 23, no. 1 (2003): 176–7.

35 For an account of the role of women within the movement see Barbara Metcalf, 'Tablighi Jama'at and Women', in *Travellers in Faith: Studies of the Tablighi Jama'at as a Transnational Islamic Movement for Faith Renewal*, ed. Muhammad Khalid Masud (Boston: Brill, 2000).

36 Ali, 'Islamic Revivalism: The Case of the Tablighi Jamaat'.

37 Barbara Metcalf, '"Traditionalist" Islamic Activism: Deoband, Tablighis, and Talibs', *ISIM Paper*, no. 4 (2002): 1–24.

38 See G. Hoffstaedter, *Modern Muslim Identities: Negotiating Religion and Ethnicity in Malaysia* (Copenhagen: Nordic Institute of Asian Studies, 2011).

39 Ali, 'Islamic Revivalism: The Case of the Tablighi Jamaat'.

God and renounced his worldly possessions can achieve a more spiritual nature. In other words, for the Tablighis there is spiritual wealth in poverty.[40]

In line with this thinking the poor have become an important part of the movement's constituency, as they strive for social reform. Typically, when the Tablighis move into a new country to set themselves up they establish operations in poorer urban and rural districts. For example, in 1957 when they moved into Jakarta they based themselves in a Mosque that no one else wanted in the red light district,[41] while in Thailand in the 1960s they worked predominantly in rural Muslim villages in the south recruiting poor farmers and fishermen.[42] As a result of this focus on the poor the movement has had, and continues to have, a great deal of success with those in need of guidance, such as unemployed youth, drug addicts, alcoholics and others from marginalized groups that lacked support networks in South-East Asia.[43] A similar pattern has also played out in the Western context of Australia when the Tablighis arrived in 1972. Ali found that by the 1980s the movement had struck a chord with poor Muslim migrant workers who were forced to work in unskilled jobs or perform highly skilled jobs for significantly reduced rates of pay, as the Australian government tended not to recognize foreign qualifications. He also found that, like in South East Asia, the Tablighis were also appealing to the Muslim youth on account of high unemployment, racial discrimination and rising Islamophobia.[44]

This all leads to the question, what is it that Muslims seek and find in the Tablighi Jama'at? According to Hoffstaedter it is the strict life model that is offered that provides them with a sense of connectedness to the Muslim community through shared symbolic and ritual practice, and the face-to-face interaction granted from preaching door-to-door. Further, he notes that it also grants an escape from the outside, from the incursions of the hedonistic lifestyle of the West.[45] This is particularly clear when one takes into account that it is not just the poor that join the Tablighis. It is also common to hear narratives from members who were doing well professionally but felt lost and un-sustained by their material existence. For example, Noor in his ethnography of the Tablighis in South-East Asia recounts the story of Ustaz Zulman who, despite having a DVD business, felt low and aimless

---

40 Farish A. Noor, *Islam on the Move: The Tablighi Jama'at in Southeast Asia* (Amsterdam: Amsterdam University Press, 2012).

41 Ibid.

42 Joseph Chinyong Liow, 'Islamic Education in Southern Thailand: Negotiating Islam, Identity, and Modernity', in *Making Modern Muslims: The Politics of Islamic Education in Southeast Asia*, ed. Robert W. Hefner (Honolulu: University of Hawaii Press, 2009).

43 Hoffstaedter, *Modern Muslim Identities: Negotiating Religion and Ethnicity in Malaysia*; Noor, *Islam on the Move: The Tablighi Jama'at in Southeast Asia.*

44 Jan Ali, 'Islamic Revivalism: A Study of the Tablighi Jamaat in Sydney'.

45 Hoffstaedter, *Modern Muslim Identities: Negotiating Religion and Ethnicity in Malaysia.*

and upon joining decided to ultimately abandon his business in Brigen and give his belongings away:

> Slowly I gave up my business. I was glad to leave the DVD business because it meant I didn't have to deal with *kafirs* anymore. I only wanted to be with good Muslims from now on. I sold my things, my property I gave to my family along with my cars and other stuff.[46]

His reasoning was not only that he wanted to escape the bad Muslims, but also that he wanted to be happy and peaceful like the smiling Tablighis that turned up on his doorstep, who he initially mistook for wandering beggars.[47] Similarly, Hoffstaedter tells the story of one Tablighi who as an engineer is able to earn enough money in six months to support his family and allow him to undertake the mission for the rest of the year.[48]

Thus, what begins to emerge here is that the movement provides those things that Narayan et al., Alkire and Nussbaum found to be of higher value to the poor. Rather than material wealth, they provide the other side of the development conundrum, namely, connectedness to the community through shared rituals and practice that allow people to find social solidarity, solace and peace. In other words, the Tablighis provide an 'alternative sensibility' to the God of materialism and consumption driven by the West that enables people to more effectively manage their life situation, and the Gülen movement, although more mercantilist than the Tablighis, operates in a very similar way.

The Gülen Movement

> People of heart are monuments of humility and modesty who are devoted to a spiritual life, determined to stay away from all the material and spiritual dirt, always vigilant to corporeal desires of the body, and ready to struggle with such evils as hatred, resentment, greed, jealousy, selfishness and lust. They always endeavour to give what is right the highest esteem, to convey to others what they feel about this world, as well as the next, and they are always patient and cautious. People of faith and action who, rather than talking and making noise, live as they believe, present an exemplary personality for others. Such people move on, never pausing, teaching those who are walking toward God how to do so.[49]

---

46 Noor, *Islam on the Move: The Tablighi Jama'at in Southeast Asia*, 120.

47 Ibid.

48 Hoffstaedter, *Modern Muslim Identities: Negotiating Religion and Ethnicity in Malaysia*.

49 Fethullah Gülen, *Toward a Gobal Cvilization of Love & Tolerance* (Somerset, N.J.: Light, Inc., 2004), 84.

For Fethullah Gülen the world is suffering from a dearth of spirituality and is in need of the people described above, namely the ideal person; one who is not governed by material and worldly concerns, but rather seeks to instil the spirit in others through pious behaviour. He sees that many of the ills of this world are the result of unchecked positivism and science. Thus, his ultimate aim is to create a *yeni nesil* (new generation) of Muslims that are educated but morally upright who have the wisdom to better guide society. This desire led Gülen in the late 1960s and 70s, guided by the teachings of Said Nursi, to develop education programmes, comprising of both the physical sciences (chemistry, physics, biology etc.) and the religious sciences. His view was that Muslims needed to be educated to be in the world, but also needed to be provided with the necessary moral education to help guide them. In other words, Gülen sought to create what he sees as holistic education that focuses not just on the development of the individual intellectually but also spiritually.

In the 1990s, when the movement began to open schools abroad, Gülen expanded his approach to include non-Muslims as well through the introduction of 'universal values'. That is teachers were to follow the practice of *temsil* (representation). This means that the teachers need not speak of their faith, but simply represent it through their actions, such as being respectful to their elders, respecting the importance of family, not smoking, drinking or drug taking, and praying when it is time to pray. In this way they look to impart a dual message of good values to non-Muslims, but also present a pious example to their fellow (nominal) Muslims with the hope of guiding them on the path towards God. Typically this practice is supplemented by informal *ahlak dersleri* (morality classes), in the place of religious studies, which remains general if non-Muslims are present to avoid offending those that are of a different religious persuasion.[50]

Effectively, in Gülen's ontology the teacher has become a revered individual and their work has become an act of *hizmet* (service) to humanity.[51] In other words, those that are working in the schools are undertaking God's work and therefore the teaching of physical sciences and representing faith through model behaviour has become an act of piety. This is not to say Gülen devalues other professions. One can be a pious example whatever one's profession. However, for those within the movement that do not become teachers, they undertake *hizmet* through both *zakat* (alms) and *himmet* (voluntary giving) to fund the building of schools (amongst other projects) and support the work undertaken by the teachers. There is a widespread acceptance that the amount given varies from person to person, with some giving 5 per cent, others 10 per cent and some as much as 20 per cent of their income. Indeed, a select few wealthier movement members donate as much as $1 million a year.[52]

---

[50] David Tittensor, *The House of Service: The Gülen Movement and Islam's Third Way* (New York: Oxford University Press, 2014).

[51] Agai, 'The Gülen Movement's Islamic Ethic of Education'.

[52] Ebaugh, *The Gülen Movement: A Sociological Analysis of a Civic Movement Rooted in Moderate Islam*.

Further, an important part of undertaking *hizmet* for the teachers, like the pilgrims of Tablighi Jama'at, is sacrifice. Teachers, when they travel abroad often do so for a reduced wage compared to what could be earned if they remained in Turkey, as the schools, particularly in their start-up phase, have limited income streams. Indeed, of schools in both Central Asia and Afghanistan, teachers reported that they either forwent their salaries for a time or donated part of their salaries back to the school so that it could continue to run, for the schools often provided a scholarship stream and subsidies to enable students from lower socio-economic brackets to attend.[53] Moreover, the teachers often went above and beyond the normal requirements and provided additional tuition after hours to help the students succeed in their studies. As Yusuf Doger, a student from a Gülen school in Australia recounted: 'Our teachers stayed back after school and held special classes on weekends … I know if it were not for them I would not have gotten such a high score'[54]. This is because Gülen actively counsels that people of service are those:

> Preferring the sacred cause over all worldly and animal desires … seeking happiness, not in material or even spiritual pleasures, but in the happiness and well-being of others; never seeking to obtain any posts or positions; and preferring oneself to others in taking on work but preferring others to oneself in receiving wages – these are the essentials of this sacred way of serving the truth.[55]

Thus, in the same vein as the Tablighi pilgrims the act of conveying the message is reward enough for their endeavours. They do not seek monetary gain from their activities. Rather, the chief objective is to both bring spirituality to non-Muslims and to return Muslims to the community of believers who will then take up the mantle after them, and for some the lifestyle they offer is precisely what they were looking for. For example, the dedication and sacrifices displayed by the teachers leads students to want to follow the lifestyle presented. Indeed, it moved Yusuf Doger, the dux of Işık College[56] in 2008, to want to become a teacher so that he could give back to other students in the way the teachers gave to him and he began

---

53 David Tittensor, *The House of Service: The Gülen Movement and Islam's Third Way*.

54 Çemen Polat, 'Gülen Inspired Schools in Australia and Their Funding', in *The Gülen Hizmet Movement and its Transnational Activities: Case Studies of Altruistic Activism in Contemporary Islam*, ed. Sophia Pandya and Nancy Elizabeth Gallagher (Boca Raton: BrownWalker Press, 2012), 175.

55 Fethullah Gülen, *Pearls of Wisdom* (Somerset, N.J.: The Light, 2005), 104.

56 The School in 2013 changed its name to Sirius College. The name change from Isik which means light and illumination in Turkish, was changed to Sirius, after the star, as it is seen as better reflecting the multicultural base of the school. *Northern Weekly* 'When Isik became Sirius about a new name' (2013) http://www.northernweekly.com.au/story/1382480/when-isik-became-sirius-about-new-name/ (accessed 7 March 2014).

to tutor students in junior classes at his old high school for free.[57] The principal of Işık, in an interview with the *Hume Leader*, feels that this behaviour is driven by the sense community that is derived from the teachers mentoring practices.[58] Thus, we are again confronted with a different sensibility that is not about improving their personal material wealth or that of others, but rather about behaving in a way that is directed towards the well-being of others through improving their capacity to function through the provision of education and a particular spiritual outlook on life; one that is driven by a sense of community.

Concluding Thoughts

It is important to note that I am not advocating rampant and unchecked proselytism. Rather, through the above discussion and examples from the Muslim world – which is much maligned – I simply wish to convey that we need to keep a more open mind to the value that religious organizations bring to the development sector, particularly in relation to their own faith communities. As can be seen from the brief case studies of Tablighi Jama'at and the Gülen Movement, they operate in very different ways to their secular counterparts and strive to provide people with many of the things that traditional development strategies overlook. Namely, they provide them with community, solidarity, faith and purpose, all of which lend themselves to social and psychological well-being, which is not necessarily achieved simply through improved material and financial means. Basically, both provide alternative lifestyles or sensibilities that are very much focused on individual development and could complement more traditional aid practice, as it goes some of the way to rectifying the missing person factor inherent in economic aid.

References

ACFID. 'Code of Conduct' (2010). http://www.acfid.asn.au/code-of-conduct/files/code-of-conduct.

Agai, Bekim. 'The Gülen Movement's Islamic Ethic of Education'. In *Turkish Islam and the Secular State: The Gülen Movement*, edited by M. Hakan Yavuz and John L. Esposito. Syracuse, N.Y.: Syracuse University Press, 2003.

Ali, Jan. 'Islamic Revivalism: A Study of the Tablighi Jamaat in Sydney'. Unpublished PhD Thesis, University of New South Wales, 2006.

———. 'Islamic Revivalism: The Case of the Tablighi Jamaat'. *Journal of Muslim Minority Affairs* 23, no. 1 (2003): 173.

[57] Polat, 'Gülen Inspired Schools in Australia and Their Funding'.

[58] Kelly Sammut 'Isik tops study list' *Hume Leader* 23 June, 2009.

Alkire, Sabina. 'Dimensions of Human Development'. *World Development* 30, no. 2 (2002): 181–205.

Alterman, Jon B., and Karin Von Hippel. *Understanding Islamic Charities*. Washington, D.C.: Center for Strategic and International Studies, 2007.

Bellion-Jourdan, Jerome. 'Islamic Relief Organizations: Between "Islamism" and "Humanitarianism"'. *ISIM Newsletter* 5, no. 1 (2000): 15.

Benthall, Jonathan, and Jerome Bellion-Jourdan. *The Charitable Crescent: The Politics of Aid in the Muslim World.* London: I.B. Taurus, 2003.

Bornstein, Erica. *The Spirit of Development: Protestant NGOs, Morality and Economics in Zimbabwe*. Religion in History, Society & Culture. London; New York: Routledge, 2003.

Burr, J. Millard, and Robert O. Collins. *Alms for Jihad: Charity and Terrorism in the Islamic World.* New York: Cambridge University Press, 2006.

Clarke, Gerard. 'Faith-Based Organisations and International Development: An Overview'. In *Development, Civil Society and Faith-Based Organisations*, edited by Gerard Clarke and Michael Jennings. New York: Palgrave Macmillan, 2008.

Diamond, Sara *Spiritual Warfare: The Politics of the Christian Right* Boston: South End Press, 1989.

———. *Roads to Dominion: Right-Wing Movements and Political Power in the United States* New York: The Guilford Press, 1995.

Ebaugh, Helen Rose. *The Gülen Movement: A Sociological Analysis of a Civic Movement Rooted in Moderate Islam*. New York: Springer, 2010.

Gaborieau, Marc. 'The Transformation of Tablighi Jama'at into a Transnational Movement'. In *Travellers in Faith: Studies of the Tablighi Jama'at as a Transnational Islamic Movement for Faith Renewal*, edited by Muhammad Khalid Masud. Boston: Brill, 2000.

Ghandour, Abdel-Rahman. "Humanitarianism, Islam and the West: Contest or Cooperation?," *Humanitarian Exchange Magazine* no. 25 (2003). http://www.odihpn.org/humanitarian-exchange-magazine/issue-25/humanitarianism-is lam-and-the-west-contest-or-cooperation.

Gülen, Fethullah. *Pearls of Wisdom*. Somerset, N.J.: The Light, 2005.

———. *Toward a Gobal Cvilization of Love & Tolerance*. Somerset, N.J.: Light, Inc., 2004.

Hoffstaedter, G. *Modern Muslim Identities: Negotiating Religion and Ethnicity in Malaysia*. Copenhagen: Nordic Institute of Asian Studies, 2011.

Johnson, Todd M. 'Christianity in Global Context: Trends and Statistics'. (n/d). http://www.pewforum.org/uploadedfiles/Topics/Issues/Politics_and_Elections /051805-global-christianity.pdf.

Levitt, Matthew. *Hamas: Politics, Charity, and Terrorism in the Service of Jihad.* New Haven: Yale University Press, 2006.

Liow, Joseph Chinyong. 'Islamic Education in Southern Thailand: Negotiating Islam, Identity, and Modernity'. In *Making Modern Muslims: The Politics of*

Islamic Education in Southeast Asia, edited by Robert W. Hefner. Honolulu: University of Hawaii Press, 2009.

Metcalf, Barbara. 'Tablighi Jama'at and Women'. In *Travellers in Faith: Studies of the Tablighi Jama'at as a Transnational Islamic Movement for Faith Renewal*, edited by Muhammad Khalid Masud. Boston: Brill, 2000.

———. '"Traditionalist" Islamic Activism: Deoband, Tablighis, and Talibs'. *ISIM Paper*, no. 4 (2002): 1–24.

Mirakhor, Abbas, and Hossein Askari. *Islam and the Path to Human and Economic Development*. 1st ed. New York: Palgrave Macmillan, 2010.

Narayan, Deepa, Raj Patel, Kai Schafft, Anne Rademacher, and Sarah Koch-Schulte. *Can Anyone Hear Us? Voices of the Poor*. New York: Published by Oxford University Press for the World Bank, 2000.

Noor, Farish A. *Islam on the Move: The Tablighi Jama'at in Southeast Asia*. Amsterdam: Amsterdam University Press, 2012.

Northern Weekly, 'When Isik became Sirius about a new name' *Northern Weekly* (2013) Published electronically 25 March http://www.northernweekly.com.au/story/1382480/when-isik-became-sirius-about-new-name/.

Nussbaum, Martha Craven. *Women and Human Development: The Capabilities Approach*. Cambridge; New York: Cambridge University Press, 2000.

Petersen, Marie Juul. 'For Humanity or for the Umma? Ideologies of Aid in Four Transnational Muslim NGOs'. Unpublished Doctoral Thesis, University of Copenhagen, 2011.

———.'Islamizing Aid: Transnational Muslim NGOs after 9.11'. *VOLUNTAS: International Journal of Voluntary and Nonprofit Organizations* 23, no. 1 (2012): 126–55.

Pew Forum on Religion & Public Life. 'The Future of the Global Muslim Population: Projections for 2010–2030'. Washington DC: Pew Research Center, 2011.

———. 'Global Christianity: A Report on the Size and Distribution of the World's Christian Population'. Washington DC: Pew Research Center, 2011.

———. 'The Global Religious Landscape: A Report on the Size and Distribution of the World's Major Religious Groups as of 2010'. Washington DC: Pew Research Center, 2012.

Polat, Çemen. 'Gülen Inspired Schools in Australia and Their Funding'. In *The Gülen Hizmet Movement and Its Transnational Activities: Case Studies of Altruistic Activism in Contemporary Islam*, edited by Sophia Pandya and Nancy Elizabeth Gallagher. Boca Raton: BrownWalker Press, 2012.

Ray, Anil Baran. 'Communal Attitudes to British Policy: The Case of the Partition of Bengal 1905'. *Social Scientist* 6, no. 5 (1977): 34–46.

Sammut, Kelly 'Isik tops study list' *Hume Leader* 23 June, 2009.

Sen, Amartya. 'Capability and Wellbeing'. In *The Quality of Life*, edited by Martha Craven Nussbaum and Amartya Sen. New York: Oxford University Press, 1993.

Sikand, Yoginder. 'Muslim Reactions to the Shuddhi Campaign in Early Twentieth Century North India'. *The Milli Gazette*, January 15, 2001.

Sugden, Robert. 'Welfare, Resources, and Capabilities: A Review [Inequality Reexamined]'. *Journal of Economic Literature* 31, no. 4 (1993): 1947–62.

Talib, Mohammad. 'Tablighis in the Making of Muslim Identity'. In *Islam, Communities and the Nation: Muslim Identities in South Asia and Beyond*, edited by Mushirul Hasan. New Delhi: Manohar Publishers & Distributors, 1998.

Tittensor, David. *The House of Service: The Gülen Movement and Islam's Third Way*. New York: Oxford University Press, 2014.

UNDP. *Human Development Report*. New York: Oxford University Press, 1990.

Wiktorowicz, Quintan, and Suha Taji Farouki. 'Islamic NGOs and Muslim Politics: A Case from Jordan'. *Third World Quarterly* 21, no. 4 (2000): 685–99.

Chapter 3
Islamic International Aid Flows for Poverty Alleviation

Matthew Clarke

Introduction

Islam is based upon the direct revelation of Allah's word through the Supreme Prophet Muhammad. The word 'Islam' is based on the root *s-l-m*, which has two connotations – peace and surrender. Thus, Islam is the peace found when one surrenders one's life to Allah.[1] Islam has four basic theological premises. At its base, there is one God, Allah. The second premise is that Allah created the earth and through this act of creation all that is created is good. The third belief is that each one of us has a soul that is fashioned by Allah. As we are created by Allah, we must first give thanks to Allah for this existence, but also surrender ourselves to him. Finally, there is a judgment day, at which time we are held to account for our earthly existence. Adherents of Islam are known as Muslims, and are the third 'people of the book', sharing a common Abrahamic ancestry with Judaism and Christianity.

There are 1.3 billion Muslims worldwide (20 per cent of the global population) with Islam being the state religion of 25 countries. Nearly 70 per cent of all Muslims live in Asia (including the Middle East), while just over a quarter live in Africa. Indonesia's 200 million Muslims make it the country with the highest number of adherents to this religion. Only a small percentage of Europe's population are Muslim (around 2.5 per cent), and there are even fewer in North America (0.5 per cent of the population), Latin America (0.15 per cent) and Oceania (0.05 per cent).[2]

Within Islam there is a close affiliation between faith and action. The Arabic term for righteousness is *birr*, which also translates as social justice and love. Therefore a righteous Muslim is also a Muslim who loves others and seeks social justice for the poor and disempowered.

> Righteousness is not to turn your faces towards the East and the West; the righteousness is he who believes in Allah, the Last Day, the angels, the Book and the Prophets; who gives of his money, in spite of loving it, to the near of kin, the

---

[1] H. Smith, *The World's Religions* (New York: HarperOne, 1991).

[2] Joanne O'Brien and Martin Palmer, *The Atlas of Religion* (Berkeley: University of California Press, 2007).

> orphans, the needy, the wayfarers and the beggars, and for the freeing of slaves; who performs the prayers and pays the alms-tax. Such are those who keep their pledges once they have made them, and endure patiently privation, adversity and times of fighting. (Qur'an 2: 177)

In this sense, Islam requires more than faith; it requires action based upon that faith. Given the very practical nature of Islam,[3] there are very clear teachings on the charitable expectations of Muslims. Much of these charitable expectations do involve significant alms-giving – known as *zakat* (the poor-due) – directed at aiding those in need. While these private acts of giving have primarily focused on addressing local deprivation of neighbours or family members, the increased globalization of the last century has resulted in an increased spread of charitable flows to include international poverty alleviation. Thus, it is not surprising that, in concert with the rise of international flows of financial assistance from wealthy Western nations to less wealthy countries, similar flows are now increasingly originating in what might be termed Muslim-majority countries and being provided to low-income nations.

Understanding the donor motivations of these non-traditional donors is equally important as understanding the efficacy of their aid. In addition to increasing aid from China and Brazil, aid flows from the Muslim-majority world are becoming increasingly significant. This chapter reviews the history of this aid and its particular characteristics to shed light on this development. For, like other non-traditional aid flows, there is a level of unease amongst traditional Western donors concerning this aid on account of the limited understanding of its motivation, and the fear that it is encroaching on what they might consider their own spheres of influence. This chapter will also consider the value of aid flows and its characteristics, noting, of course, that this data is not as complete or accessible as that of aid originating from traditional western donors. This chapter therefore will consider some explanation as to the motivations of these aid flows as well as some description of how these aid flows compare and contrast to that of traditional donors. Consideration will be given to both aid that originates from Muslim-majority governments as well as aid flows through private Muslim-based non-governmental organizations (NGOs). The next section will consider the theological impetus of charitable giving by Muslims. This will be followed in turn by a discussion of wider international aid flows, and the final section will examine Muslim aid flows, both private and public.

Islamic Action: Charity and Development

In 570 CE the great prophet Muhammad was born into a chaotic and strife-torn society in which rolling tribal battles were on-going, living standards were

[3] See Matthew Clarke, *Development and Religion: Theology and Practice* (Cheltenham, UK; Northampton, MA, USA: Edward Elgar, 2011).

low, and it was common to assault neighbours to secure food and other material comforts. As descendants of Abraham, belief in *Allah* (the God of Abraham) did exist during this time, however there had also grown alongside this belief a rise in the worship of a pantheon of other gods. These gods largely were called upon to offer protection against the terrors of the desert which Mohammed and other descendants of Abraham inhabited. While Mohammed struggled to live a righteous life in these circumstances, it was not until he was aged around 40 that Allah sent an angel to tell him to proclaim his greatness to the world (Qur'an 96: 1–3).

Allah revealed to the illiterate Muhammad his infallible revelation over two decades. These revelations were retold by Muhammad and transcribed and collated. These collated words are known as the Qur'an. Muslims believe the Qur'an is divine – it is Allah's direct word, not spoken through prophets but spoken directly to the ultimate prophet, Muhammad.[4] In addition to Allah's word in the Qur'an, Muhammad's own words, deeds, and silence on issues, were recorded in the hadith, which is also revered as a sacred teaching (though having slightly less authority than the Qur'an). Built upon the basic theological premises of monotheism, divine creation, having a soul, and judgement day, there is also a significant focus on providing practical expressions of how these four premises translate to living a righteous life. Based firstly on the Qur'an and secondly upon the hadith, local clergy (*khatib*) do assume responsibility for teaching and delivering moral education within Islam. These sermons generally address issues such as 'justice, equality, obligations towards the family, respect for parents, asking forgiveness, observing modesty, the reconciliation of estranged friends'.[5]

The Islamic teaching that is most relevant to poverty alleviation is that of equality.[6] This sense of equality is clearly evident in its approach to the allocation of scarce resources. Therefore, it is argued that Islam is 'directed towards the creation of a meaningful and positive equality among human beings. As such, the Islamic purpose cannot be realized until genuine freedom to human beings is restored and freedom from all forms of exploitation – social, spiritual, political and economic – assured'.[7] Just before his death, Muhammad made it clear that all Muslims are equal and deserving of respect: 'You know that every Muslim is the brother of another Muslim. You are all equal'. The very marked shift in social relations during Muhammad's rule is a clear indication of how powerful this sense of equality was. Moreover, the Qur'an specifically relates the neglect of the poor to the neglect of religion. 'Have you observed him who denies religion? That is he who repels the orphan, and urges not the feeding of the needy' (Qur'an 107: 1–3).

4 Smith, *The World's Religions*.

5 F. Peters, 'Broadcasting the World: Prophet, Preacher and Saint', in *The Meaning of Life in the World Religions*, ed. Joseph Runzo and Nancy M. Martin (Oxford: Oneworld, 2001), 101.

6 William E. Shepard, *Introducing Islam* (London ; New York: Routledge, 2009).

7 Fazlur Rahman, 'Some Reflections on the Reconstruction of Muslim Society in Pakistan', *Islamic Studies* 6, no. 2 (1967): 103.

Fighting for the poor is considered as fighting for Allah's cause and is equivalent to fasting or prayer.[8] The importance of meeting basic needs was very evident to the desert dwelling Arabs of this time. Water, food and shelter are necessary for subsistence and so access to these goods was vital. It was also evident that people had to work hard to be able to gain these goods. Life was hard and living conditions difficult; hard work was required to survive.

In this way, economic life is recognized as a central component to existence. Moreover, economic participation is considered not a necessary evil, but as simply necessary. No moral judgements are made regarding participating in economic activities. If anything, the implicit assumption is that one cannot exclude oneself from the economy and economic participation. Both the Qur'an and hadith are very clear in how this free flow of wealth must be supported. Thus, Islamic social teaching supports entrepreneurial activity, the profit motive and economic competition. Those who work harder should be rewarded for this hard work and be free to enjoy the material goods this brings. However, the Qur'an also calls for frugality, that is, to avoid extravagance. 'Give the kinsman his due, and the needy, and the wayfarer, and squander not [your wealth] wantonly. Lo! the squanderers were ever brothers of the devils, and the devil was ever ungrateful to his Lord' (Qur'an 17: 26–7). There must be a balance struck so that one enjoys the fruits of one's toil without conspicuous consumption. Moreover, money is simply a tool to facilitate this simple enjoyment; it should not be an overriding driver of action. This frugality is also expressed in how Muslims are required to respond to those in need, as in Islam there is also a need for compassion towards those less well off. Certainly, teaching contained within the Qur'an directly resulted in improvement in the status of women and other disadvantaged groups in society, including slaves and the poor.[9]

This compassion within Islam is actually formalized as an annual charitable donation. Along with accepting Allah as the one true God, saying prayers five times a day, observing Ramadan (the month of fasting) and undertaking a pilgrimage to Mecca, the giving of *zakat* is one of the five obligatory aspects of Islam. Islam accepts that distribution of wealth will not be equal. 'We have apportioned among them their livelihood in the life of the world, and raised some of them above others in rank so that some of them take labour from others' (Qur'an 43: 32). So while it does not set out to achieve the goal of complete equity, it does require its adherents to respond to this inequality. This response is mandated through the payment of 2.5 per cent (or one fortieth) of total wealth. While this amount may not appear overly large, it is set against one's entire wealth, not simply income. Moreover, payment of this tax must not simply be a financial transaction made without thought. If the reasons for fulfilling this obligation are not the right reasons it cannot be considered to have satisfied the obligation of prayer as set out in the Qur'an (53: 34). However,

[8] Oliver Leaman, 'Money', in *The Qur'an: An Encyclopedia*, ed. Oliver Leaman (New York: Routledge, 2005).

[9] Abdullah Saeed, *Interpreting the Qur'an: Towards a Contemporary Approach* (Abingdon, England; New York: Routledge, 2006).

having said that, it is clear in Islam that acts of charity should also remain at reasonable levels and themselves should not be grandiose displays. Moderation is therefore all important for both charity and enjoying the fruits of one's hard work. Thus, the Qur'an (25: 67) approves those 'who, when they spend, are neither prodigal nor grudging; and there is always a clear line between the two'.

Rather than being used to support religious institutions, as can be found within tithing associated with Christianity or merit-making associated with Buddhism, this *zakat* is directly used to improve the material living standards of the poor. Those eligible to receive this charity include: the needy, whether they be Muslim or not; the extremely poor, whether they be Muslim or not; those employed to collect and distribute the *zakat* itself; those who may be converted to Islam; those who are captive; those in debt; and those travelling, whether they be Muslim or not. Without doubt, the Qur'an is very clear as to the protection of the poor and acts of charity.

As discussed previously, the provision of this charitable giving has predominantly been to those in need at the local level (indeed, a number of chapters contained within this book do consider how domestically raised Islamic charitable aid is being spent in those very same countries). This was simply a matter of practicality, whereby the provision of assistance was largely constrained by locality. For much of its millennium and a half history, this aid has had a very limited area of distribution, centred around the actual giver. Such a constrained focus was perfectly reasonable throughout this time, however the process of globalization from the middle of the last century has widened not only our awareness of deprivation experienced in other parts of the globe, but has also enhanced our ability to communicate with and transfer funds to these once distant places. Given this focus on assisting the poor, and the lessening of constraints around addressing poverty in non-local areas, it is not surprising that there are now increasing international financial flows from those with greater wealth to those with lesser wealth.

International Aid Flows

International aid flows from wealthy to poorer countries date their modern incarnation to the reconstruction of Europe following World War Two. This injection of (primarily) trans-Atlantic capital became known as the Marshall Plan and quite quickly enhanced the economic recovery of those war-damaged countries. The success of this response coupled with American political expansion culminated in a rapid rise of capital flowing from developed to developing countries. The motivation for this move to provide foreign assistance to developing countries is best illustrated by President Truman's Inauguration Speech in 1949:

> More than half the people of the world are living in conditions approaching misery. Their food is inadequate. They are victims of disease. Their economic

> life is primitive and stagnant. Their poverty is a handicap and a threat both to them and to more prosperous areas … Our aim should be to help the free peoples of the world, through their own efforts, to produce more food, more clothing, more materials for housing, and more mechanical power to lighten their burdens.[10]

Following their own recovery, other (Western) nations soon joined the United States in addressing global poverty alleviation. Nearly seven decades later, official development assistance (ODA) provided by 'traditional' donors was valued at USD134 billion in 2012. These traditional donors comprise 23 Western nations: Australia, Austria, Belgium, Canada, Denmark, Finland, France, Germany, Greece, Ireland, Italy, Japan, Korea, Luxembourg, Netherlands, New Zealand, Norway, Portugal, Spain, Sweden, Switzerland, United Kingdom, and United States. This group of nations are collectively known as the Development Assistance Committee (DAC) and co-ordinate their roles as aid donors through the Organization of Economic Cooperation and Development (OECD). As such, data on these aid flows is well reported and analysed.[11]

A primary focus of ODA from these nations has been the alleviation of human suffering and the humanitarian principle has been central to the commitment to and allocation of these funds. However, it is naive to attribute these substantial aid flows solely to this altruistic motivation. As President Truman also made clear in the Inauguration Speech quoted above, there was an equally pragmatic reason for providing aid funds, which was to directly combat the (then) spread of communist ideology within the developing world.

In the interceding seven decades the consideration of donor national interests has remained central to (and has perhaps dominated) humanitarian needs in the allocation of ODA. As Feeny and McGillivray state: 'DAC bilateral aid donors consider *both* recipient need *and* donor interests in determining the amounts of aid allocated over time to almost all the recipients under specific consideration'.[12] The OECD defines official development assistance as those funds which, as their primary purpose, promote the economic development and welfare of developing countries. Moreover, these funds must also have a concessional character, that

---

[10] H. Truman, 'Inaugural Address, January 20', (1949), http://www.presidency.ucsb.edu/ws/index.php?pid=13282. This commitment to international assistance was also reiterated by Truman's successor, President Eisenhower, in his 1953 Inauguration Speech.

[11] See http://www.oecd.org/dac/stats/.

[12] Simon Feeny and Mark McGillivray, 'What Determines Bilateral Aid Allocations? Evidence From Time Series Data', *Review of Development Economics* 12, no. 3 (2008): 522. Early work in this field found that donors' needs were prioritized in allocation determination. For example Maizels and Nissanke argued that 'bilateral aid allocations are made … solely … in support of donors' perceived foreign economic, political and security interests'. Alfred Maizels and Machiko K. Nissanke, 'Motivations for Aid to Developing Countries', *World Development* 12, no. 9 (1984): 891.

is, they must in part be a grant or discounted loan to a developing country. There is no requirement that these funds be allocated in particular ways or that humanitarian needs be prioritized over donor national interests.

This point is made to illustrate that aid flows – as defined above – that may be provided from countries other than the 23 members of the DAC can be considered quite 'legitimate' even if the reasons for allocation do not align with those of traditional DAC donors. These non-traditional donors are increasing their aid flows and in some instances 'challenging' the dominance of traditional donors, giving rise to a level of competition between donors perhaps not seen since the end of the Cold War.[13]

Muslim Aid: Donors and NGOs

Motivations for providing aid differ between all donors. While the two primary explanatory drivers are national interest and humanitarian need, it is not the case that these two drivers are mutually exclusive. Indeed, it is more accurate to describe allocation decisions by donors as being along a continuum that stretches between these motivations. Indeed, it is further the case that allocation decisions by donors will be continuously shifting along this continuum in response to both changes in national circumstances and recipient needs. Such variations in donor determinations result in volatility in aid flows.[14]

Understanding Muslim aid flows demands acknowledgement that aid from these countries has occurred over a long period of time and, like DAC-donors, is neither driven solely by self-interest nor by altruistic responses to need in recipient countries. Understanding these aid flows also demands acceptance that Muslim-majority aid-donors' national interests are not naturally aligned to the set of national interests that could be ascribed to DAC-donors. For example, Bellers shows that Saudi Arabia has provided development assistance since at least 1973 (in line with the significant funds made available through petroleum exports). Over this time, the primary focus on Saudi aid has been the promotion of mainly non-revolutionary Arab and Islamic countries, and is therefore highly politicized. Bellers also notes that, in addition to aid flows from the Saudi government, there is also a quantity of aid that is provided by the Saudi Royal Family. However, the actual quantity and purpose of this aid is not publically known.[15] Utilizing econometric techniques more familiarly used to understand traditional DAC-donors' aid allocation

---

[13] See for example S. Wilson, C. Pan, and M Clarke, 'New Aid, New Leadership? Implications of Increasing Chinese Aid to PNG and Melanesi', *ADRI Working Paper Series* (Geelong: Deakin University, forthcoming).

[14] See Matthew Clarke, Tim Fry, and Sandra Mihajilo, 'Aid Allocation and Volatility to Small Island States', *Pacific Economic Bulletin* 23, no. 2 (2008): 179–202.

[15] J. Bellers, 'Aiding Their Moslim Friends: Saudi Arabia's Development Policy'', *Development and Cooperation*, no. 4 (1993): 28–9.

decision-making, Neumeyer examined the factors determining the pattern of aid allocation by Arab countries and multilateral agencies using Heckman's two-step estimator. He found that countries that are poor, Arab, Sub-Saharan African and Islamic, as well as countries that vote similarly to Saudi Arabia in the UN General Assembly, were statistically significantly more likely to receive aid. Among the countries chosen to receive aid, the more populous Arab and Islamic countries receive a greater share of the total aid from Arab countries. Thus, Neumeyer finds the existence of a preferential treatment based on Arab solidarity.[16] A similar consideration of Muslim aid is provided by Villanger, who examines Muslim aid flows and aid policies, and contrasts them with the broad picture of Western practice in these areas and then assesses whether Muslim and Western aid can complement each other. He shows that Muslim aid is very generous and at the same time very volatile. Muslim aid simultaneously supports donors' political, commercial, and religious interests. He also recommends a number of ways in which Western donors can learn from Muslim-majority donors and how both parties can better cooperate with each other.[17]

Aid flows from Muslim majority countries are not as significant in total value as those from traditional DAC-donors. In absolute terms, the United States provides the largest amount of official development assistance of all countries. Other significant donors include EU Institutions, the United Kingdom, Germany, Japan, France, and the Netherlands (see Table 3.1).

Table 3.1 Top 10 ODA Donors (constant 2010 USD Million)

Ranking	Five-year period (2006–2010)	Ten-year period (2001–2010)
1	United States 132,255	United States 227,843
2	EU Institutions 60,676	EU Institutions 110,190
3	Germany 52,937	Japan 102,018
4	United Kingdom 50,508	Germany 89,952
5	Japan 48,699	France 82,668
6	France 47,826	United Kingdom 82,474

[16] Eric Neumayer, 'What Factors Determine the Allocation of Aid by Arab Countries and Multilateral Agencies?', *Journal of Development Studies* 39, no. 4 (2003): 134–47.

[17] E. Villanger, 'Arab Foreign Aid: Disbursement Patterns, Aid Policies and Motives', *CMI Report No.2* (Bergen: Chr Michelsen Institute, 2007).

Table 3.1 Continued

7	Netherlands 29,877	Netherlands 54,958
8	Spain 26,398	Canada 40,303
9	Canada 23,312	Spain 39,968
10	Norway 20,292	Sweden 37,912

Source: GHA. 'Global Humanitarian Assistance Report', 2012.

The top-ranking Muslim-majority countries for ODA are Saudi Arabia and UAE. During the period 2006 to 2010, for example, Saudi Arabia provided USD 15,377 million (2010 constant). In terms of Muslim-majority, there are a number that do feature within the top 30 donors of humanitarian assistance (as compared to total ODA). These include Saudi Arabia, the United Arab Emirates and Turkey (see Table 3.2).

Table 3.2 Top Muslim-Majority Countries in Top 30 of Humanitarian Assistance (constant 2010 USD Million) – Top 30 Ranking in Brackets

2006	**2007**	**2008**	**2009**	**2010**
Saudi Arabia (17) 131	Saudi Arabia (14) 212	Saudi Arabia (8) 566	UAE (12) 353	Saudi Arabia (15) 256
UAE (23) 44	UAE (22) 45	UAE (20) 110	Saudi Arabia (20) 82	UAE (20) 114
Kuwait (26) 24	Turkey (27) 11	Kuwait (21) 96	Kuwait (24) 40	Turkey (22) 61
Turkey (30) 11	Kuwait (28) 11	Kazakhstan (30) 10	Qatar (30) 13	Kazakhstan (30) 25

Source: GHA. 'Global Humanitarian Assistance Report', 2012.

It is evident from Table 3.2 that, as Villanger observed, there is a fair degree of volatility in these humanitarian aid flows. For example, during the five-year period 2006 to 2010, humanitarian aid from Saudi Arabia fluctuated from a low of

USD 131 million (2010 constant) to USD 566 million (2010). In terms of rankings, this volatility of aid saw Saudi Arabia's ranking also shift from the seventeenth largest donor to the eighth largest donor over this five-year period. Similarly, ODA from the UAE rose as high as USD 353 million (2010 constant) from USD45 million (2010 constant) in just two years (2007 to 2009).

Muslim-majority countries do feature in the top rankings of recipient countries. For the five-year period 2006 to 2010, Muslim-majority countries comprised half of the top 10 recipient nations in terms of ODA (see Table 3.3). These countries include Afghanistan, Iraq, Pakistan, Palestine/OPT, and Sudan. Non-Muslim majority countries that are also commonly found within the top 10 of ODA recipient nations include Ethiopia, Vietnam, Tanzania, India and Mozambique.

Table 3.3 Top Muslim-Majority Countries in Top 10 Receiving ODA (constant 2010 USD Million) – Top 10 Ranking in Brackets

2006	2007	2008	2009	2010
Iraq (1) 5,964	Afghanistan (1) 5,067	Afghanistan (1) 4,850	Afghanistan (1) 6,330	Afghanistan (1) 6.369
Afghanistan (2) 3.252	Iraq (2) 4,563	Iraq (2) 3,299	Iraq (5) 2,838	Pakistan (3) 2,999
Pakistan (3) 2,425	Pakistan (5) 2,311	Sudan (5) 2,523	Palestine/OPT (6) 2,829	Palestine/OPT (8) 2,517
Sudan (4) 2,246	Sudan (7) 2,163	Palestine/OPT (6) 2,390	Pakistan (7) 2,804	Iraq (9) 2,164
Palestine/OPT (10) 1,531	Palestine/OPT (9) 1,767	Bangladesh (9) 2,007	Sudan (9) 2,384	Sudan (10) 2,046

Source: GHA. 'Global Humanitarian Assistance Report', 2012.

In a similar vein, Muslim-majority countries also feature prominently in rankings of funds received for humanitarian assistance. Sudan, Pakistan, Palestine/OPT, Iraq and Afghanistan rank alongside non-Muslim countries such as Ethiopia, Democratic Republic of Congo, Zimbabwe and Sri Lanka as the top-ranking recipients of humanitarian aid.

The fact that these Muslim-majority countries do receive considerable funding relative to other developing countries, combined with the fact that Muslim-majority countries rank amongst the top 30 donors – but in the lower part of this ranking – does suggest that much of the aid received by Muslim-majority aid does not originate in Muslim-majority countries. Of course, this is not entirely unsurprising given that there are few Muslim-majority countries who are donors – but it does suggest that the divide between Muslim and non-Muslim is not a deterrent to ODA flows to Muslim-majority countries. Indeed, De Cordier suggests that Muslims or those having Muslim backgrounds are 'over represented' in terms of aid received in relation to the global population. For example, while Muslims or those from a Muslim background make up just over 20 per cent of the world's population, (around 1.3 billion people), they do receive more than a quarter of humanitarian aid, and nearly half of all UNHCR beneficiaries are Muslim or from a Muslim background, while nearly 45 per cent of World Food Programme beneficiaries are also Muslim or from a Muslim background.[18]

In addition to donor-provided Muslim aid, there is also Muslim-inspired non-governmental organizations (NGOs, or perhaps more correctly, faith-based organizations (FBOs). Unlike donor aid, the determinant of aid allocation of these NGOs is more focused on responding to humanitarian needs. In the late 1970s, in response to the humanitarian consequences of famines in Africa and the war in Afghanistan, many Islamic aid organizations came into existence.[19] The appearance of these organizations was claimed to be specifically rooted in Islamic faith and they were a reflection of 'Islamic solidarity'. As a result, and more particularly early on in their existence, these Islamic NGOs did give preference to development interventions whose primary beneficiaries were Muslim communities. Unease regarding such preferences or biases reflects a 'naivety about all forms of organised charity and aid – Islamic, Western, and other'.[20] Aid flows bereft of any self-interest or political influence is, according to Benthall and Bellion-Jourdan, a universal ideal that is not practice in reality.[21] There is of course a significant number of Muslim NGOs that now subscribe to a policy of non-differentiation in aid delivery – which does not conflict with aid allocation still having dual determination of national interest and humanitarian need. Indeed, the provision of Islamic charity to non-Muslims may very directly serve certain political purposes.[22]

Perhaps more so than aid originating from Muslim-majority countries, aid flows from Muslim-based or Muslim-inspired NGOs is difficult to assess

---

18 Bruno De Cordier, 'Faith-Based Aid, Globalisation and the Humanitarian Frontline: An Analysis of Western-Based Muslim Aid Organisations', *Disasters* 33, no. 4 (2009): 608–28.

19 Jerome Bellion-Jourdan, 'Islamic Relief Organizations: Between "Islamism" and "Humanitarianism"', *ISIM Newsletter* 5, no. 1 (2000): 15.

20 Jonathan Benthall and Jerome Bellion-Jourdan, *The Charitable Crescent: The Politics of Aid in the Muslim World* (London: I.B. Taurus, 2003), 23.

21 Ibid.

22 Abu El Ela Mady, 'How do Islamic Organisations See Their Social Role? An Islamic Perspective (from Egypt)', in *Religion, Politics, Conflict and Humanitarian Action Faith-Based Organisations as Political, Humanitarian or Religious Actors: Proceedings of the Workshop, May 18–19 2005, Geneva, Switzerland* (Graduate Institute of International Studies, 2005).

accurately (though this is also true to some extent of the wider NGO sector). This is partly due to the large amount of funds provided for charitable purposes as required by Muslim doctrine but is also due to the sheer number of Muslim charities. For example, there are around 1,500 registered charities regulated by the Charity Commission for England and Wales alone. However, more than half have annual budgets of less than £10,000. While much of these funds are used to address the needs of the poor close to home, many also do 'have charitable objectives including the relief of poverty overseas'.[23] There are of course larger Islamic NGOs that do have sizeable annual budgets approaching USD100 million per annum, including Muslim Aid, Islamic Relief, and the Aga Khan Foundation.[24]

While these substantial funds are often used to support 'development' projects that directly address the needs of the poor and are very similar to those projects funded and implemented by secular NGOs, Muslim NGOs do also provide assistance to the poor to assist with their religious duties. For example, Muslim Aid uses funds raised to facilitate participation of the poor in religious celebrations. Approximately 70 days following the end of Ramadan, Muslims celebrate the Eid-ul Adha to commemorate Abraham's obedience to God and his willingness to sacrifice his son. There are two aspects of this that Muslim Aid (UK) raises funds for. The first is for donors to purchase an Eid gift, which is a livelihood gift. Eid Gifts can be selected from the education, health, food and income generation sectors. The second is to donate funds to allow the slaughter of an animal in line with religious duties – known as the *qurbani*:

> Muslim Aid carries out sacrifices in over 47 of the poorest countries in the world, allowing you not only to fulfil your obligation but contribute to our wider goal of fighting poverty. For many, it is the first opportunity they get all year to taste meat, providing respite from the months of hunger they're forced to endure … To make the Eid gift of Qurbani last longer for families in certain countries, Muslim Aid cans the meat immediately after the animal is slaughtered. These are then distributed at times of need, allowing the meat to benefit the poor long after Eid.[25]

Such confluence of religious charitable giving and the use of it for religious purposes does suggest an advantage for Muslim NGOs in working in Muslim-majority countries or with Muslim communities. Benthall compares an Islamic NGO (Islamic Relief) and a Christian NGO (Norwegian Church Aid) to evaluate where there is a natural advantage to Islamic NGOs operating in Islamic contexts. Benthall found that this advantage does exist, with Islamic Relief being better

---

[23] M. Kroessin, 'Mapping UK Muslim Development NGOs', *Religions and Development Working Paper 30* (International Development Department: University of Birmingham, 2009), 7.

[24] Ibid.

[25] Muslim Aid, 'Muslim Aid's Qurbani Programme', http://www.muslimaid.org/index.php/what-we-do/qurbani/.

able to involve itself within the daily, religious, and tradition life of communities with whom it was working. In contrast, Norwegian Church Aid found it difficult to make a 'connection' with the local communities and whilst held in esteem by the communities in which they work, they were considered distant from the local population and unable to effectively bridge both religious and social divides. So evident was this inability to work effectively with the local Muslim community that in the case study examined by Benthall, Norwegian Church Aid withdrew.[26] De Cordier further explores the impact of 'religiosity' of NGOs operating in the humanitarian sector. De Cordier defines the operational context, where humanitarian actors are perceived by local communities and authorities have been key players in hidden religious and political agendas, as the 'humanitarian frontlines'. He suggests that whilst there are certain opportunities for religious NGOs operating on this frontline, equally there are limitations or constraints. Moreover, De Cordier argues that religious NGOs remain largely ambivalent towards both the potential advantages and risks.[27] In connection with Benthall's study, it is interesting to note therefore that successful relations between Islamic NGOs and the Muslim communities within which they work cannot be naturally assumed. Benthall also provides evidence in which other (Saudi-based) Islamic NGOs failed to effectively partner with local communities, which was primarily explained by the NGOs' seeking to 'correct' local Islamic doctrines and practices.[28] A more 'successful' model might be that identified in Kalimullah and Fraser which examines the work of three Islamic NGOs in Bangladesh: Rabitat Al-Alam al-Islam, Islam Prochar Samity, and the Raghikhali Islamic Centre. This examination looks at their organizational structures, the nature of their programmes and finances, and their external relationships. Kalimullah and Fraser show that these Islamic NGOs in Bangladesh were involved in preaching, charitable work, and development activities and were able to command both government and party support – should they need it.[29]

Public standing of Islamic NGOs is of importance as there is within the literature a level of suspicion regarding Islamic aid, especially that provided by Islamic NGOs utilizing charitable donations of *zakat*. Burr and Collins, for example, examine the work of certain Islamic NGOs purported to be supportive of terrorist activities in Sudan, the Balkans, Russia, Central Asia, Southeast Asia

---

[26] Jonathan Benthall, 'Islamic Aid in a North Malian Enclave', *Anthropology Today* 22, no. 4 (2006): 19–21.

[27] Bruno De Cordier, 'The 'Humanitarian Frontline', Development and Relief, and Religion: What Context, Which Threats and Which Opportunities?', *Third World Quarterly* 30, no. 4 (2009): 663–84; 'Faith-Based Aid, Globalisation at the Humanitarian Frontline: An Analysis of Western-Based Muslim Aid Organisations'.

[28] Benthall, 'Islamic Aid in a North Malian Enclave'.

[29] Nazmul A. Kalimullah and Caroline B. Fraser, 'Islamic Non-Government Organisations in Bangladesh with Reference to Three Case Studies', *Islamic Quarterly* 34, no. 2 (1990): 71–92.

and within Israel. They further make claims that these charities are undertaking the 'Islamization' of Europe and North America.[30] According to Kohlmann the practice of supporting terrorist organizations through Islamic NGOs goes back to the period of the Soviet-Afghan war. This financing model has been used from that time in different parts of the world.[31]

It would be inaccurate to characterize all Islamic NGOs as operating in similar ways. Examining two of the world's largest transnational Islamic NGOs – International Islamic Relief Organization (IIRO) based in Saudi Arabia and Islamic Relief based in the United Kingdom – Petersen analyses the ways in which these organizations Islamize aid and the kinds of Islam they construct in the process. For example, Petersen argues that IIRO promotes an all-encompassing Islam, encouraging an Islamized aid and blocking integration into mainstream development and humanitarian aid where Islamic Relief demonstrates a quasi-secular invisible Islam, accompanied by an almost secularized aid which facilitates integration into the aid field. She concludes that the positions of these NGOs are best understood as poles in a continuum, stretching from an embedded Islam to an invisible Islam.[32] This analysis is supported by Saeed, who argues that Islamic NGOs play a very important role for Muslims who must provide charitable donations as part of their religious duties but may not wish these donations to be channelled through their government, but also that there is not necessarily any contradiction between being a Muslim, being a humanitarian and working in a highly politicized climate. Indeed, given this political environment, Saeed concludes that standard regulations and monitoring of Muslim NGOs would enhance their efficacy and public standing.[33] Clarke et al. provide evidence of Muslim NGOs operating within the HIV and AIDS sector and providing assistance that can be considered best-practice.[34]

Conclusion

A central tenet of Islamic faith is that of providing assistance to those in need. The practical nature of Islam mandates that those of means pay an annual wealth tax

---

30 J. Millard Burr and Robert O. Collins, *Alms for Jihad: Charity and Terrorism in the Islamic World* (New York Cambridge University Press, 2006).

31 E. Kohlmann, 'The Role of Islamic Charities in International Terrorist Recruitment and Financing', *DIS Working Paper*, no. 7 (2006).

32 Marie Juul Petersen, 'Islamizing Aid: Transnational Muslim NGOs After 9.11', *VOLUNTAS: International Journal of Voluntary and Nonprofit Organizations* 23, no. 1 (2012): 126–55.

33 Saeed, *Interpreting the Qur'an : Towards a Contemporary Approach.*

34 Matthew Clarke, Simone Charnley, and Juliette Lumbers, 'Churches, Mosques, and Condoms: Understanding Successful HIV and AIDS Interventions by Faith-Based Organisations', *Development in Practice* 21, no. 1 (2011): 3–17.

of 2.5 per cent. In recent decades, the use of these funds has shifted from century-old practices of local funds being used to address local needs. More recently we have observed an increase in the use of these charitable alms to alleviate poverty across the globe. Reflecting the rise of international aid flows, Muslims are now increasingly using their religious charitable obligations to fund poverty alleviation activities in both Muslim-majority countries as well as non-Muslim countries. These funds are flowing through both nation aid programmes as well as through Muslim NGOs.

Understanding the motivations of this aid is important for 'traditional' Western donors, who to date have expressed high levels of suspicion as to why this aid is being provided and to whom. The questioning of these aid programmes, however, sits uncomfortably with the origins and firmly entrenched practices of Western aid that sets out to address both humanitarian needs as well as the donors' own national interests. While data on Muslim-originated aid is not as publicly available or easily assessable as that of aid flows from non-Muslim countries, empirical evidence does suggest that Muslim-majority donors do determine their aid flows according to both humanitarian needs as well as national interests. It is perhaps true to say though that these donors do not share the same national interests as their traditional donor counterparts. There is also evidence that whilst Muslim NGOs can provide aid that is less focused on addressing issues of poverty, there is evidence that – like all civil society organizations – there is a range of practices, with the work of some Muslim NGOs closely resembling that of non-Muslim NGOs.

Aid flows from Muslim-majority countries addressing poverty alleviation are likely to continue to increase. It is important therefore that further work is undertaken to better understand not just the motivations of these aid flows but also to ensure the efficacy of this aid is as positive as possible. This is equally important for recipient nations, traditional donors, Muslim-majority donors and Muslim NGOs.

References

Bellers, J. 'Aiding Their Moslim Friends: Saudi Arabia's Development Policy'. *Development and Cooperation*, no. 4 (1993): 28–9.

Bellion-Jourdan, Jerome. 'Islamic Relief Organizations: Between "Islamism" and "Humanitarianism"'. *ISIM Newsletter* 5, no. 1 (2000): 15.

Benthall, Jonathan. 'Islamic Aid in a North Malian Enclave'. *Anthropology Today* 22, no. 4 (2006): 19–21.

Benthall, Jonathan, and Jerome Bellion-Jourdan. *The Charitable Crescent: The Politics of Aid in the Muslim World.* London: I.B. Taurus, 2003.

Burr, J. Millard, and Robert O. Collins. *Alms for Jihad: Charity and Terrorism in the Islamic World.* New York: Cambridge University Press, 2006.

Clarke, Matthew. *Development and Religion: Theology and Practice*. Cheltenham, UK; Northampton, MA, USA: Edward Elgar, 2011.

Clarke, Matthew, Tim Fry, and Sandra Mihajilo. 'Aid Allocation and Volatility to Small Island States'. *Pacific Economic Bulletin* 23, no. 2 (2008): 179–202.

Clarke, Matthew, Simone Charnley, and Juliette Lumbers. 'Churches, Mosques, and Condoms: Understanding Successful HIV and Aids Interventions by Faith-Based Organisations'. *Development in Practice* 21, no. 1 (2011): 3–17.

De Cordier, Bruno. 'Faith-Based Aid, Globalisation and the Humanitarian Frontline: An Analysis of Western-Based Muslim Aid Organisations'. *Disasters* 33, no. 4 (2009): 608–28.

———. 'The 'Humanitarian Frontline', Development and Relief, and Religion: What Context, Which Threats and Which Opportunities?' *Third World Quarterly* 30, no. 4 (2009): 663–84.

Feeny, Simon, and Mark McGillivray. 'What Determines Bilateral Aid Allocations? Evidence from Time Series Data'. *Review of Development Economics* 12, no. 3 (2008): 515–29.

GHA. 'Global Humanitarian Assistance Report', 2012.

Kalimullah, Nazmul A, and Caroline B. Fraser. 'Islamic Non-Government Organisations in Bangladesh with Reference to Three Case Studies'. *Islamic Quarterly* 34, no. 2 (1990): 71–92.

Kohlmann, E. 'The Role of Islamic Charities in International Terrorist Recruitment and Financing'. *DIS Working Paper*, no. 7 (2006).

Kroessin, M. 'Mapping UK Muslim Development NGOs'. *Religions and Development Working Paper 30*. International Development Department: University of Birmingham, 2009.

Leaman, Oliver. 'Money'. In *The Qur'an: An Encyclopedia*, edited by Oliver Leaman. New York: Routledge, 2005.

Mady, Abu El Ela. 'How Do Islamic Organisations See Their Social Role? An Islamic Perspective (from Egypt)'. In *Religion, Politics, Conflict and Humanitarian Action Faith-based Organisations as Political, Humanitarian Or Religious Actors: Proceedings of the Workshop, May 18–19 2005, Geneva, Switzerland*: Graduate Institute of International Studies, 2005.

Maizels, Alfred, and Machiko K. Nissanke. 'Motivations for Aid to Developing Countries'. *World Development* 12, no. 9 (1984): 879–900.

Muslim Aid. 'Muslim Aid's Qurbani Programme'. http://www.muslimaid.org/index.php/what-we-do/qurbani/

Neumayer, Eric. 'What Factors Determine the Allocation of Aid by Arab Countries and Multilateral Agencies?'. *Journal of Development Studies* 39, no. 4 (2003): 134–47.

O'Brien, Joanne, and Martin Palmer. *The Atlas of Religion*. Berkeley: University of California Press, 2007.

Peters, F. 'Broadcasting the World: Prophet, Preacher and Saint'. In *The Meaning of Life in the World Religions*, edited by Joseph Runzo and Nancy M. Martin. Oxford: Oneworld, 2001.

Petersen, Marie Juul. 'Islamizing Aid: Transnational Muslim NGOs after 9.11'. *VOLUNTAS: International Journal of Voluntary and Nonprofit Organizations* 23, no. 1 (2012): 126–55.

Rahman, Fazlur. 'Some Reflections on the Reconstruction of Muslim Society in Pakistan'. *Islamic Studies* 6, no. 2 (1967): 103–20.

Saeed, Abdullah. *Interpreting the Qur'an : Towards a Contemporary Approach*. Abingdon, England; New York: Routledge, 2006.

Shepard, William E. *Introducing Islam*. London; New York: Routledge, 2009.

Smith, H. *The World's Religions*. New York: HarperOne, 1991.

Truman, H. 'Inaugural Address, January 20'. (1949). http://www.presidency.ucsb.edu/ws/index.php?pid=13282.

Villanger, E. 'Arab Foreign Aid: Disbursement Patterns, Aid Policies and Motives'. *CMI Report No.2*. Bergen: Chr Michelsen Institute, 2007.

Wilson, S., C. Pan, and M. Clarke. 'New Aid, New Leadership? Implications of Increasing Chinese Aid to PNG and Melanesi'. *ADRI Working Paper Series*. Geelong: Deakin University, forthcoming.

Chapter 4
Development by Muslims, with Muslims and among Muslims: Prospects and Challenges for Christian Aid Agencies

Peter Riddell

Introduction

The attention of development theorists and practitioners has been turning increasingly towards the world's Muslim population for some time. Two factors are at work here. First, the number of Muslims as a proportion of the world's population is increasing rapidly. In 1950 Muslim-majority countries accounted for 6.25 per cent of the population of the top 30 nations,[1] but by 2050 this proportion will have risen to 19.5 per cent. And this statistic does not even take account of India, which already includes a Muslim minority that dwarfs most Muslim-majority countries. Taking a different angle but reaching similar conclusions on population projections, the Pew Research Center Report of 2011 notes that '[i]f current trends continue, Muslims will make up 26.4% of the world's total projected population of 8.3 billion in 2030, up from 23.4% of the estimated 2010 world population of 6.9 billion'.[2]

The second factor accounting for increasing attention towards the world's Muslims by development specialists is that not only are Muslims growing rapidly in numbers, but they also constitute some of the most socially and economically disadvantaged communities in the world. In 2008 Muslim-majority countries represented five (Sudan, Afghanistan, Palestine, Somalia, Iraq) of the top seven recipients of humanitarian aid, with another, Ethiopia, having a large Muslim minority. Compounding this story of disadvantage is that Muslims have long represented around 80 per cent of the world's refugees and displaced persons.[3]

In the above context, Christian development agencies will be increasingly involved in providing humanitarian relief and development in Muslim contexts in the future, supplementing a long track record of the same for certain agencies.

---

[1] Though at the time Pakistan and Bangladesh were one country.

[2] Pew Forum on Religion & Public Life, 'The Future of the Global Muslim Population: Projections for 2010–2030', (Washington DC: Pew Research Center, 2011), 13.

[3] Jerome Bellion-Jourdan, 'Islamic Relief Organizations: Between "Islamism" and "Humanitarianism"', *ISIM Newsletter* 5, no. 1 (2000): 15.

Increasingly Christian agencies will therefore be faced by a series of questions and key decisions. In the following pages, we will consider 10 major issues for Christian development agencies and workers as they explore ways of addressing development needs among Muslim communities.

Issue 1: Muslim Communities and the Spiritual Expectation

One issue presents itself from the outset: the spiritual expectations of Muslim recipient communities. Beek considers this in a generic sense, but his observations are especially relevant to Islamic communities:

> Spirituality is central to many of the daily decisions people in the 'South' make about their own and their community's development, including that of whether or not to participate in risky but potentially beneficial social action. Despite the evident centrality of spirituality to such decisions, the subject is conspicuously under-represented in the development discourse.[4]

Beneficiaries in Muslim communities will often expect a spiritual dimension to development work. Repeated field reports by development workers record that Muslim recipient communities see a close connection between the problem statement, be it drought, deforestation, illness and so forth, and the sovereignty of Allah. This view is grounded in Islamic Scripture and is reinforced by popular belief and practice.

So in the Qur'an, we often find a close connection drawn between the human condition and the divine will. In the Qur'anic narrative of Jonah, for example, the prophet emerges from the belly of the fish in the following condition:

فَنَبَذْنَـٰهُ بِٱلْعَرَآءِ وَهُوَ سَقِيمٌ

Q37:145 Then We cast him on a desert shore while he was sick

In this short excerpt, Jonah's illness is portrayed as part of God's sovereign plan. In fact, the following verses reinforce the overriding sense of God (speaking as 'We') being in control: *And We caused a tree of gourd to grow above him;* (146) *And We sent him to a hundred thousand (folk) or more* (147) *And they believed, therefor We gave them comfort for a while.* (148)

This sense of divine sovereignty determining the state of the world is reinforced in the hadith collections, as seen in the following hadith account from the authoritative Sunni collection of Abu Dawud:

---

[4] Kurt Alan Ver Beek, 'Spirituality: A Development Taboo', *Development in Practice* 10, no. 1 (2000): 31.

> Narrated Abu Bakrah: Abdur Rahman ibn Abu Bakrah said that he told his father: O my father! I hear you supplicating every morning: 'O Allah! Grant me health in my body. O Allah! Grant me good hearing. O Allah! Grant me good eyesight. There is no god but Thou'. You repeat them three times in the morning and three times in the evening.
>
> He said: I heard the Apostle of Allah (peace be upon him) using these words as a supplication and I like to follow his practice ... [5]

This also confirms the Muslim understanding of the power of God to provide good health, with the prophet Muhammad himself embracing this view in this particular hadith.

With such repeated scriptural emphasis upon the sovereignty of God, it is little wonder that Muslim communities receiving humanitarian assistance look for spiritual explanations to their problems, and seek a link with the spiritual in planning for solutions. A case study from Mauritania that I personally experienced will illustrate this.

Case Study: In the Sahara Desert, Mauritania[6]

Our development team visited a Muslim village in an oasis in the middle of the desert. The survival of the village was being threatened by the desert, which was slowly but steadily advancing, and gradually restricting the fertile area surrounding the village.

We spoke with the villagers about their crop growing activities. They informed us that their village had undergone a substantial reorientation in their income-generating activities in recent times, because of the gradual drying up of the local area. The village had traditionally grown date palms, but in recent times had moved away from this in favour of crops which could survive in drier soils, such as melons and eggplant.

The perimeter of the fertile area where the village was located was marked by a fence. In addition, other fences were erected around the various crops, to prevent livestock from straying into the crops. The sand dunes were slowly encroaching onto the fertile area. Several small trees beyond the perimeter fence were half submerged by the dunes, and the fence itself was, in parts, slowly disappearing under the advancing sands, which moved forward a little each year.

We discussed with the village leadership various possibilities for development activities. One possibility which we suggested was a reforestation project to try to hold back the desert. This would be based on planting specially selected shrubs and trees at strategic locations to try and stop the advancing sands. It was argued

[5] Sunan Abu Dawud Book 41 Number 5071.

[6] This meeting occurred in the Sahara desert, 90 minutes by 4WD from Kiffa, 25 November 1993.

that such a project might provide longer term sustainability for the community, which would otherwise be overrun by the desert.

The village leadership was not favourably disposed to the suggestion of a reforestation project, or indeed anything which was aimed at holding back the desert. The villagers felt that the advance of the desert was God's will, and it would not therefore be appropriate to interfere in God's predestined plan for the village.

Case Study: Health Education and the Will of Allah

In another case study from the Horn of Africa, expatriate Community Development Workers (CDW) developed a Health Education curriculum in an Islamic community. Infants in the village were suffering from hygiene- and nutrition-related illnesses, due to poor knowledge of good hygiene practices and nutrition by local mothers. The CDWs gave basic lessons to local mothers, stressing the importance of personal hygiene and good all-round nutrition, as well as the need to consider nutrients of food and strategies to circumscribe germs. The local mothers reportedly responded with suspicion, because neither germs nor nutrients could be seen, and they regarded the CDW explanations as fabrications designed to explain away what was really the will of Allah. After one lesson in which the causes of relevant illnesses were explained, a CDW asked the question 'Why then do children get diarrhoea?' Rather than receiving a response such as 'Because we have not been boiling the water to kill the germs before drinking', the development worker received the response 'My baby has diarrhoea because Allah sends it'.[7]

Issue 2: Changing Attitudes among Government and Multilateral Donors

Western governments and multilateral agencies have been reluctant in the past to combine aid with faith activities. Clarke provides a context to this:

> Western official donors have traditionally been ambivalent about the relationship between faith and development and the activities of faith-based organisations. They were heavily influenced by the legal separation of church and state in liberal democracies. They felt that religion was counter to development, that religious discourses with strong historical resonance were inflexible and unyielding in the face of social and political change.[8]

However, increasing flexibility on this score has been evident since the hardline stance of the 1990s, especially in the wake of the 9/11 terrorist attacks in America,

[7] Bruce Bradshaw, *Bridging the Gap: Evangelism, Development and Shalom*, Innovations in Mission (Monrovia, Calif.: MARC, 1993), 59–60.

[8] Gerard Clarke, 'Agents of Transformation? Donors, Faith-Based Organisations and International Development', *Third World Quarterly* 28, no. 1 (2007): 79.

which convinced all but the most sceptical that faith needed to be considered in addressing the big development issues of the modern world. Petersen explained this changing context:

> Failures in mainstream aid provision, among other things, have forced actors in the field to look for alternative ways of doing aid – and in this, many have turned to religious NGOs, or faith-based organizations as they are often called, seeing them as the new panacea.[9]

The UK Department for International Development (DfID) commissioned research into the role of faith groups in poverty alleviation from 2004 onwards.[10] Across the Atlantic, USAID passed a ruling on 'Participation by Religious Orders in USAID Programs', effective from October 2004, which determined that 'USAID can not discriminate against organisations which combine development or humanitarian activities with "inherently religious activities" such as worship, religious instruction or proselytisation'.[11] This ruling reflected in part the Bush administration initiative that led to the establishment of the USAID Center for Faith-Based and Community Initiatives in 2002.[12]

Nevertheless, greater openness to faith-based development by governments does not necessarily translate to endorsement of evangelism. Berger's definition of the goals of his research neatly state the view of typical Western donor governments that consider supporting Faith-Based Organizations (FBO): ' … it is assumed that the use of religion in development aid, regardless of the form it takes, is to serve the development of the recipient and not the religion of the donor'.[13]

So with Christian development agencies no longer needing to apologize to government and multilateral donors for seeing spiritual issues as inextricably intertwined with physical development – and indeed with Islamic development groups similarly benefiting from changing times and attitudes – the whole question of spirituality as part of development activity has become increasingly evident in development discourse.

---

[9] Marie Juul Petersen, 'Islamizing Aid: Muslim NGOs after 9.11' (paper presented at the 60th Political Studies Association Annual Conference, Edinburgh UK, 29 March–1 April 2010).

[10] Tamsin Bradley, 'Does Compassion Bring Results? A Critical Perspective on Faith and Development', *Culture and Religion* 6, no. 3 (2005): 339.

[11] Clarke, 'Agents of Transformation? Donors, Faith-Based Organisations and International Development', 82.

[12] Amy Gambrill, 'From Practice to Policy to Practice: Connecting Faith and Conservation in Africa', (Washington DC: International Resources Group for USAID Bureau for Africa, 2011), 3.

[13] Maurits Berger, 'Religion and Development Aid: The Special Case of Islam', *Clingendael Diplomacy Papers*, no. 8 (2006), 6. See http://www.clingendael.nl/sites/default/files/20061000_cdsp_pap_berger.pdf (accessed 12 January, 2012).

Issue 3: The Question of Christian–Muslim Co-operation

The above-mentioned case studies suggest that Christian development workers should not ignore spiritual factors in undertaking development activities among such Muslim communities. But this leads to a key question: how should they build a spiritual component into their development activities?

Three options present themselves. First, Christian development workers could build a Christian spiritual component into their activities, drawing on their own knowledge and religious perspectives. Second, Christian development workers could recruit Muslim workers to add an Islamic spiritual dimension to the development activities in question. Third, Christian development agencies could outsource the responsibility for spiritual activities to Muslim development agencies through formal partnerships.

The first of the above options is highly controversial, not least among Christian development agencies themselves, with some arguing that development and evangelism should under no circumstances be combined. The second option already operates in part, with many Christian development agencies such as World Vision recruiting Muslim workers in Muslim locations, though not necessarily for the purpose of providing spiritual inputs to development projects. It is the third of the above options – that of Christian development agencies joining forces with Muslim NGOs where feasible – that I will mainly focus on in the following discussion.

Issue 4: What Kinds of Muslims to Partner With?

With the opening up of the discourse regarding faith in development, there has been an increasing openness to the notion of development agency partnerships across faith lines. Indeed, in situations such as the case studies described above, a Christian–Muslim partnership makes a lot of sense. But for the Christians concerned, it is not sufficient to choose any Muslim partner, given the great diversity of Muslim agencies and associated methods. In 2010, there were approximately 400 Muslim NGOs representing 2.4 per cent of a total of 16,700 international NGOs.[14] Indeed, for development inputs to be effective, it would be essential that partnering agencies worked well together. So the choice of a partner is vital for development effectiveness and sustainability. Berger stresses the importance of making wise choices in forming agency partnerships:

> The introduction of religion into development issues has created such enthusiasm on the Western part that an initial refusal to cooperate with any Islamic organizations at all may be substituted by an uncritical welcoming of *all* Islamic organizations.[15]

[14] Petersen, 'Islamizing Aid: Muslim NGOs after 9.11'.

[15] Berger, 'Religion and Development Aid: The Special Case of Islam', 16.

What kind of Muslim agency should Christian development projects partner with?[16] Muslims are diverse in numerous ways, offering diverse interpretations on questions and issues related to faith. Berger considers dilemmas facing Western donors in choosing Muslim partners, but the same issues face Christian donor agencies:

> Should one listen to the [Islamic] interpretation of the farmer whose well one is drilling, or the local imam, or the state officials, or the state *mufti*? Or is the donor allowed and entitled to study the Koran and religious literature itself to determine what Islam is?[17]

While it is helpful up to a point for Christian development agencies to consider generic typologies of Muslims – according to Traditionalists, Islamists, Modernizers, Secularists and so forth – it is far more relevant to consider different Muslim approaches to development in seeking potential partners.

In this context, Petersen's research is helpful. She differentiates between, firstly, embedded Islam and invisible Islam, and secondly, Gulf-based and West-based Islamic NGOs. On the former, embedded Islam for Petersen is seen in the work of the Islamic International Relief Organization (IIRO), which promotes 'an understanding of Islam as all-encompassing and pervasive, influencing all aspects of aid provision – what we may call an embedded Islam … strongly embedded in all spheres of organizational life'.[18]

In contrast, invisible Islam for Petersen is seen in the work of Islamic Relief Worldwide, which 'explicitly dissociates itself from missionary activities, rejecting traditions of mixing *da'wa* and aid'. So rather than placing emphasis on mosque building, such agencies prefer to focus on poverty alleviation.

Petersen adds a cautionary note at the end of her article to the effect that agencies cannot be completely pigeonholed in terms of embedded or invisible Islam, with policies and practices evolving over time.

On the distinction between Gulf-based and West-based Islamic NGOs, a notion also supported by Yaylaci,[19] Petersen cites development worker sources in observing that:

> … while Gulf-based NGOs do a valuable job helping the poor, they are also … missionary and discriminatory, presenting a 'fundamentalist' and sometimes

[16] Of course, Muslims would want to address the same question of Christian agencies, but consideration of that angle is not within the scope of this chapter.

[17] Berger, 'Religion and Development Aid: The Special Case of Islam', 17.

[18] Petersen, 'Islamizing Aid: Muslim NGOs after 9.11'.

[19] Ismail Yaylaci, 'Communitarian Humanitarianism: The Politics of Islamic Humanitarian Organisations' (paper presented at the Workshop on Religion and Humanitarianism, American University of Cairo, June 3–5 2008), 37.

'extremist' image of Islam. Western [based Muslim] NGOs, on the other hand, are neutral, universalist, and tolerant, promoting a moderate image of Islam.[20]

On the one hand, there is a sense of a caricature about Petersen's distinctions between embedded versus invisible Islam and Gulf-based versus Western-based Islamic NGOs; rarely do such clear-cut dichotomies reflect total truth. At the same time, stereotypes often carry an element of fact at their core, and Christian development workers seeking Muslim agency partners would do well to consider these distinctions in going about the process of building their partnerships.

Issue 5: Recipients: Muslim or Anyone?

A further issue that Christian agencies must give thought to in forming partnerships with Muslim NGOs is highlighted by Ismail Yaylaci, who asserts that although Islamic Humanitarian Organizations (IHO) declare their neutrality regarding beneficiary communities,

> ... only a small portion of the budget is allocated for non-Muslims. Most Islamic humanitarian organizations are explicit about the fact that they develop projects primarily for the benefit of the Muslim populations.[21]

This theme recurs repeatedly in the development literature. In his widely published research, Bellion-Jourdan affirms the above point,[22] while Espen Villanger relates it to the activities of the Islamic Development Bank:

> The Islamic Bank, which is the single biggest Arab donor agency measured by cumulative disbursements up to the end of 2005 and is funded mostly by official aid from the Arab countries, is restricted to lending only to member countries of the Organisation of the Islamic Conference.[23]

Yaylaci cites the example of the Human Rights and Liberties Humanitarian Relief Foundation (IHH),

> which was founded in Germany by Turkish people in 1995 with the original aim to distribute relief to the Bosnian and Chechen Muslims. IHH delivers aid

---

[20] Petersen, 'Islamizing Aid: Muslim NGOs after 9.11'.

[21] Yaylaci, 'Communitarian Humanitarianism: The Politics of Islamic Humanitarian Organisations', 40.

[22] Bellion-Jourdan, 'Islamic Relief Organizations: Between "Islamism" and "Humanitarianism"'.

[23] E. Villanger, 'Arab Foreign Aid: Disbursement Patterns, Aid Policies and Motives', *CMI Report No.2* (Bergen: Chr Michelsen Institute, 2007), 19–20.

> almost exclusively to Muslim people. What is quite striking in terms of the kind of umma-centric identity politics it pursues, IHH delivers aid not only to the Muslims in countries where they constitute the majority, but they also go to most of the countries where they are minority.[24]

On the one hand, the disproportionate degree to which Muslim communities suffer from deprivation and displacement around the world explains to a considerable extent the reason for high levels of Muslim agency development inputs to Muslim communities. But if, on top of that, there is a clear policy to favour Muslims as recipients, rather than being determined primarily by need rather than creed, then that would call for consideration and discussion among Christian agencies to determine compatibility for potential partnerships.

On a related issue, UN Millennium Development Goals (MDGs) set the halving of people living in poverty as a key aim. Hence OECD funding decisions take account of the extent to which development projects contribute to poverty reduction, and hence central to Western secular, and mainstream Christian, development activities is poverty reduction, without discrimination with regard to recipients. Ismail Yaylaci's following observation prompts a number of questions regarding the compatibility between the MDGs and the priorities of much development work by Islamic agencies:

> a close analysis of [Islamic Humanitarian Organisations'] places of action reveals that their humanitarian action is predominantly focused on the Islamic world … What is embedded in most of these IHOs' actions is a clear appeal to, and call for, Islamic solidarity (*al-ta'awun al-islami*) through the notion of umma.[25]

Issue 6: The Islamization Dimension

Petersen's reference to some Islamic NGOs taking an embedded Islam approach bears further thought in planning inter-religious agency partnerships. Using IIRO as her case study, she observes that:

> [t]he provision of aid is explained and legitimated with reference to Muslim traditions and concepts such as zakat, sadaqa and hadiths rather than the Millennium Development Goals, the Universal Human Rights Declaration or the Human Development Index.

Anticipating a dysfunction in approach between IIRO and Western (and indeed Christian) agencies, Petersen adds that IIRO 'insists on the intimate connection

---

[24] Yaylaci, 'Communitarian Humanitarianism: The Politics of Islamic Humanitarian Organisations', 21–2.

[25] Ibid., 19.

between Islam and aid, presenting a pervasive organizational religiosity embedded in and influencing all aspects of aid provision, from staff environment to activities and funding, and as such colliding with mainstream European and North American donor expectations of religion and aid as largely separate categories'.[26]

While Christian development agencies may well wish to outsource the spiritual dimension of aid activities to a Muslim partner agency, they may equally wish to avoid a partner who promotes an approach where a literalist reading of the Islamic primary texts serves as the starting point for all aid activities.

It may well come down to choosing between a partner who seeks to use the development activities as a means for Islamization and a partner who embodies Islamic values as a broad and fairly subtle framework for carrying out the activities; i.e. the ultimate goal being Islamization or development. The comfort zone for Christian development agencies is far more likely to be the latter kind of partner.

De Kadt reminds us of the need to closely monitor the balance between religious and other activities, with a statement that bears consideration by both Christian and Islamic agencies:

> Taking religion seriously is one matter, but it becomes seriously problematic when it is promoted as the only identity that counts, disregarding the many other components of identity that should be salient in different situations, thereby truncating a broader sense of self. As a result, people become blinkered.[27]

Indeed, devout adherents of religion at the far end of the conservative spectrum can be a force for undermining rather than enhancing the development process. In Muslim-majority Bangladesh, many Western and Christian NGOs identified empowerment of women as one of their key objectives, to address a situation where up to one in five women have their first child before the age of 15, and two thirds before the age of 18, resulting in 40 per cent of female deaths before the age of 18 being related to pregnancy. World Vision developed its couples programme to address this situation, placing well-trained Community Development Worker married couples, Christian Bangladeshis, in the poorest communities in Bangladesh to help the poor with health, basic literacy and income generation skills.[28]

Far more prominent than the World Vision Couples Programme is the Grameen Bank, which has set the empowerment of Bangladeshi women at the centre of its microfinance operations for over a generation, with resounding success. But such programmes have attracted a backlash from conservative

---

26 Petersen, 'Islamizing Aid: Muslim NGOs after 9.11'.

27 Emanuel De Kadt, 'Should God Play a Role in Development?', *Journal of International Development* 21, no. 6 (2009): 784.

28 Morris Stuart, *Stories of Transformation: A Theological Reflection from the Christian Resource Unit, World Vision Australia (with a Response from Ian Breward)*, ed. Ian Breward (Burwood East, Vic: Christian Resource Unit, World Vision Australia, 1994).

Islamic groups, some of whom responded to the activities of the Grameen Bank with hostility, burning down microcredit banks, attacking borrowers, condemning microcredit as un-Islamic, and threatening and beating women participants in the Bank programmes.[29]

Nevertheless, a decision to shun traditionalist Islamic authorities and groups involved in Islamization risks throwing out the baby with the bathwater. Some traditionalist organizations may in fact be crucial to development, such as madrasas in some countries. Clarke observes insightfully:

> Most madrassas … play an important role in educating children in countries where the state lacks the resources to fund universal primary education and where parents lack a choice of schools. The better-resourced madrassas often provide free food and accommodation for the children of the poor, and employment for a significant minority who go on to work in madrassas or mosques. Where they combine secular and religious education, Islamic schools can play a potentially important role in providing poor children with a basic primary school education, and as a significant social safety net.[30]

Issue 7: Aid for Political Purposes?

A further issue for Christian agencies to consider as they seek Muslim agency partners is the extent to which aid might be seen as a vehicle to realize certain political goals on the part of some Muslim agencies. Neumayer commented on the vast funds put into the aid sector by Saudi Arabia: 'more Arab aid flows to countries that do not maintain diplomatic relations with Israel as well as to those with similar voting patterns in the UN General Assembly as Saudi Arabia'.[31] Similarly Yaylaci, referring in 2008 to the German-based Human Rights and Liberties Humanitarian Relief Foundation (IHH), notes that 'IHH also engages in various sorts of political activism for the political and also economic and social improvement of the Muslims worldwide. Apart from organizing massive relief rallies, it organizes conferences and lobbies for Palestine, Kosovo, Kashmir, Iraq, Afghanistan and Chechnya'.[32]

---

29 Alan Jolis, 'Microcredit: A Weapon In Fighting Extremism', *International Herald Tribune*, 19 February 1997. See also Chapter 9 in this volume by Mohammad Musfequs Salehin for a critical account of the Grameen Bank on the issue of women's empowerment.

30 Clarke, 'Agents of Transformation? Donors, Faith-Based Organisations and International Development', 82.

31 G. Mavrotas and E. Villanger, 'Multilateral Aid Agencies and Strategic Donor Behaviour', *Discussion Paper No. 2* (Helsinki: World Institute for Development Economics Research, United Nations University, 2006), 3.

32 Yaylaci, 'Communitarian Humanitarianism: The Politics of Islamic Humanitarian Organisations', 24.

Referring again to Bangladesh, Sayeed Iftekhar Ahmed, doctoral researcher at North Arizona University observes:

> It is alleged that the Islamic NGO Rabita Trust has been used by the Jamaat as a platform to preach their political ideals. A good number of Jamaat activists have been working as undercover NGO workers there. For example, Mir Kasem Ali, the secretary general of Rabita Bangladesh, was president of the student wing of Jamaat in 1980. He was also a Chittagong area regional commander of Al Badar, a militant group formed by the Jamaat's student wing in 1971 to assassinate the Bangladesh freedom fighters and intellectuals of the country. This armed group was mainly responsible for killing many intellectuals on 14 December 1971, just prior to the independence of Bangladesh.[33]

Sometimes the discourse from Muslim writers can involve a kind of Westophobia, where Westerners can be held responsible for all the ills of the Muslim world, and Western NGOs are portrayed as a second wave of colonialism. Christian NGOs can get caught up in this Westophobic discourse. So while foreign NGOs might be accused of corruption, proselytising, diverting funds away from approved projects,[34] Christian NGOs are accused of diverse sins: spreading pornography; establishing an indigenous mercenary army; setting up parallel government; indoctrinating employees; involving themselves in the drug trade; infiltrating their lackeys into academic positions in local universities; and establishing newspapers to promote their views and values.[35]

This kind of anti-Westernism can also come from more respectable NGOs. Petersen points out that IIRO discourse on the War on Terror is that it is a war between Muslims and the West. The agency calls for cooperation between Muslim agencies rather than broad-based cooperation across the faith lines to tackle development issues and crises.

Issue 8: The Terrorist-Financing Controversy

No consideration of partnering can ignore a controversy that preoccupied much official discussion about Islamic development agencies during the first decade of the twenty-first century: the funding of terrorism issue. During that decade US and European governments accused a range of Islamic development groups of funding jihadist militants, with the assets of some agencies frozen by Western

33 Sayeed Iftekhar Ahmed, 'Resurgence of Islam in Bangladesh Politics', *South Asian Journal*, no. 11 (2006), 161. See http://www.southasianmedia.net/Magazine/Journal/11_resurgence_of_islam.htm.(accessed 17 July 2010).

34 Nuruzzaman, 'NGOs-The Web of New Colonialism: Aid Merchant Buying up Sonar Bangla', *Impact International* (London) 1994.

35 Mohammad Abul-Hayat Jalal-Abadi, 'NGOs spread pornography in Muslim Bangladesh', *Crescent International* August 1–15, 1998, 8–10.

governments, such as the al-Haramain Islamic Foundation branches in Somalia and Bosnia-Herzegovina.[36]

Saudi Arabia especially was the target of biting criticism and Western government pressure. The 2004 report of the US Council on Foreign Relations stated: 'Through the support for *madrassas*, mosques, cultural centers, hospitals, and other institutions, and the training and export of radical clerics to populate these outposts, Saudi Arabia has spent what could amount to hundreds of millions of dollars around the world financing extremism'.[37]

Berger articulates the dilemma surrounding this issue very well, leaving open the door for cooperation with groups attracting suspicion:

> Another dilemma is that of Islamic organizations that are very active in humanitarian projects and at the same time have a militant political agenda. Examples are Hamas and Hizbollah, which run extensive humanitarian programmes for their communities, participate in local and parliamentarian elections, but also maintain a paramilitary wing that has put them on international lists as 'terrorist organizations'. There are no clear-cut solutions for these politically and morally complex problems, but rejecting any kind of cooperation outright seems sometimes short-sighted. Careful analysis of the linkage between the paramilitary and social and humanitarian activities may provide solutions.[38]

The government that has attracted most criticism on this score, that of Saudi Arabia, moved to address these concerns. In mid-2003, the Saudi Arabian Monetary Agency implemented new regulations governing Saudi aid organizations, requiring them to obtain official approval prior to transferring funds abroad.[39] The following year the Saudi government established the National Commission for Relief and Charity Work Abroad tasked with monitoring private Saudi funding for charitable activities overseas.[40]

Christian agencies need to be nuanced in considering this issue, not giving in to simplistic stereotypes regarding supposed links between aid and terrorism.

Issue 9: The Issue of Transparency

Transparency is something of a sacred cow in Western and Christian development sectors, with donors, both government and private, expecting detailed feedback on

[36] BBC, 'US Freezes Saudi Charity Assets', *BBC News* (2002), http://news.bbc.co.uk/2/hi/americas/1868306.stm. (accessed 4 July 2013).

[37] Independent Task Force on Terrorist Financing, 'Update on the Global Campaign Against Terrorist Financing', (New York: Council on Foreign Relations, 2004), 21.

[38] Berger, 'Religion and Development Aid: The Special Case of Islam', 16.

[39] Petersen, 'Islamizing Aid: Muslim NGOs after 9.11'.

[40] Clarke, 'Agents of Transformation? Donors, Faith-Based Organisations and International Development', 89.

the method of disbursement of aid support. So repeated references in the development literature to less-than-complete transparency among Islamic development agencies is bound to raise questions when potential partnerships are being considered.

Anthony Bubalo and Greg Fealy relate the question of transparency to the thorny issue of the funding of terrorism:

> Saudi Arabia has provided considerable legitimate humanitarian and development assistance to Muslim causes around the world. The difficulty is trying to disentangle genuine charity from the funding of terrorist groups and the propagation of ideas that cross the line between purely religious and a more political activism. This difficulty is reinforced by the lack of Saudi transparency.[41]

Similarly, Villanger poses questions about access to information about Saudi-sourced funding, commenting that 'much of the Arabic resource flows have traditionally been channelled in private through the ruling families, and through government channels that are not necessarily transparent in the public domain',[42] and further that '[t]he Ministry of Finance is the major aid agency in Saudi Arabia, but little is known about how it operates'.[43]

Ismail Yaylaci provides Muslim comment on this issue, arguing that '[o]ne prominent organizational difference between IHOs and Western organizations is the former's lack of a tradition of accountability and transparency. Most Islamic agencies do not provide detailed account of their financial transactions as to how much they collected as revenues and how much and where they were spent'.[44]

Yaylaci offers an explanation for the accountability issue, arguing that the hadith collections call on Muslims to make charitable gifts secretly in order to gain greater merit. He points out that those INGOs more motivated by *da'wa* among Christian communities 'are not interested in releasing account of their actions'. In contrast, he says, 'the UK-based Islamic Relief and Muslim Aid, and Switzerland-based Agha Khan Foundation fully adopted their Western counterparts' standards of accountability and transparency through publicizing their income and expenditure accounts'.[45]

Issue 10: Grants vs Loans

Discussion of potential bridges and stumbling blocks to Christian–Muslim cooperation in development activities would not be complete without addressing

---

[41] Anthony Bubalo and Greg Fealy, 'Joining the Caravan? The Middle East, Islamism and Indonesia', *Lowy Institute Paper* 05 (Sydney: Lowy Institute 2005), 55.

[42] Villanger, 'Arab Foreign Aid: Disbursement Patterns, Aid Policies and Motives', 1.

[43] Ibid., 8.

[44] Yaylaci, 'Communitarian Humanitarianism: The Politics of Islamic Humanitarian Organisations', 17.

[45] Ibid., 37.

the issue of grants versus loans. Western, and Christian, development agencies have long attached importance to microfinance activities that involve small, often token, interest payments by the borrowers in order to grow the activity start-up fund.

On the side of Islamic development activities, a steady increase in shari'a awareness and the shari'a lobby has made itself felt during the first decade of the twenty-first century. This will work against interest payments as part of Islamic development. Nevertheless, this need not necessarily be a deal breaker in cooperation discussions between Christian and Muslim agencies. Petersen reports an interesting statement by the Chief Executive Officer of Islamic Relief Worldwide (IRW) on how his Islamic-values based organization handles microfinance activities:

> IRW offers vulnerable communities … microfinance loans based upon Islamic banking principles. These livelihood programmes deploy zero-interest financial support, shared risk with beneficiaries and practical skills training for ethically sound income generation activities.[46]

IRW claims an almost 100 per cent pay back rate on loans which, however, are not in the form of cash but rather take the form of training together with an asset, such as a cow, to initiate the microfinance activity. This offers good potential as a basis of Christian–Muslim cooperation in the microfinance area.

Conclusion

Is there an elephant in the room in these discussions? Beek hints at such in pointing out that '[s]pirituality and religion have often been sources of conflict and oppression rather than development and liberation'.[47] What if the spiritual dimension that development agencies seek to address is in fact part of the problem rather than the solution?

Ron Sider is not coy about being politically incorrect in arguing both that 'Hinduism's complex theology and practice of the caste system is a major cause of poverty' and that 'Confucian culture perceived innovation and technology as a threat rather than an opportunity'.[48]

Is such a notion relevant to some Muslim communities? Ibrahim Musliyar Bekal, a religious judge in Udupi District, Karnataka, India, reportedly said in interview that '[it] is very important to eradicate the dowry system and other such evils prevailing in the Muslim community. [These undermine] its overall

46 Petersen, 'Islamizing Aid: Muslim NGOs after 9.11'.

47 Ver Beek, 'Spirituality: A Development Taboo', 32.

48 Ronald J. Sider, *Rich Christians in an Age of Hunger: Moving from Affluence to Generosity* (Nashville: Thomas Nelson, 2005), 122–3.

development'.[49] Moreover, *The Arab Human Development Report 2005* refers to problems facing women, including high rates of morbidity and mortality connected with pregnancy and reproductive functions, and high rates of illiteracy, across the Arab World, due to 'general life styles that discriminate against women'.[50]

Such problems may well be seen as the fruit of cultural practice rather than faith and doctrine, but whatever the case, it would be easier for Muslim than non-Muslim agencies to address such questions in the field. This provides another argument in favour of Christians and Muslims exploring avenues for co-operation and sometimes partnership in aid and development.

This paper has mostly presented issues bearing consideration when Christian development agencies explore partnerships with Muslim development agencies. Many of the same questions could be asked in reverse if our angle of approach was from the perspective of the Muslim agencies. Some of the issues considered are quite sensitive, even uncomfortable. But that should not provide a reason to avoid these issues. On the contrary, mature partnership should be able to cope with difficult issues of sensitivity. The need for Christian–Muslim co-operation in the development sector is patently clear and it is incumbent upon both Christian and Muslim development theorists and practitioners to grapple with obstacles to partnership in order to overcome them for the benefit of communities in need.

References

Ahmed, Sayeed Iftekhar. 'Resurgence of Islam in Bangladesh Politics'. *South Asian Journal* no. 11 (2006). http://www.southasianmedia.net/Magazine/Journal/11_resurgence_of_islam.htm.

BBC. 'US Freezes Saudi Charity Assets'. *BBC News* (2002). Published electronically 12 March. http://news.bbc.co.uk/2/hi/americas/1868306.stm.

Bellion-Jourdan, Jerome. 'Islamic Relief Organizations: Between "Islamism" and "Humanitarianism"'. *ISIM Newsletter* 5, no. 1 (2000): 15.

Berger, Maurits. 'Religion and Development Aid: The Special Case of Islam'. *Clingendael Diplomacy Papers* no. 8 (2006). http://www.clingendael.nl/sites/default/files/20061000_cdsp_pap_berger.pdf.

Bradley, Tamsin. 'Does Compassion Bring Results? A Critical Perspective on Faith and Development'. *Culture and Religion* 6, no. 3 (2005): 337–51.

---

[49] Nirmala Carvalho, 'Some Muslim Practices Cause Poverty, Muslim Religious Leader Says', *AsiaNews.it* (2010), http://www.asianews.it/news-en/Some-Muslim-practices-cause-poverty,-Muslim-religious-leader-says-18719.html. (accessed 19 June, 2010)

[50] UNDP Regional Bureau for Arab States (RBAS), 'The Arab Human Development Report 2005: Towards the Rise of Women in the Arab World', (New York: United Nations Development Program, 2006), 7.

Bradshaw, Bruce. *Bridging the Gap: Evangelism, Development and Shalom*. Innovations in Mission. Monrovia, Calif.: MARC, 1993.

Bubalo, Anthony, and Greg Fealy. 'Joining the Caravan? The Middle East, Islamism and Indonesia'. *Lowy Institute Paper* 05. Sydney: Lowy Institute 2005.

Carvalho, Nirmala 'Some Muslim Practices Cause Poverty, Muslim Religious Leader Says'. *AsiaNews.it* (2010). Published electronically 18 June. http://www.asianews.it/news-en/Some-Muslim-practices-cause-poverty,-Muslim-religious-leader-says-18719.html.

Clarke, Gerard. 'Agents of Transformation? Donors, Faith-Based Organisations and International Development'. *Third World Quarterly* 28, no. 1 (2007): 77–96.

De Kadt, Emanuel. 'Should God Play a Role in Development?'. *Journal of International Development* 21, no. 6 (2009): 781–86.

Gambrill, Amy. 'From Practice to Policy to Practice: Connecting Faith and Conservation in Africa'. Washington DC: International Resources Group for USAID Bureau for Africa, 2011.

Independent Task Force on Terrorist Financing. 'Update on the Global Campaign against Terrorist Financing'. New York: Council on Foreign Relations, 2004.

Jalal-Abadi, Mohammad Abul-Hayat 'NGOs Spread Pornography in Muslim Bangladesh'. *Crescent International*, August 1–15, 1998, 8–10.

Jolis, Alan. 'Microcredit: A Weapon in Fighting Extremism'. *International Herald Tribune*, 19 February 1997.

Mavrotas, G., and E. Villanger. 'Multilateral Aid Agencies and Strategic Donor Behaviour'. *Discussion Paper No. 2*. Helsinki: World Institute for Development Economics Research, United Nations University, 2006.

Nuruzzaman. 'NGOs-the Web of New Colonialism: Aid Merchant Buying up Sonar Bangla'. *Impact International* (London), 1994, 8–12.

Petersen, Marie Juul 'Islamizing Aid: Muslim NGOs after 9.11 ' Paper presented at the 60th Political Studies Association Annual Conference, Edinburgh UK, 29 March–1 April 2010.

Pew Forum on Religion & Public Life. 'The Future of the Global Muslim Population: Projections for 2010–2030'. Washington DC: Pew Research Center, 2011.

Sider, Ronald J. *Rich Christians in an Age of Hunger: Moving from Affluence to Generosity*. Nashville: Thomas Nelson, 2005.

Stuart, Morris. *Stories of Transformation: A Theological Reflection from the Christian Resource Unit, World Vision Australia (with a Response from Ian Breward)*. edited by Ian Breward Burwood East, Vic: Christian Resource Unit, World Vision Australia, 1994.

Sunan Abu Dawud Book 41 Number 5071.

UNDP Regional Bureau for Arab States (RBAS). 'The Arab Human Development Report 2005: Towards the Rise of Women in the Arab World'. New York: United Nations Development Program, 2006.

Ver Beek, Kurt Alan. 'Spirituality: A Development Taboo'. *Development in Practice* 10, no. 1 (2000): 31–43.

Villanger, E. 'Arab Foreign Aid: Disbursement Patterns, Aid Policies and Motives'. *CMI Report No.2*. Bergen: Chr Michelsen Institute, 2007.

Yaylaci, Ismail 'Communitarian Humanitarianism: The Politics of Islamic Humanitarian Organisations'. Paper presented at the Workshop on Religion and Humanitarianism, American University of Cairo, June 3–5, 2008.

Chapter 5
Riba-Free Finance and *Zakat*-Induced Economic Aid: The Political Economy of Two Developmental Initiatives in the Muslim World

Ameer Ali

Introduction

Riba-free finance in the shape of an institutionalized Islamic banking and finance industry (IB&F) and *zakat*-induced economic/financial aid from affluent Arabs to poorer Muslim nations emerged as alternative faith-based economic initiatives in a world of economic rationalism and secular humanism. IB&F and Arab economic/financial aid emerged in the 1970s in the wake of an oil-based economic boom and a wave of Islamic religious resurgence in the Arab Middle East, which coincided with the collapse of Keynesian-Neoclassical Macroeconomic Consensus (KNMC) and rise of neo-liberal market fundamentalism. In a global economy ruled by secular ideologies the appearance of a faith-based financial sector was initially viewed as bizarre and ridiculous. However, such secular antipathy was not evident when affluent Arab nations came together to institutionalize an Islamic religious obligation, *zakat* or charity, into a distinct category of foreign aid. Over the last four decades however, IB&F has grown as a resilient alternative to conventional banking and finance and has captured a niche market both within and outside Muslim countries, while Arab foreign aid after a meteoric rise in the 1970s and 1980s appears to have taken a back seat allowing IB&F to become the leading facilitator of economic development, mostly amongst Muslim communities. What follows is a two-part analysis of the political economy of IB&F and Arab economic/financial aid. After a brief outline of the political and economic background that produced these developmental agencies, the main section of this chapter will dwell on the growth and role of IB&F, followed by a short section of Arab economic/financial assistance. The chapter will conclude with some comments on the critical role of these two agencies in the economic development of the Muslim world.

Political and Economic Environment of the 1970s

Internationally, IB&F as a specialized and faith-based industry, and Arab bilateral aid as an independent source of economic/financial assistance to poorer Muslim nations, emerged in the 1970s and flourished in an environment of momentous economic and political challenges; and within the Muslim world these developments overlapped with a new wave of religious awakening. The collapse of *dirigisme*, the re-emergence of the classical free-market ideology, and the ushering in of the 'Third Wave' of technological revolution set the stage for the advent in the 1980s of economic globalization. The progressive loosening of restrictions for capital to move across national borders coincided with an era of accelerated capital accumulation in petroleum-rich Muslim nations. The partial victory of Egypt in the 1973 Ramadan War, and six years later in 1979 with the 'Islamicized'[1] Revolution in Iran, reinvigorated Islamic religious fervour, which until then had remained quiescent, initially under the repressive political hegemony of Western colonial powers and then, in the 1950s and 1960s, under an equally repressive but militaristic secular nationalism with a socialist face.[2] Lavishly funded and organizationally supported by several of the affluent Arab countries led by Saudi Arabia, this rekindled religious awakening, apart from its outward expressions of regularized religious rituals, construction of new and renovation of old mosques, establishment of religious schools, and the drive for halal food and clothing, generated a series of Islamic conferences and colloquiums for Muslim intellectuals and academics with the specific purpose of producing a blueprint or programme for Islamizing a perceived un-Islamic world order that reigned supreme. The demand for an interest-free economic and financial system and the resolve to assist financially poorer Muslim countries and communities, through soft loans and outright grants, based on the principle of *zakat* (obligatory wealth tax) and *sadaqa* (voluntary charity) were the products of this grand Islamization project.

From the point of view of the history of the IB&F industry, the year 1979 was momentous for its political impact in the Muslim and Western worlds. The *shia*-Islamized revolution in Iran in February that year, followed by the Mecca rebellion in Saudi Arabia in November, and the Soviet invasion of Afghanistan in December, created an international political ambience within which IB&F could operate quietly without provoking undue attention from any quarters. Khomeini's resolve to export the revolution to other parts of the Muslim world obviously sent shock waves to autocratic Muslim regimes and among them to the Saudi monarchy in particular. When a group of armed religious zealots occupied the mosque in Mecca and demanded the overthrow of the Saudi regime Khomeini's wish seemed to have

[1] Hamid Dabashi, *The Arab Spring: The End of Postcolonialism* (New York: Zed Books, 2012), 40.

[2] Leila Ahmed, *A Quiet Revolution: The Veil's Resurgence, From the Middle East to America* (New Haven: Yale University Press, 2011).

almost come to fruition. Although the rebellion was brutally crushed by the Saudi regime with the approval of Wahhabi clerics, it soon realized its vulnerability and sought to fortify its position partly through allying with the West more closely and partly through economic generosity. Fortunately for the Saudis the Soviet invasion of Afghanistan and US's determination to drive out the 'Evil Empire' from Asia came as a blessing in disguise. The congruence of interests between the Saudi regime and the United States – oil and money in exchange for technology and protection, and their common interest against the Soviet threat – created an opportunity for the forces of resurgent Islam with its Islamization project to penetrate the West without much resistance. Arab foreign aid, especially its Saudi component, was similarly used as a political weapon in that country's international contest for Muslim leadership against a radicalized *shia*-Iran.

The end of the 1970s and beginning of the 1980s also witnessed another development, which was to facilitate IB&F penetration into the West even further. This was the collapse of KNMC which was structured on the edifice of independent national economies, but monitored through the Bretton Woods economic arrangements. The 1970s stagflation induced economic recession in the industrialized nations and the serial collapse of command economies led by the former Soviet Union, and the revolutionary breakthrough in electronic and communication technologies opened the way for the re-birth of unfettered economic liberalism that hitherto remained somewhat constrained by KNMC. Economic liberalism, which rolled back the state from economic management and freed the invisible hand, forced open the doors for economic globalization. It was in this global economic environment that the idea of an interest-free financial sector was to become a reality.

Economic globalization and the ensuing freedom for cross-border movement of finance capital meant a two-way traffic as far as IB&F industry was concerned. While conventional banking and financial institutions could enter the hitherto 'unbanked' Muslim sector and compete with nascent IB&F intermediaries, the latter also had the same freedom to do likewise outside its home ground. Yet, in the 1980s and 1990s IB&F activities remained overwhelmingly a Muslim-country phenomenon. With accommodative regulatory arrangements by home governments and with flexible administrative arrangements by interested institutions, even conventional banks operating in Muslim countries entered the faith-based industry by opening 'Islamic windows'. By the end of the 1990s virtually every conventional bank in the Middle East was an IB&F business. While Malaysia was fast emerging as the IB&F hub, international banks, such as Citicorp and HSBC, had entered the field by the end of the century.

Arab bilateral aid as a newly found arm of economic development was also the product of the tumultuous 1970s. The decision by the Organization of Petroleum Exporting Countries (OPEC) to take control of the production, consumption, and distribution of their natural resources, and among the members of OPEC the resolution by Saudi Arabia to use oil as a weapon against the United States and Europe for their support of Israel in the Arab–Israeli conflict, not only strangled the growth and prosperity of all industrialized economies but also brought economic hardship to poorer nations of the developing world that were import-dependent for their consumption of most manufactured products. In order to mitigate the growing anger of the developing world and to win the support of its members in the United Nations the petroleum-rich Arab countries initiated a bilateral aid programme whose scale of generosity, which will be discussed shortly, was unique in the annals of international altruism. The Arab aid was indeed *The Other Face of OPEC*.[3]

Islamic Banking and Finance

The State of Play

Although the ideological debate about an Islamized economy and finance was first raised by Abul-ala Maududi in pre-partition India, and although a few but sporadic experiments in that area were tried out in Malaysia and Egypt in the 1950s and 1960s,[4] IB&F as an independent and unique model of money and credit business came into existence only in the mid-1970s with the establishment of the first private Islamic bank in Dubai in 1975. Since then the growth of IB&F has been robust and it has earned itself a specific identity and a niche market in an otherwise volatile environment of banking and financial activities. *The Banker* magazine of the *Financial Times* and Group HSBC Amanah listed in the November 2007 issue the top 500 Islamic financial institutions that were operating in 47 countries with a total shari'a-compliant asset value of $500.5 billion at the end of the year 2006. According to that source, 'in addition to 292 banks, both fully Islamic and those offering Islamic windows or selling Islamic products, there are 115 Islamic investment banks and finance companies, and 118 insurance companies, adding up to a global total of 525 institutions … '.[5] According to the Ernst & Young World Islamic Banking Competitiveness Report of 2011, Islamic banking assets with commercial banks globally were expected to reach US$1.1 trillion in 2012, a 33 per cent jump from US$826 billion in 2010. This was obviously an underestimate because, according to another source, by the end of 2011 itself the total had reached US$1.3 trillion.[6] The HSBC Group alone

[3] Ibrahim F.I. Shihata, *The Other Face of OPEC: Financial Assistance to the Third World*, Energy Resources and Policies of the Middle East and North Africa (London; New York: Longman, 1982).

[4] H. Visser, *Islamic Finance: Principles and Practice* (Cheltenham, UK; Northampton, MA: Edward Elgar, 2009).

[5] Brian Caplen and Joseph DiVanna, 'Top 500 Islamic Financial Institutions', *The Banker*, 24 November 2007.

[6] Anjuli Davies, 'Global Islamic Finance Assets Hit $1.3 Trillion – Study', (2012), http://www.reuters.com/article/2012/03/29/islamic-finance-growth-idUSL6E8ET3KE20120329.

has a global network comprising 'about 10,000 offices with almost 110 million customers in 77 countries and territories in Europe, the Asia-Pacific region, the Americas, the Middle East and Africa'.[7]

Among the non-Muslim countries, in India for example, due to financial exclusion of a large section of the Muslim community 'because of a certain mindset prevailing in the banking sector' the demand for Islamic banking appears to have won the sympathy of the Indian Banks' Association and is awaiting an amendment to the Banking Regulation Act to make Islamic banking and finance a reality.[8] The State of Kerala appears to be leading the way. In Australia, there is already one private institution, the Muslim Community Cooperative Australia (MCCA) established in 1989 'to provide a comprehensive Islamic alternative for all financial needs of the Muslim community',[9] and within the conventional banking industry, the National Bank of Australia recently announced its intention to engage in shari'a-compliant financial business.[10]

Thus, in the 'global village' where conventional banking and financial institutions are grappling with periodic currency crises, financial meltdowns and institutional bankruptcies, the IB&F industry appears to be 'Islam's collective answer to the failures of Adam Smith's invisible hand'.[11] A strong demand for shari'a-compliant products in Muslim countries, the progressive strengthening of regulatory framework within IB&F, a growing demand from conventional investors in search of asset diversification, the relative resilience that the IB&F industry has shown during the 1997 financial crisis in Asia and the 2008 financial meltdown in the US and Europe, and the capacity of the industry to innovate and structure financial instruments to satisfy the needs of both corporate and individual investors, have combined to provide the necessary impetus to the robustness of IB&F.[12] Yet, in terms of its size and scale IB&F is still minuscule. The entire $820 billion shari'a-compliant assets cited above is not even one per cent of the $196 trillion worth of global financial assets, as reported by McKinsey & Company in 2008.[13] Even in Malaysia where IB&F has the support of the government only 10

---

7 Caplen and DiVanna, 'Top 500 Islamic Financial Institutions'.

8 Purnima S. Tripathi, 'Inclusive Banking', *Frontline* 26, no. 21 (2009): 43–6.

9 Abdullah Saeed, 'The Muslim Community Co-operative of Australia as an Islamic Financial Service Provider', in *Muslim Communities in Australia*, ed. Shahram Akbarzadeh and Abdullah Saeed (Sydney: UNSW Press, 2001), 189.

10 Ameer Ali, 'NAB May Lose Interest But Keep the Faith', *The Australian Financial Review*, 1 July 2009.

11 Loretta Napoleoni, *Terrorism and the Economy: How the War on Terror is Bankrupting the World* (New York: Seven Stories Press, 2010), 17.

12 Maher Hasan and Jemma Dridi, 'The Effects of the Global Crisis on Islamic and Conventional Banks: A Comparative Study', *IMF Working Paper WP/10/201* (Washington: International Monetary Fund, 2010).

13 Diana Farell et al., 'Mapping Global Capital Markets: Fifth Annual Report', (San Francisco: McKinsey & Company 2008).

per cent of all banking assets were held in shari'a-compliant accounts in 2005.[14] Yet, as a religiously legitimized financial institution to promote economic growth and development IB&F has proved its stability, permanency and robustness.

The Religious Rationale

IB&F is a prohibition-driven industry. It is the religious ban on (a) *riba*, translated as usury by some and interest by many; (b) *gharar*, meaning risk and uncertainty; and (c) *maysir*, literally meaning games of chance where one party faces the possibility of total loss – and therefore, in general, referring to gambling – that provides the divine rationale for IB&F. Jurists of all schools of Islamic jurisprudence consider *riba*, *gharar*, and *maysir* immoral and unjust and therefore deem them to be detrimental not only to the welfare of the individuals and institutions that indulge in them, but also to the societies in which they operate. In the jurists' view these activities contradict the Islamic principles and objectives of economic fairness and social justice.

Riba, the prohibition of which preceded long before the revelation of the Qur'an in the seventh century, is not confined to monetary transactions alone, but rather covers a broad range of economic exchanges including gold, silver, wheat, dates, barley, and so on, where the economic return to one party in the involvement exceeds what is considered to be a fair market norm. In this sense, all monopoly profits would fall under the category of *riba*. In addition, and in the context of conventional bank lending however, it is argued that it is unfair and unethical for capital, as a factor of production, to claim a pre-determined rate of return before that factor enters the process of production and shares the outcome.

Historically, the ban on *riba* predates Islam and was imposed by all Abrahamic faiths at a time when money was considered purely as a medium of exchange, and therefore an unproductive asset. The modern interpreters of shari'a and IB&F practitioners, however, accept that money is a productive resource and a store of value, but insist on the ethical imperative that any resource should share equally in both the risks and benefits that accrue from an enterprise. Thus, while conventional banking intermediation is largely debt-based and allows for risk transfer, Islamic banking mediation is asset-based and risk-sharing. In short, IB&F activities are based on the principle of profit-loss-sharing (PLS). While, according to Tawney , the two elder siblings of the Abrahamic family in Judaism and Christianity, gave up the prohibition and surrendered totally to the forces of mammon,[15] Islam, the youngest of them, after centuries of silent resistance has now taken the fight

[14] KPMG, 'Making the Transition from Niche to Mainstream: Islamic Banking and Finance: A Snapshot of the Industry and its Challenges Today', (2006), http://us.kpmg.com/microsite/FSLibraryDotCom/docs/Islamic%20Banking%20and%20Finance%20-%20A%20Snapshot%20of%20the%20Industry%20and%20Its%20Challenges%20Today.pdf.

[15] See R.H. Tawney, *Religion and the Rise of Capitalism: A Historical Study* (London: J. Murray, 1926).

to a new level. IB&F is the present battleground on which this confrontation is taking place.

Diaspora Muslims, the Housing Market, and IB&F

The pre-1970 industrialization and economic affluence in the Western countries encourgaed a relaxed attitude towards immigration. The need for cheap labour and a political interest in keeping the former colonies under economic tutelage made it desirable for Western powers to grant at least temporary resident permits to Muslim migrants from the Middle East and South Asia. The size of the Muslim population living in the West swelled significantly and the latest estimates of their number vary between 12 and 24 million.[16] This Muslim diaspora living mostly in the United States, Canada, Britain, France, Germany, and the Netherlands presented a potential target niche market for IB&F. The religious resurgence of the 1970s in the Muslim-majority countries and the rise of Islamism under the leadership of Ikhwan-al Muslimeen in Egypt, Jama'at-e-Islami in Pakistan, and Tablighi-Jamaat in India all had an impact on immigrant Muslims in the West.[17] A significant segment of these immigrants who flocked to the West in the sixties and seventies were already living in virtual parallel societies and remained largely disconnected socially and culturally from mainstream communities. After the seventies however, the second generation of these immigrants came increasingly under the influence of resurgent Islam. A significant number of this community became members of several Islamic organizations, like the Islamic Society of North America and the Council on American-Islamic Relations, which were generously funded by Saudi Arabia and other Gulf countries, and became centres for the propagation of Islamist ideals.[18]

The Islamic prohibition of interest kept many Muslim families in the West away from the housing-mortgage market. Many of them preferred to live in rental properties rather than purchasing their own through bank loans. Even though the European Council for Research and Fatwas and the League of Scholars for Shari'a in the USA had allowed, on the basis of the Hanafi school of Islamic jurisprudence, interest-based borrowing from banks for financing homes, the more orthodox Muslims, like the Moroccans in the Netherlands and *salafis* in the US and in other parts of Europe, kept aloof from conventional mortgage markets.[19] It was this unmet need within the immigrant Muslim community that initially offered a lucrative opportunity for IB&F to enter the West. Several so-called

[16] Pew Forum on Religion & Public Life, 'Mapping the Global Muslim Population', (Washington DC: Pew Research Center, 2009); Hussein Kettani, '2010 World Muslim Population' (paper presented at the Hawaii International Conference on Arts and Humanities, January 12–16 Honolulu, 2010).

[17] Ahmed, *A Quiet Revolution: The Veil's Resurgence, From the Middle East to America.*

[18] Ibid.

[19] Visser, *Islamic Finance: Principles and Practice*, 106, 142–4.

shari'a-compliant financial products were devised, such as *murabaha* or cost-plus sale, where the financier buys the house and resells it to the ultimate buyer with a mark-up against periodic payments; *ijara wa iqtina* or deferred payment sale, where the client finds a home and asks the financier to buy it, the financier then sells the house to the client against deferred payment, possibly at the same price, but holds on to the title until the last payment is made; *musharaka mutanaqisah*, or partnership contract, where the financier and the home buyer jointly own the home and over time the fancier's share diminishes continuously as the home buyer's share increases; and *istisna*, or sale with deferred delivery, which involves financing of home construction.[20] Although these shari'a-compliant products are more expensive and complex to transact than conventional ones, and therefore were criticized by some scholars as Islamic only in name,[21] to the religiously committed, those products are deemed qualitatively better and are therefore spiritually rewarding. The Al-Baraka Islamic Bank in Britain until its closure in 1993, and the United Bank of Kuwait concentrated their business mainly in the housing market.[22]

Another shari'a-compliant product, the *sukuk* or asset-backed Islamic bonds, which originated outside the immigrant communities, and which were to draw high demand after 2000, had its religious legitimation in the 1980s when the Fiqh Academy of the Organization of the Islamic Conference (OIC) gave its approval in 1988.[23] *Sukuks* are 'certificates that represent ownership of an underlying pool of assets, or the usufruct … of such assets, and therefore, entitle their holders to return resulting from the sale or lease of the assets'.[24] There are about 14 different types of *sukuk* described as permissible in the AAOIFI (Accounting and Auditing Organization for Islamic Financial Institutions) shari'a standards on *sukuk*. Most *sukuk* issues have been sponsored by sovereign and quasi-sovereign issuers in Islamic countries. Currently, Malaysia is the pacemaker and leader for the development of *sukuks* when in 2002 the Malaysian Government kick-started the market with a US$600 million issuance backed by lease payments.[25] In 2003, Qatar followed with an issuance of US$700 million. Bahrain and Pakistan did the

---

[20] Ibid., 107–12.

[21] Mahmoud A. El-Gamal, *Islamic Finance: Law, Economics, and Practice* (New York: Cambridge University Press, 2006).

[22] M. Fahim Khan and Mario Porzio, eds, *Islamic Banking and Finance in the European Union : A Challenge*, Studies in Islamic Finance, Accounting and Governance Series (Northampton, MA: Edward Elgar Pub., 2010), 213–15.

[23] Andreas A. Jobst, 'The Effects of the Global Crisis on Islamic and Conventional Banks: A Comparative Study', *IMF Working Paper, WP/07/117* (Washington: International Monetary Fund, 2007).

[24] Ibrahim Warde, *Islamic Finance in the Global Economy* (Edinburgh: Edinburgh University Press, 2010), 150.

[25] Jobst, 'The Effects of the Global Crisis on Islamic and Conventional Banks: A Comparative Study'.

same for US$250 million and US$600 million in 2004 and 2005 respectively.[26] According to the London based IFIS (Islamic Finance Information Service), the total value of *sukuk* issued in the first half of 2010 had exceeded US$20 billion.[27]

Conventional insurance is another prohibited area for Muslims according to a majority of shari'a experts. The Fiqh Council of the World Muslim League in 1978 and the Fiqh Academy of the OIC in 1985 declared conventional insurance as *haram* or prohibited. This led to the birth of *takaful*, or cooperative or mutual insurance, in which an insurer agrees with other participants in the fund to mutually help each other by way of providing financial assistance should any member of the fund suffer a catastrophe or disaster. The *takaful* fund invests the contributions in a shari'a-compliant manner. Any surplus earned will be distributed to the participants.

With these shari'a-compliant innovations the IB&F industry with better standards of accounting and supervision carried out by the Accounting and Auditing Organization for Islamic Financial Institutions (AAOIFI) set up in Algiers in 1990, operated as an alternative and well integrated financial institution within and outside many Muslim countries in the 1980s and 1990s. Occasional financial scandals, such as the international investigation into the money laundering activities of the Bank of Credit and Commercial International (BCCI), which eventually led to the bank's collapse in 1991, did not seem to have much impact on the organic growth of IB&F.

The Impact of 9/11

The al-Qaeda sponsored terrorist attack on New York and Washington in 2001 and the decision by President George Bush Junior to declare an un-winnable war on terrorism spelt disaster to the life and security of all Muslim communities living in the West. However, the President's declaration of a 'financial war on terror' became an unexpected blessing for the growth of IB&F. 'This morning', announced President Bush on September 24, 2001, 'a major thrust of our war on terrorism began with a stroke of a pen. Today, we have launched a strike on the financial foundation of the global terror network'.[28] Following the President's announcement, the United Nations Security Council passed Resolution 1373 on September 28 requesting all nations to keep their financial system clean and free of terrorist funds. The G7 countries, the World Bank, and the International Monetary Fund introduced stringent measures of financial control to satisfy the UN stipulated conditions.[29]

---

[26] Ibid.

[27] AJP, 'Global Sukuk Markets', *Sukuk.net* (2011), http://www.sukuk.net/news/articles/73/Global-sukuk-markets.html.

[28] Quoted in Ibrahim Warde, *The Price of Fear: The Truth Behind the Financial War on Terror* (Berkeley: University of California Press, 2007), vii.

[29] Ibid.

The US Government's clampdown on the operation of all Muslim charities and its close surveillance over the activities of Islamic banks,[30] and similar actions by the British and European authorities, dealt a blow to the IB&F industry. It was in this hostile atmosphere that Sheikh Saleh Kamel, the founder of the Al-Baraka International Bank, called the Muslim financial institutions and individuals to withdraw their money from the West and invest in Muslim countries and develop the IB&F industry in the region.[31] Thus began a short exodus of Muslim investments from the West to Asia and the Middle East. According to Napoleoni, Muslim investors who held about $1,000 trillion in the US deserted the greenback and switched to safer destinations, which ultimately hurt the US dollar.[32] The rapid rise of Malaysia as the chief centre of Islamic banking coincides with this exodus.

In spite of the 9/11 infamy and subsequent clampdown on Islamic charities and finances, the rising disenchantment against a global turbo-capitalist economy, 'liberated from government regulation, unchecked by effective trade unions, unfettered by sentimental concerns over the fate of employees or communities, unrestrained by customs barriers or investment restrictions, and unmolested as little as possible by taxation',[33] had already produced several anti-globalization protests starting in Seattle in November 1999. The common cry in all such protests was 'economic justice'. In the world of banking and finance it meant a call for limits on investing in risky assets and making greedy profits.

The financial meltdown triggered by the sub-prime mortgage crisis in the United States in 2008 was only the severest of more than one hundred economic and financial crises over the last four decades. Excessive and imprudent lending by banks, high leverage enabling such lending, greed and speculation, lack of managerial and accounting transparency, and weak regulatory mechanisms are some of the reasons that may have contributed to these crises. However, even before the 2008 crisis there had been calls for ethical investments and socially responsible behaviour of investors and corporations, from economists like Joseph Stiglitz and financial experts like George Soros who had become increasingly critical of market fundamentalism. Above all, and surprisingly, in a joint report authored by Loretta Napoleoni and Claudia Segre, the Abaxbank Spa fixed income strategist, and published in the official newspaper of the Vatican *L'Osservatore Romano* on 5 March 2009, Islamic finance was cited as the solution to the global financial crisis. 'The ethical principles on which Islamic finance (are) based', said the authors, 'may bring banks closer to their clients and to the true spirit which should mark every financial service'. 'Western banks', they continued, 'could use tools such as the Islamic bonds, known as sukuk, as collateral'. Giovanni Maria

30 Ibid., 74.

31 Warde, *Islamic Finance in the Global Economy*, 86.

32 Napoleoni, *Terrorism and the Economy: How the War on Terror is Bankrupting the World*, 76.

33 Edward Luttwak, *Turbo-capitalism: Winners and Losers in the Global Economy*, 1st US ed. (New York: HarperCollins Publishers, 1999), 27.

Vian, the editor of the paper, in an effort to include Christianity in the picture added that 'great religions have always had a common attention to the human dimension of the economy'.[34] This endorsement from the most powerful Christian quarter is another testimony to the changed global attitude towards the IB&F industry.

The participation of non-Muslim governments and institutions in the IB&F industry is the most interesting development after 2001. Their participation is noteworthy in the property market and *sukuk* issuance. In the property market, for example, the Singapore-listed Cambridge Industrial Trust has been transformed into an Islamic property trust. The National Australia Bank has also shown interest in investing US$35 million for a stake in the world's first listed shari'a-compliant industrial property trust. It will be the first publicly listed shari'a-compliant Real Estate Investment Trust in Singapore. In *sukuk* issuance, the World Bank, for example, issued its first local-currency dominated 760 million Malaysian Ringgits *sukuk* in 2005. In Germany the provincial government of Saxony Anhalt raised €100 million from both Middle East and European investors through *sukuk*. In Japan, the Financial Services Authority has proposed an amendment to the banking law to allow Japanese banks to offer Islamic products through a subsidiary.[35]

Intellectual Debate on IB&F

Between the 1970s, when IB&F was at its experimental stage, and the 1990s, when it received recognition as a separate and unique entity by the global financial industry, intellectual debate on Islamic economics in general, and IB&F in particular, had swung from theological generalities and euphoric support to simplistic secular reductionism and outright condemnation. While the supporters were mainly concerned with implementing the shari'a-prohibition of *riba*, *gharar*, and *maysir*, and therefore redesigned and renamed some of the conventional financial products to circumvent religious prohibition, the opponents criticized those products solely on the basis of legal trickery and economic inefficiency. El-Gamal, a prominent critic of IB&F, underlines this dichotomy when he writes that 'the primary emphasis in Islamic finance is not on efficiency and fair pricing. Rather, the emphasis is on contract mechanics and certification of Islamicity by "Shari'a Supervisory Boards"'.[36] The entire IB&F industry, to another Muslim thinker, is 'a prolonged exercise in artful delusion' and an 'oxymoron'.[37] Even Ibrahim Warde, an expert on international business and a supporter of IB&F, concedes the fact that the industry '[r]ather than being a different financial system, based on partnership finance … ha[s] generally mirrored conventional finance and concentrated on

[34] Lorenzo Totaro, 'Vatican Says Islamic Finance May Help Western Banks in Crisis', *Bloomberg*, 4 March 2009.

[35] AJP, 'Global Sukuk Markets'.

[36] El-Gamal, *Islamic Finance: Law, Economics, and Practice*, 1.

[37] Ali A. Allawi, *The Crisis of Islamic civilization* (New Haven, Conn.: Yale University Press, 2009), 214–15.

short-term financial transactions'.[38] However, he attributes this shortcoming to the relative immaturity and therefore the growing pains of the industry. In spite of its double digit growth, from an average of 14 per cent a year between 1994 and 2002 to 26 per cent a year between 2003 and 2009, the industry 'did not … quite live up to its original billing'.[39]

The argument that IB&F products are expensive and therefore economically inefficient should be balanced against the fact that it is qualitatively a better product, at least in the eyes of the beholders. To the Muslim faithful who want to be guided by shari'a, the higher cost is the price for keeping their financial matters clean of *riba*, *maysir*, and *gharar*. Still, one has to confront the other criticism of El-Gamal about the actual Islamicity of the products. With at least four different major schools of jurisprudence in *sunni* Islam, namely Shafii, Hanafii, Maliki and Hanbali, and with an altogether separate *shia* school, there is a multiplicity of legal opinion on every single issue that affects a Muslim. In matters of economics and finance, the Islamicity or otherwise of a certain product or service will ultimately depend on the verdict of the board of scholars or shari'a boards who advise various governments and financial institutions. Experts on Islamic shari'a equipped with equal expertise on banking and finance are in short supply. According to a 2008 report there are only 60 such scholars worldwide.[40] On top of that there is also a serious shortage of skilled personnel who could innovate and introduce new shari'a-compliant products and make them marketable. Conflict of interest and pecuniary motives among the innovators, approvers, and suppliers of shari'a-compliant products may threaten the credibility of the industry and will make it supply-driven rather than demand-driven. Even though organizations like the Islamic Financial Services Board (IFSB)[41] and AAOIFI are striving towards creating shari'a-convergent standards, the hardline Wahhabi school in Saudi Arabia and its supporters in other parts of the world may present a problem for the sustainability of some of the shari'a-compliant products. The influence of Wahhabi orthodoxy from Saudi Arabia, in extending bilateral economic and financial assistance through microfinancing, has recently become evident, especially in the light of Iran's entry into the same arena.

Mutual Accommodation and Convergence

When IB&F emerged as a possible alternative to conventional banking and finance in the 1970s it was like David challenging Goliath. Even after four decades of respectable growth amidst a tumultuous political and economic environment IB&F, as pointed out at the beginning, is tiny in size and in no way a threat to the conventional sector. However, after the 2008 sub-prime mortgage collapse

---

[38] Warde, *Islamic Finance in the Global Economy*, 247.

[39] Ibid., 247.

[40] Sharmila Devi, 'Scholars and Harmony in Short Supply', *Financial Times*, 18 June 2008.

[41] See www.ifsb.org.

in the United States, which triggered a banking and financial crisis worldwide producing the 'Great Recession',[42] there was immense pressure from governments, inter-governmental organizations and NGOs for the banking and finance industry to radically change its business behaviour by making it socially responsible, less risky and more transparent and accountable. A worldwide demand for an efficient regulatory mechanism to control the reckless behaviour of mega-banks and other financial institutions, especially in the United States and Europe, is bound to impose limits on risky operations. The need to control leverage, to restructure banking and financial assets by shifting from asset-based to asset-backed assets, and to improve institutional governance are measures promoted as part of the banking and financial reforms. Ironically these are the pillars on which IB&F claims to have built itself.

On the side of IB&F it has been observed that a number of its products that are marketed as shari'a-compliant differ only in their Arabized names but not in substance. For example, in the case of *murabaha* contracts in mortgage financing 'the result looked a lot like interest, and some argue that murabaha is simply the thinly veiled version of it. … The bank officials argue that God is in the details'.[43] Similarly El-Gamal finds not much difference between the *sukuk* and conventional bonds.[44] In fact he agrees with other observers that there is 'tension between attempts to be essentially similar to conventional finance … and attempts to preserve a distinctive Islamic character …'.[45] In this tension the bank officials and financiers who design and market various shari'a-compliant products and the shari'a-boards that approve those products are indulging in an age old practice of *hiyal* or legal trickery in order to circumvent the religious prohibition of *riba*, *maysir*, and *gharar*. It should also be stated that Islamic banking is acting like a money laundering mechanism to religiously legitimize wealth earned otherwise in non-halal sectors.

The advice of Muzzam Ali, the founder of the Institute of Islamic Banking and Insurance (IIBI), to the experts in both IB&F and conventional banking and finance quoted in the brochure of the 2012 Annual Three-day Residential Workshop in Cambridge, UK, captures the evolving convergence between *hiyal*-based IB&F and secular banking and finance industry. 'If Islamic banking has to develop', according to Ali, 'one has to take advantage of the innovative products wherever available. For your own sake, accept anything good wherever you find it. Do not stick to stereotyped philosophies. Western bankers and financial experts should also look at the Islamic parameters with an open mind'.[46]

---

42 Robert W. Kolb, *The Financial Crisis of our Time*, Financial Management Association Survey and Synthesis Series (New York: Oxford University Press, 2011).

43 J. Useem, 'Banking on Allah', *Fortune*, 10 June 2002.

44 El-Gamal, *Islamic Finance: Law, Economics, and Practice*, 97.

45 Useem, 'Banking on Allah', 2.

46 Quoted in Institute of Islamic Banking & Insurance, '6th Annual Three Day Residential Workshop Brochure', (2012), http://www.islamic-banking.com/resources/1/Cambridge%20Ws%202012/IIBI%20Workshop%20Cambridge%20for%202012%20website_withspons.pdf.

Thus, what one finds in the development of the faith-based and secular banking and finance industries is a progressive movement towards accommodating each other. While the latter undertakes to reform its business behaviour by incorporating some of the ethical values enshrined in Islamic Banking and Finance, the former, by borrowing the conventional products and adding an Islamic veneer to them, is virtually blurring the line of demarcation between the two. In globalized economies in which institutional structures are increasingly losing their rigidities, such borrowing and blending become unavoidable. Finally, the regime changes brought upon by the Arab Spring created more opportunities for the expansion of Islamic finance. The majority of the new regimes that followed the uprisings were, until recently, headed by Islamist parties like the Muslim Brotherhood in Egypt and the Ennahda Party in Tunisia; but all of them are sympathetic towards an Islamized economic structure which opens up more opportunities for IB&F.

Arab Foreign Aid

Although the immediate cause for the upsurge of Arab aid in the 1970s and 1980s was partly to mitigate the negative developmental impact of skyrocketing oil prices in the 'Third World' and partly to garner support from the poorer members of the United Nations for the Arab use of oil as a strategic weapon in the Arab–Israeli conflict,[47] one cannot ignore the religious underpinnings of this new phenomenon. Unlike in other religions Islam has made charity compulsory for those who have excess to spare. While *riba* is prohibited, *zakat* is promoted and is one of the five pillars of Islam. The 2.5 per cent *zakat*, imposed by the shari'a upon the wealthy, cannot be dismissed as irrelevant to the collective generosity of affluent Arab nations. In a sense, the prohibition of *riba* and the duty of giving *zakat* are both cleansers. The former cleanses financial transactions from unethical impurities and the latter does the same for capital. Thus, while IB&F claims to cleanse the financial sector of *riba*, Arab aid on the other hand, motivated by the principle of *zakat*, purifies the remaining Arab wealth from any unethical taint. This link between *zakat* and Arab aid has elevated that religious institution to an exemplary international arm of Muslim development assistance,[48] though '[t]he religious motive for giving aid is somewhat neglected in the literature, and plays an important role both for Arab donors and the recipient societies'.[49]

The amount of Arab aid grew in terms of both absolute dollar volume and as a ratio of donors' respective gross national product (GNP). This ratio surpassed

---

47 Debra Shushan and Christopher Marcoux, 'The Rise (and Decline?) of Arab aid: Generosity and Allocation in the Oil Era', *World Development* 39, no. 11 (2011): 1969–80.

48 Saudi Aramco, 'Arab Aid: An Introduction', *Saudi Aramco World Magazine* 30, no. 6 (1979), http://www.saudiaramcoworld.com/issue/197906/arab.aid-an.introduction.htm.

49 E. Villanger, 'Arab Foreign Aid: Disbursement Patterns, Aid Policies and Motives', *CMI Report No.2* (Bergen: Chr Michelsen Institute, 2007), 19.

the minimum target of 0.70 per cent of GNP set by the United Nations in 1970. Robert McNamara, the then President of the World Bank, by adding a 30 per cent 'depleting factor' to oil resources, estimated in 1974 that the United Arab Emirates (UAE) and Qatar donated 13 and 7 per cent of their respective GNP to foreign aid.[50] These were undoubtedly 'unprecedented ratios in the history of economic assistance by the richer countries to the poorer ones'.[51]

It is difficult to quantify the scale of Arab foreign aid partly because of paucity of data supplied by national aid organizations, and partly because of 'additional unreported transfers by Arab governments which bypass the bilateral organizations'.[52] Arab foreign aid operates through both multilateral and bilateral organizations. Among the former, the main organizations are the Arab Fund for Economic and Social Development (AFESD), established in 1974 and located in Kuwait; the Islamic Development Bank (IDB), established in 1975 and headquartered in Jeddah, Saudi Arabia; the OPEC Fund for International Development (OFID) established in 1976 and based in Vienna; the Arab Bank for Economic Development in Africa (BADEA), established in 1975 and based in Khartoum in Sudan; the Arab Monetary Fund (AMF) founded in 1976 and headquartered in Abu Dhabi; and the Arab Gulf Program for United Nations Development Organizations (AGFUND), founded in 1980 and based in Riyadh, Saudi Arabia. Among the bilateral aid organizations, the Kuwait Fund for Arab Economic Development (KFAED) established in 1961, the Abu Dhabi Fund for Development (ADFD) founded in 1971, and the Saudi Fund for Development (SFD) started in 1974 are the more notable.

According to a 2007 study by Espen Villanger of the CHR Michelsen Institute, it appears that since the inception of all but one of these organizations, the AGFUND, a total of $90.5 billion worth of aid had been disbursed for various development projects within and outside the Arab world.[53] If one was to add donations by private Arab individuals and non-government organizations, which normally go unrecorded, the total amount may increase severalfold.

Shushan and Marcoux in their study of Arab generosity have noted that the scale of the aid has declined in recent years and has not kept up with rising national income in the Arab donor countries. Kuwait and Saudi Arabia, according to their findings, clearly demonstrate this declining generosity. A greater emphasis on multilateral rather than bilateral aid and an increasing propensity to spend domestically are two reasons they attribute to this decline.[54] There is also a third reason, which is linked to the growth of IB&F and changing economic philosophy

[50] Saudi Aramco, 'Arab Aid: An Introduction'.

[51] Ibid.

[52] Shushan and Marcoux, 'The Rise (and Decline?) of Arab Aid: Generosity and Allocation in the Oil Era'.

[53] Villanger, 'Arab Foreign Aid: Disbursement Patterns, Aid Policies and Motives', 2.

[54] Shushan and Marcoux, 'The Rise (and Decline?) of Arab Aid: Generosity and Allocation in the Oil Era'.

about the effectiveness of aid. Generally speaking, the rise of economic liberalism in the 1980s and policies associated with it de-emphasized the role of official development assistance and stressed the importance of free trade, private enterprise, and open markets as assured means of reducing poverty and promoting economic growth in developing countries. Foreign direct investment, and not foreign aid, became the prescribed cure for poverty alleviation and economic prosperity. Economic recession and consequent domestic problems in the donor countries added further to a mood of aid weariness among international donors. In 22 of the donor countries the ratio of ODA to Gross National Income (GNI), which never met the UN target of 0.7 per cent, declined from 0.35 per cent in 1985 to 0.23 per cent in 2002.[55] This shift in economic thinking did not fail to impact Arab donors too. While the Arab donor economies themselves were successfully embracing the principles of market liberalism and private enterprise they saw no reason why those principles could not work for the aid recipients. Thus, in their view what was needed for poorer nations and communities was access to recoverable institutionalized halal funds to encourage private initiative, which IB&F provided, rather than to make them depend outright on charity.

There was also another reason for the decline in bilateral aid. This is related to the lack of an efficient institutional structure to monitor the effectiveness of funds disbursed to recipients through direct aid. This structural shortcoming was highlighted by the *Arab Human Development Report 2002* as a general weakness that militated against Arab development.[56] In fact, even among development economists there is a significant number who argue for more foreign investment than foreign aid. It is in this climate of liberal economic thinking that the supply of cheap and *riba*-free finance through IB&F was thought to be a more effective way of promoting economic development than to provide concessional loans and outright grants to poorer Muslim countries. This explains the robust growth of Islamic banking and finance and the relative decline of Arab bilateral aid. However, this argument does not apply to private donations from individuals and Arab NGOs. For example, the International Islamic Relief Organization, an arm of the Rabita al-Alam al-Islami (RABITA), or Muslim World League of Saudi Arabia, had a budget of $47 million in 2009; similarly, three other transnational Muslim NGOs, Islamic Relief, Muslim Aid and International Islamic Charitable Organization, had budgets of $96 million (1984), $73 million (1985) and $30 million (1984) respectively. Among these RABITA is accused of spreading Wahhabi orthodoxy through economic assistance.[57]

---

55 Michael P. Todaro and Stephen C. Smith, *Economic Development*, 9th ed. (Boston: Pearson Addison Wesley, 2006), 720.

56 UNDP Regional Bureau for Arab States, 'Arab Human Development Report 2002', (New York: UNDP, 2002).

57 See Marie Juul Petersen, 'For Humanity or for the Umma? Ideologies of Aid in Four Transnational Muslim NGOs' (Unpublished Doctoral Thesis, University of Copenhagen, 2011), 171.

Conclusion

The aim of this chapter has been to provide an overview of the development of the IB&F sector, its various core elements and its relationship with foreign aid and charity. As has been shown, the sector, although small, and despite the attack on the industry following 9/11 that saw an exodus of Islamic finance from the West, has continued to grow at a rapid rate, with double digit growth going as high as 26 per cent a year. A further indication of the sector's future is the fact that many mainstream banks have recognized the emergent sector and opened Islamic banking windows to meet the needs of increasingly affluent Muslim countries, as exemplified by Malaysia.

Interestingly, the emergence of the IB&F sector has not seen a concomitant growth in economic aid and charity. Rather, as touched on above, it has led Muslim economists to suggest that the solution is not to provide direct bilateral assistance through ad hoc loans and charity, but rather for the IB&F sector to provide poorer nations and communities with access to recoverable institutionalized halal funds that encourage private initiative, rather than to make them depend on outright charity. This is leading to interesting intersections between IB&F and the development sectors. For an insight into the burgeoning relationship between IB&F and aid see the contribution by Aimatul Yumna in this volume.

References

Ahmed, Leila. *A Quiet Revolution: The Veil's Resurgence, from the Middle East to America*. New Haven: Yale University Press, 2011.

AJP. 'Global Sukuk Markets'. *Sukuk.net* (2011). http://www.sukuk.net/news/articles/73/Global-sukuk-markets.html.

Ali, Ameer. 'NAB May Lose Interest but Keep the Faith'. *The Australian Financial Review*, 1 July 2009.

Allawi, Ali A. *The Crisis of Islamic Civilization*. New Haven, Conn.: Yale University Press, 2009.

Caplen, Brian, and Joseph DiVanna. 'Top 500 Islamic Financial Institutions'. *The Banker*, 24 November 2007.

Dabashi, Hamid. *The Arab Spring: The End of Postcolonialism*. New York: Zed Books, 2012.

Davies, Anjuli. 'Global Islamic Finance Assets Hit $1.3 Trillion – Study'. (2012). http://www.reuters.com/article/2012/03/29/islamic-finance-growth-idUSL6E8ET3KE20120329.

Devi, Sharmila 'Scholars and Harmony in Short Supply'. *Financial Times*, 18 June 2008.

El-Gamal, Mahmoud A. *Islamic Finance: Law, Economics, and Practice*. New York: Cambridge University Press, 2006.

Farell, Diana, Susan Lund, Oskar Skau, Charles Atkins, Jan Philipp Mengeringhaus, and Moira S. Pirece. 'Mapping Global Capital Markets: Fifth Annual Report'. San Francisco: McKinsey & Company 2008.

Hasan, Maher, and Jemma Dridi. 'The Effects of the Global Crisis on Islamic and Conventional Banks: A Comparative Study'. *IMF Working Paper WP/10/201*. Washington: International Monetary Fund, 2010.

Institute of Islamic Banking & Insurance. '6th Annual Three Day Residential Workshop Brochure', (2012). http://www.islamic-banking.com/resources/1/Cambridge%20Ws%202012/IIBI%20Workshop%20Cambridge%20for%202012%20website_withspons.pdf.

Jobst, Andreas A. 'The Effects of the Global Crisis on Islamic and Conventional Banks: A Comparative Study'. *IMF Working Paper, WP/07/117*. Washington: International Monetary Fund, 2007.

Kettani, Hussein. '2010 World Muslim Population'. Paper presented at the Hawaii International Conference on Arts and Humanities, January 12–16 Honolulu, 2010.

Khan, M. Fahim, and Mario Porzio, eds. *Islamic Banking and Finance in the European Union: A Challenge*, Studies in Islamic Finance, Accounting and Governance Series. Northampton, MA: Edward Elgar Pub., 2010.

Kolb, Robert W. *The Financial Crisis of Our Time*. Financial Management Association Survey and Synthesis Series. New York: Oxford University Press, 2011.

KPMG. 'Making the Transition from Niche to Mainstream: Islamic Banking and Finance: A Snapshot of the Industry and Its Challenges Today'. (2006). http://us.kpmg.com/microsite/FSLibraryDotCom/docs/Islamic%20Banking%20and%20Finance%20-%20A%20Snapshot%20of%20the%20Industry%20and%20Its%20Challenges%20Today.pdf.

Luttwak, Edward. *Turbo-Capitalism: Winners and Losers in the Global Economy*. 1st US ed. New York: HarperCollins Publishers, 1999.

Napoleoni, Loretta. *Terrorism and the Economy: How the War on Terror Is Bankrupting the World*. New York: Seven Stories Press, 2010.

Petersen, Marie Juul. 'For Humanity or for the Umma? Ideologies of Aid in Four Transnational Muslim NGOs'. Unpublished Doctoral Thesis, University of Copenhagen, 2011.

Pew Forum on Religion & Public Life. 'Mapping the Global Muslim Population'. Washington DC: Pew Research Center, 2009.

Saeed, Abdullah. 'The Muslim Community Co-operative of Australia as an Islamic Financial Service Provider'. In *Muslim Communities in Australia*, edited by Shahram Akbarzadeh and Abdullah Saeed, xii. Sydney: UNSW Press, 2001.

Saudi Aramco. 'Arab Aid: An Introduction'. *Saudi Aramco World Magazine* 30, no. 6 (1979). http://www.saudiaramcoworld.com/issue/197906/arab.aid-an.introduction.htm.

Shihata, Ibrahim F.I. *The Other Face of Opec: Financial Assistance to the Third World*. Energy Resources and Policies of the Middle East and North Africa. London; New York: Longman, 1982.

Shushan, Debra, and Christopher Marcoux. 'The Rise (and Decline?) of Arab Aid: Generosity and Allocation in the Oil Era'. *World Development* 39, no. 11 (2011): 1969–80.

Tawney, R.H. *Religion and the Rise of Capitalism: A Historical Study*. London: J. Murray, 1926.

Todaro, Michael P. and Stephen C. Smith. *Economic Development*. 9th ed. Boston: Pearson Addison Wesley, 2006.

Totaro, Lorenzo 'Vatican Says Islamic Finance May Help Western Banks in Crisis'. *Bloomberg*, 4 March 2009.

Tripathi, Purnima S. 'Inclusive Banking'. *Frontline* 26, no. 21 (2009): 43–6.

UNDP Regional Bureau for Arab States. 'Arab Human Development Report 2002'. New York: UNDP, 2002.

Useem, J. 'Banking on Allah'. *Fortune*, 10 June 2002.

Villanger, E. 'Arab Foreign Aid: Disbursement Patterns, Aid Policies and Motives'. *CMI Report No.2*. Bergen: Chr Michelsen Institute, 2007.

Visser, H. *Islamic Finance: Principles and Practice*. Cheltenham, UK; Northampton, MA: Edward Elgar, 2009.

Warde, Ibrahim. *Islamic Finance in the Global Economy*. Edinburgh: Edinburgh University Press, 2010.

———. *The Price of Fear: The Truth Behind the Financial War on Terror*. Berkeley: University of California Press, 2007.

PART II
Islam in Practice

Chapter 6
Applying Islamic Finance Principles to Microfinance

Aimatul Yumna

Introduction

Financial exclusion is one of the major factors that inhibit the poor from being able to actively participate in the development process. Financial exclusion is defined as a situation where a proportion of the population has limited access to mainstream financial services.[1] It often constrains the ability of the poor to acquire assets, start a business, finance their emergency needs and increase their welfare.[2] The implications of financial exclusion include not only financial consequences, but also social consequences, which have disadvantageous effects and push the excluded further into the poverty cycle. Financial exclusion has been cited as one of the obstacles in the achievement of the first six out of the eight Millennium Development Goals (MDGs) 2015.[3]

Microfinance is a development strategy to enhance financial inclusion. It is designed to provide a full range of financial services for low income people. The Consultative Group to Assist the Poor (CGAP) defines microfinance as the supply of loans, savings and other basic financial services to the disadvantaged.[4]

---

[1] Muhamed Hersi Warsame, 'The Role of Islamic Finance in Tackling Financial Exclusion in the UK' (PhD Thesis, Durham University, 2009).

[2] Manfred Zeller and Richard L. Meyer, *The Triangle of Microfinance: Financial Sustainability, Outreach and Impact* (Johns Hopkins University Press, 2002).

[3] Jonathan and Barbara Haley Morduch, 'Analysis of the Effects of Microfinance on Poverty Reduction', *NYU Wagner Working Paper 2002*. The MGDs 2015 are: reduce people living in poverty by half between 1990 and 2015; enrol all children in primary school by 2015; make progress toward gender equality and empowering women by eliminating gender disparities in primary and secondary education by 2015; reduce infant and child mortality rates by two-thirds between 1990 and 2015; reduce maternal mortality ratios by three quarters between 1990 and 2015; provide access to all who need reproductive health services by 2015; and to implement national strategies for sustainable development by 2005 so as to reserve the loss of environmental resources by 2015, and lastly, global partnership and development.

[4] CGAP, 'Introducing Savings in Microcredit Institutions: When and How?', *Focus Note* April, no. 8 (1997), http://www.cgap.org/sites/default/files/CGAP-Focus-Note-Introducing-Savings-in-Microcredit-Institutions-When-and-How-Apr-1997.pdf.

The poor are often excluded from mainstream financial institutions due to their inability to meet the minimum standard lending requirements. Microfinance with its unique characteristics of joint liability and a group lending mechanism has been successful in providing the poor with microproducts such as microsaving, microlending and other microfinancial transactions. The data from the Microcredit Summit Campaign 2007 shows it has served 154.8 million poor clients in 3,352 Microfinance Institutions (MFIs) worldwide.[5]

However, while microfinance is making some headway towards alleviating poverty, many MFIs still face a range of limitations in providing effective services for the poor. The main problem is the lack of economic viability of the institutions, on account of a lack of mobilized funds to expand the operation as well as high levels of non-performing loans.[6] Microfinance clients are usually perceived as high risk borrowers due to their inability to provide physical collateral. Furthermore, microfinance requires high operational costs for loan distribution, monitoring and enforcement. Additional problems such as poor infrastructure, illiteracy and health problems also contribute to the poor performance of microfinance.

Another limitation of microfinance is that it only targets the upper levels of the poor. According to The World Bank, two-thirds of the people defined as poor by the $1 a day standard are classified as extremely poor, and would not be served by microfinance. Poor households – the target clients of microfinance – face multiple constraints on earning. They often lack marketable skills and education or suffer from illnesses that impact on their productivity. Hence, microfinance has to identify the nonfinancial constraints of their clients and provide them with various training and education facilities to enhance their ability to generate income.[7] Most MFIs have subsidized social development programmes that run alongside their credit programme, which provide periodical training and workshops to enhance the skills of its members. Subsequently, the cost of running such support programmes increases the cost of providing microfinance services.[8]

Considering the limitations of microfinance outlined above, it is clear that there is scope to create more effective and widespread distribution in the microfinance sector, and it to this end that this chapter strives. It argues that the application of Islamic finance principles to the delivering of microfinance will achieve better outcomes in poverty alleviation. Islamic finance has unique characteristics that are ideologically and practically similar to microfinance. To begin, the chapter introduces the current limitations of microfinance, then examines the concept of microfinance and Islamic

---

[5] Sam Daley-Harris, 'State of the Microcredit Campaign Report 2009', (Washington: Microcredit Summit Campaign, 2009).

[6] Joanna Ledgerwood and Victoria White, *Transforming Microfinance Institutions: Providing Full Financial Services to the Poor* (Washington, DC: The World Bank, 2004).

[7] Zeller and Meyer, *The Triangle of Microfinance: Financial Sustainability, Outreach and Impact*.

[8] Habib Ahmed, 'Financing Microenterprises: An Analytical Study of Islamic Microfinance Institutions', *Islamic Economic Studies* 9, no. 2 (2002): 27–64.

finance, before outlining the similarities and differences between microfinance and Islamic finance principles in creating financial services. The application of Islamic finance concepts to microfinance is outlined in the following section, and is followed by two case studies that exemplify its application in Indonesia.

The Nexus of Microfinance and Islamic Finance

The Concept of Microfinance

Microfinance is not a new concept. The practice of non-formal microfinance, such as money lenders and rotating saving and credit associations (ROSCA), existed before the development of a formal financial system.[9] The first formal financial institutions that served poor people were developed in Europe in the 1800s.[10] The Irish Loan System was a sustainable system that served about 300 funds in the 1840s in Ireland. The development was continued in Germany when a more formal institution was developed under the financial cooperative system. The success of microfinance in the early 1800s in Ireland and Germany promoted the development of regulated microfinance institutions that mobilized savings from the poor and distributed loans through a credit cooperative. The root of the cooperative nowadays is based on the European movement. Another type of microfinance provider was that of the village banks that were established in Indonesia during the Dutch Colonial period.[11] The village banks became one of the major providers of a microfinance system in Indonesia with close to 9,000 units, mostly serving agricultural credit needs. The success of the village banks was widely adapted in parts of rural Latin America in the 1900s.

Microfinance further increased its popularity in the development discourse after the Grameen Bank was developed in Jobra, Bangladesh, by Muhammand Yunus in the 1970s. Yunus witnessed that people in Jobra needed credit to secure their food and to provide working capital for their small businesses. However, due to the risks inherent in serving the poor, none of the formal financial institutions would provide credit for them. As a result this group of people was served by informal money lenders who charged unreasonable rates of interest.[12] Yunus argued that

[9] Stuart Rutherford, *The Poor and Their Money* (New Delhi: The Department of International Development, 1999).

[10] Brigit Helms, *Access for All: Building Inclusive Financial Systems* (Washington DC: Consultative Group to Assist the Poorest, The World Bank, 2006); H.D. Seibel, 'History Matters in Microfinance', *Working Paper No.5* (University of Cologne, Development Research Centre, 2003).

[11] Jay K. Rosengard et al., 'The Promise and the Peril of Microfinance Institutions in Indonesia', *Bulletin of Indonesian Economic Studies* 43, no. 1 (2007): 87–112.

[12] Muhammad Yunus and Alan Jolis, *Banker to the Poor: Micro-Lending and the Battle Against World Poverty*, 1st ed. (New York: PublicAffairs, 1999).

structural problems in the economic system could not help the poor to widen their economic capacity. This problem motivated him to develop a microcredit system for the poor.

The microcredit system introduced by the Grameen Bank is the root of modern microfinance. A focus predominantly on women clients and the application of a group lending mechanism are the two success factors of microcredit that have been replicated around the world. In its early development, microcredit focused on serving women.[13] Women were willing to work harder to get out of poverty since they suffered the most; they would use their money for family purposes and to help give their children better lives. The literature notes that women are more reliable than men regarding loan repayments. Another innovation of microcredit was the application of a group lending mechanism, where every member of the group guarantees the loan repayment of all members. As the poor generally cannot provide asset backed guarantees, this mechanism is a powerful tool in reducing the incidence of non-performing loans.[14] In addition, the application of the group lending mechanism reduces the transaction cost of credit delivery by transferring the roles of information acquisition, loan monitoring, and loan enforcement, from the bank to the group of borrowers.[15]

Initially, microfinance was mostly limited to only providing loans.[16] Most of them were funded by either government or aid agencies based on soft capital. In the period from 1980 to the 1990s, microfinance had been applied worldwide and was seen as an important tool in alleviating poverty. A new paradigm emerged in the literature which argued that in order for microfinance to serve more people it has to be a sustainable institution.[17] This period came to be known as the microfinance revolution. MFIs began to develop and establish sustainable models for lending to the poor. Commercialization of microfinance became an alternative means of raising more capital through offering saving deposits and issuing equity or debt in a capital market. In addition, the financial services of MFIs are also more varied, ranging from savings deposits, loans, insurances, and fee-based financial services.

---

[13] Ibid.; Helms, *Access for All: Building Inclusive Financial Systems*.

[14] Beatriz Armendariz and Jonathan Morduch, *The Economics of Microfinance* (Cambridge, Mass.: MIT Press, 2005).

[15] Asyraf Wajdi Dusuki, 'Lifting Barriers in Financing the Small and Poor Entrepreneurs: Lessons from Group-Based Lending Scheme and Ibn Khaldun's Social Solidarity', in *Inclusive Islamic Financial Sector Development: Enhancing Islamic Financial Services for Micro and Medium Sized Enterprises (Conference Proceedings)*, ed. Muhammad Obaidullah and Hajah Salma Haji Abdul Latiff (Brunei Darussalam: Islamic Research and Training Institute, Islamic Development Bank/Centre for Islamic Banking, Finance andManagement, Universiti Brunei Darussalam 2008).

[16] Suresh M. Sundaresan, *Microfinance: Emerging Trends and Challenges* (Cheltenham, UK; Northampton, MA: Edward Elgar, 2008).

[17] Marguerite S. Robinson, *The Microfinance Revolution* (Washington, D.C.: World Bank, 2001).

Microfinance is strikingly different from commercial financial institutions. It focuses not only on the maximization of wealth for its stakeholders, but also on the provision of financial services for the poor for poverty alleviation purposes. As providing services for the poor is a high risk and high cost investment, this may raise problems in the future with regard to balancing its dual aims: reaching the poor and achieving financial sustainability.

The Concept of Islamic Finance

Islamic finance is the most dynamic sector in the world financial industry today. This industry's assets were estimated at US$822 billion in 2009 and have been growing at a rate of more than 10 per cent per annum for more than 10 years.[18] This substantial development has been driven by many factors. One of the most important factors is the significant influence of petroleum-producing countries in the Middle East on the global economy. There is an increasing demand for shari'a-compliant investment products in the Gulf and other regions due to the high surplus of oil revenue. The second factor is the sizeable Muslim population in the world. This untapped potential will contribute to persistent growth of Islamic finance in the future. The increasing awareness of ethical business and corporate social responsibility issues worldwide is another reason behind the rise of Islamic finance. Islamic finance is considered an ethical business model due to the prohibition of speculation and exploitation of stakeholders. There are four basic concepts of Islamic finance including: the prohibition of *riba* (interest); the prohibition of uncertainty and speculation; the profit loss sharing mechanism; and prohibition of unethical investment dealing with alcohol, prostitution and gambling.

The foundations of Islamic finance are the Qur'an and sunna. The prohibition in the Qur'an against *riba* is clearly stated in several verses: 30: 39; 4: 160–61; 3: 130; 4: 29; 2: 188; and 2: 275–80. Each of these verses makes the point that any revenue derived from a lending contract, regardless of its size and its rate, is considered *riba*. The practice of charging *riba* is a form of exploitation, specifically in the case of microfinance, where the higher interest rates are charged to the lower earners.[19]

Dhumale and Shapcanin define *riba* as the additional amount that debtors have to pay above the principal, which is dependent on the predetermined rate. In addition, any return from exchange of money for money and/or any delay on payment on agreed prices is considered as *riba*.[20] *Riba* is prohibited because it exploits the borrowers by

[18] Austrade, 'Islamic Finance', (Canberra: Australian Government, 2010).

[19] Rodney Wilson, 'Why Islamic Banking Is Successful?', (n/d), http://www-stud.rbi.informatik.uni-frankfurt.de/~osman/islamic-banking.pdf.

[20] Rahul Dhumale and Amela Shapcanin, 'An Application of Islamic Banking Principles to Microfinance', *Technical Note*. UNDP with the World Bank 1999.

Figure 6.1 Islamic Finance Principles

Source: Adapted from Austrade. 'Islamic Finance' (Canberra: Australian Government, 2010), 7.

making the lender better off at the expense of the borrower.[21] Furthermore the lender will depend on the income generated by the interest rate and support accumulation of wealth of the lender but deterioration of assets of the borrower. Interest rates are considered as a form of exploitation and an injustice which is inconsistent with the Islamic principles of fairness and property rights.[22] Predetermined rates of return in financial activities are prohibited since this can cause injustice. It becomes unfair for the borrower if they have to pay a fixed rate in the case of an unsuccessful business. Conversely, it becomes inequitable on the lender's side, if they only get a small percentage rate of return when the borrower earns considerable profit.[23] Thus, the prohibition of interest is the way Islam promotes justice in financial transactions.

Siddiqi provides a different interpretation with regard to how the Qur'an defines *riba*. Taking a modernist perspective, he argues that interest is prohibited if only an excessive interest rate is charged that exploits the borrowers.[24] Therefore, according to Siddiqi, interest rates are lawful under certain conditions, namely,

[21] Abdul Rahim Abdul Rahman, 'Islamic Microfinance: A Missing Component in Islamic Banking', *Kyoto Bulletin of Islamic Area Studies* 1, no. 2 (2007).

[22] Brian Kettell, *Frequently Asked Questions in Islamic Finance* (United Kingdom: John Wiley and Sons, 2010).

[23] Ajaz Ahmed Khan, *Islamic Microfinance: Theory, Policy and Practice* (Birmingham, United Kingdom: Islamic Relief Worldwide, 2008).

[24] Kiran Siddiqi, 'Potential of Islamic Microfinance in Pakistan' (Masters Thesis, Loughborough University, 2008).

interest paid by banks on saving deposits, interest paid on government loans, and interest paid on productive loans.[25] However, other more conservative scholars argue that any form of interest charged is considered as *riba*. Recently, there has been a growing consensus that any incremental amount on a loan is defined as *riba*.

Gharar is another main principle of Islamic finance prohibited by shari'a. *Gharar* refers to entering into a contract that involves high levels of risk or uncertainty about the ultimate result of the contract.[26] A *gharar* happens because of a lack of relevant information that leads to uncertainty and exploitation of other parties in any transaction. For example, Islamic finance prohibits gambling, selling an unborn lamb in its mother's womb, and any derivative products such as futures, forwards, and options, because of the uncertainty involved in the future delivery of the underlying assets.

Islamic banks tried to remove all forms of fixed nominal interest rates and avoid any speculative transactions. Hence, the profit loss sharing mechanism (PLS) comes in and replaces the interest based transaction on resource allocation and financial intermediation. In a PLS scheme, Islamic banks do not charge any kind of interest rate but rather participate in yield resulting activities. PLS encourages partnership between banks and depositors, as well as banks and borrowers.

Islamic finance application is guided by Islamic economic objectives. The objectives of Islamic economics include three aspects: the eradication of poverty, the promotion of socio-economic justice and the distribution of equitable income in society.[27] These objectives should be unyielding features of an Islamic economic system. With this resoluteness, Islamic banking should not only maximize profit, but also promote social justice by ensuring wealth is equally distributed in society.

The Similarities and Differences Between Islamic Banking and Microfinance

A major inhibitor for many of the poor in Muslim countries is their adherence to Islam. Around 72 per cent of people living in Muslim countries do not use formal financial services since the conventional financial services apply interest rates for both lending and savings deposits.[28] Poverty is widespread in Islamic countries. Therefore, providing financial services that are compatible with Islamic values is a necessary and crucial intervention for Muslim microentrepreneurs in improving their welfare.

---

25 Loans can be used either for productive and consumptive purposes. Loans for productive purposes are used as initial capital, working capital and for business development.

26 Muhammad Ayub, *Understanding Islamic Finance* (Hoboken, NJ: John Wiley & Sons, 2007).

27 M. Umer Chapra, *Towards a Just Monetary System: A Discussion of Money, Banking, and Monetary Policy in the Light of Islamic Teachings* (Leicester, UK: Islamic Foundation, 1985).

28 Nimrah Karim, Michael Tarazi, and Xavier Reille, 'Islamic Microfinance: An Emerging Market Niche', *Focus Note* August, no. 49 (2008), http://www.cgap.org/gm/document-1.9.5029/FN49.pdf.

Islamic banking as noted earlier has seen significant growth in the last 30 years. It has several potential advantages, such as excess liquidity and human resources to create financial services for this un-served sector of the population. However, Islamic banking is run mainly through private institutions focusing on profit maximization. Islamic banking does not charge interest, but can make profit from several sources, namely 1) profit sharing under *mudharabah* and *musyarakah* schemes; 2) fees from *Qard al-Hassan*, transfers, and other fee based transactions; 3) investment in halal financial instruments; 4) mark-up sales under *murabahah* schemes. The current studies by Abdul Rahman and Siddiqi argue that Islamic banking has abandoned the poorest, since the cost of serving them is very high and can reduce the Islamic banks' profitability.[29] There is an increasing pressure for Islamic banking to put more emphasis on the achievement of Islamic economic objectives, rather than only on profit maximization. Therefore, by entering into the microfinance sector, Islamic banks may play a better role in distributing wealth for all in society. A summary of the similarities and differences between Islamic finance and microfinance is presented in Table 6.1.

Table 6.1 Similarities and Differences between Islamic Finance and Microfinance

Similarities
1. Both have a social mission to fight poverty
2. Both promote entrepreneurship
3. Both encourage risk sharing
4. Both ensure the capital is equally distributed in society
Differences
1. Conventional microfinance is interest based financing, while Islamic finance prohibits interest
2. Many conventional microfinance institutions are non-profit institutions, while Islamic banks are private institutions
3. Microfinance's major source of funds is donor funds, while Islamic banks are funded by private investors
4. Microfinance focuses on social objectives, while Islamic banks strive for profit maximization

As Islamic finance practice is guided by Islamic economic objectives, such as promoting equality and fairness in society, we can see that microfinance and Islamic finance basically share similar ideological values. Both concepts strive to allow for the participation of all people, including the poor, in the economy.

29 Abdul Rahman, 'Islamic Microfinance: A Missing Component in Islamic Banking'; Siddiqi, 'Potential of Islamic Microfinance in Pakistan'.

In this way both Islamic finance and microfinance can complement each other. Islamic finance can help microfinance to tap into the potential of the Islamic world. Although there has been some scepticism, on account of the current motive of Islamic banking being profit maximization, some scholars argue that both systems are also practically linked.[30] The example of similar practice between Islamic finance and microfinance is the disbursement of collateral free loans for their clients. To get a better understanding of how both concepts can work together, the next section will highlight the various Islamic modes of transaction, and how these can be applied to microfinance.

Islamic Schemes of Transaction and its Application to Microfinance

Islamic Schemes of Transaction

Islamic schemes of transaction include various models that can be applied to microfinance depending on the characteristic and the needs of the customer. The schemes can be classified into four categories:

1. Participatory profit loss sharing model
This is in theory the ideal scheme since it encourages the participation of both the bank as the lender and the client as the borrower. However, in practice this mode is not popular due to its complexity, since there is no predetermined rate. Furthermore, it requires high monitoring costs since the funded project is independently managed by the borrower. This scheme is used to provide working capital investment, fixed asset purchase and project financing. There are two types of this model:

a. *Mudharabah* is a partnership between two parties: the bank as the investor, who provides 100 per cent of the capital, and the borrower, who provides the entrepreneurial skill to manage the project. Generated profit will be shared between the bank and the entrepreneur on a predetermined rate and any losses are borne by the bank as the investor. However, if the losses are caused by mismanagement, the entrepreneur will be responsible for the losses. The obligations of the bank in engaging in a *mudharabah* contract are: 1) The bank should not require collateral to reduce the risk of transaction; 2) The profit loss sharing percentage must be only at a predetermined rate not in a lump sum payment; 3) Entrepreneurs control and manage the project independently, but bank monitoring is allowed.[31]

---

[30] Nashir Shahinpoor, 'The Link Between Islamic Banking and Microfinancing', *International Journal of Social Economics* 36, no. 10 (2009): 996–1007.

[31] Dhumale and Shapcanin, 'An Application of Islamic Banking Principles to Microfinance'.

b. *Musyarakah* is an equity participation contract, where banks are not always the only providers of capital. In this scheme, there are two or more parties who share the capital and expertise. Profit and losses will be shared based on the amount of capital invested. The management of the project can be run by one party or both parties. This arrangement is more flexible since the profit sharing can be negotiated by both parties.

2. Sales based model

This scheme is the most popular Islamic banking scheme, since it presents the lowest risk for the bank, in contrast with participatory profit loss sharing, for several reasons. Firstly, this model eliminates the use of written reports from customers, so t's really suitable for illiterate customers, and it reduces the risk in terms of false reporting by the customer. Secondly, this model is an asset based investment, so it will reduce the diversion of funds for consumption purposes. Lastly, it has lower administrative costs compared to the participatory based model. As such, this scheme is suitable for providing investment assets, as well as working capital assets. The types of contract available in this model are as follows:

a. *Murabahah* resells the asset on the mark-up price by the lender to the borrower on a signed contract. Repayment is made on an instalment basis to the lender. This scheme is usually used to finance working capital assets such as raw materials, machinery and equipment.[32]
b. *Bai' Muajjal* is a deferred contract in which the bank as a seller of a product accepts deferred payments in instalments or in a lump sum. The price is agreed between the buyer and seller at the time of the sale, and the seller is not allowed to include any charge for deferring payments.
c. *Bai' salam* is similar to contract sales, where the price is paid in advance and the goods are delivered in the future.
d. *Bai' al-istishna* is a contract of acquisition of goods by specification or order, where the price is paid in advance, but the goods are manufactured and delivered at a later date.

3. Leased based model

The leased based model is known as *Ijarah*, which is defined as a contract under which a bank purchases and leases out equipment required by its clients for a rental fee. The duration of the lease and rental fees are agreed in advance. The ownership of the equipment remains with the bank. Another type of *Ijarah* is *Ijarah wa Iqtina*. The instalment in *Ijarah wa Iqtina* includes the acquiring price of the product. By the end of the instalment period, the possession of goods will be transferred to the clients. This scheme is suitable for financing fixed assets and equipment such as machinery and motor vehicles.

[32] Khan, *Islamic Microfinance: Theory, Policy and Practice.*

4. Voluntary charitable contract

This contract does not allow any financial return. Although this scheme can be used for all purposes, including consumptive and productive purposes, this contract is more beneficial to the microentrepreneur in providing start-up funds to begin productive activities. The instrument is known as *Qard al-Hassan*, which is defined as an interest free loan. As suggested in the Qur'an, every wealthy Muslim should help others. In this case, banks are permitted to charge an administrative fee for loan management. A comparison of each scheme is presented in Table 6.2.

Table 6.2 Summary of all Schemes

Issues	**Participatory profit loss sharing**	**Sales based Financing**	**Lease based**	**Charitable contract**
Purposes	Fixed asset and less likely working capital	Investment capital and working capital	Equipment, machinery and motor vehicles	Consumption and productive purposes
Cost to borrowers	Higher	Lower	Lower	None
Risk to borrowers	Lower, if there is no predetermined minimum profit	Higher, since the asset is owned by the institution until the last instalment is paid	Lower	None
Risk to the institution	Higher, if there is no predetermined minimum profit, i.e. accurate reporting	Lower, as the institution owns the asset	Moderate	Low, since the loan amount is low
Administrative cost of the institution	Higher, since PLS is more complicated	High initial cost to buy the asset	High initial cost	Low
Enforcement	Requires monitoring, difficult to enforce accurate reporting	Less difficult	Less difficult	Less difficult

Source: Compiled from Rahul Dhumale and Amela Shapcanin. 'An Application of Islamic Banking Principles to Microfinance', *Technical Note*. UNDP with the World Bank 1999; Muhammad Obaidullah, *Introduction to Islamic Microfinance*. India: IBF Net Pty Ltd, 2008.

Microfinance provides a wide range of financial services, including savings deposits, lending products and other fee-based financial services. The programme is usually characterized by small transactions in rural areas, implementing an alternative approach to both collateral and simple transactions.

In implementing Islamic finance principles, initially microfinance has to develop products to comply with the prohibition on *riba* and *gharar*. These prohibitions can be translated into four basic principles: a) risk and return sharing between microfinance and its clients; b) all the transactions need to be real transactions or asset based transactions; c) to prohibit exploitation of any party in the transaction, and d) no financing on *haram* or sinful activities, such as the production of alcoholic beverages.[33] Secondly, microfinance organizations need to be overseen by a Shari'a Supervisory Board to ensure products and services are consistent with the Islamic finance principle. Lastly, and the most challenging step, is the introduction of these concepts to all stakeholders. The lack of awareness or knowledge of Islamic finance principles will reduce the performance of microfinance and possibly lead to drop out from the industry. The study by Seibel of microfinance in Indonesia found that one of the central problems of microfinance is a lack of understanding by staff about the characteristics of Islamic finance products.[34]

A wide variety of Islamic instruments can be applied to microfinance. These instruments can be implemented into microsaving, microcredits and alternative products to microfinance.[35]

1. Microsaving

Offering microsaving is important for both the microfinance institution and its clients. From a microfinance institution's perspective, saving mobilization is critical to develop sustainable institutions and strengthen microfinance's role in poverty alleviation, while for the clients these savings products are important for aiding smooth consumption, stabilizing income, and as a precautionary motive. Microsaving can be designed by several Islamic instruments such as *wadiah*, *Qard al-Hassan* and *mudharabah*.

Wadiah is safekeeping for a deposit, wherein a microfinance institution can utilize the deposits for investment purposes at its own risk. The depositors do not share any profit or losses from the investment. However, microfinancers can provide gifts for the depositors. This scheme is similar to the *Qard al-Hassan*

---

[33] Dahlia A El Hawary and Wafik Grais, 'Islamic Financial Services and Microfinance', (2005), http://siteresources.worldbank.org/EXTISLAMF/Resources/IslamicFinancialServicesandMicrofinanceJune20b.pdf.

[34] Hans Dieter Seibel, 'Islamic Microfinance in Indonesia: The Challenge of Institutional Diversity, Regulation, and Supervision', *SOJOURN: Journal of Social Issues in Southeast Asia* 23, no. 1 (2008): 86–103.

[35] Muhammad Obaidullah, *Introduction to Islamic Microfinance* (India: IBF Net Pty Ltd, 2008).

scheme or benevolent loan. The bank can utilize this loan without providing any return to the depositors.

A different model of microsaving is based on the *mudharabah* scheme. In this scheme, savings generated from the poor will be used by the institution for financing and investment purposes. In cases where there is profit, the bank will share it with the depositors, but in cases of loss, the depositor will be responsible. This scheme is rarely implemented in microfinance since it is less favourable, as it is high risk for the depositor. However, in Islamic microfinance in Indonesia, the *mudharabah* model is modified into revenue sharing rather than profit or loss sharing.

This popular microsaving product is usually characterized by high liquidity and locally oriented design.[36] The poor also require secure and convenient savings deposit processes that require only a small balance. Furthermore, most savers who select the liquid accounts are not highly sensitive to monetary return. The saving products under *mudharabah* schemes are less suitable as they include the profit loss sharing mechanism. Conversely the *wadiah* scheme is considered to be the most suitable instrument for microsaving, since it only requires a small account balance and offers high liquidity.

2. Microcredit

Microcredit is the focus of microfinance practice. Islamic microfinance can utilize the application of the group lending mechanism and joint liability to enforce creditors to pay and reduce the likelihood of non-performing loans by sharing the responsibility. The Hodaeidah Microfinance programme in Yemen successfully implemented this approach by asking the credit applicant to form a group consisting of five people who guarantee and encourage each other in their loan repayments.[37]

Participatory profit loss sharing financing, sales based financing and voluntary charity financing are all applicable to microfinance. However, in practice, the sales based modes using *murabahah* and *bai' al-muajjal* are more popular due to the simplicity of financing. The loan application is very simple. Once it is approved, the institution will provide the borrower with the required asset and resell them with a mark-up fee. Finally, a contract between the borrower and the institution will be signed indicating the agreed price, time period and the instalment amount. *Bai' al-muajjal* is a feature of *murabahah* where the payment of the required asset can be deferred to a future date. Both microfinance and its clients have to fully understand the contract, including the acquiring price and the mark-up fee.

Another scheme that is possible to implement in microcredit products is the profit loss sharing scheme. In this mechanism, microfinance and microentrepreneurs are partners. In the *mudharabah* case, microfinance will provide total funding for microentrepreneurs, while the microentrepreneurs provide the skills. The profit

---

[36] CGAP, 'Introducing Savings in Microcredit Institutions: When and How?'.

[37] Ahmed Al-ZamZami and Lorna Grace, 'Islamic Banking Principles Applied to Microfinance Case Study: Hodeidah Microfinance Program, Yemen' (New York: United Nations Capital Development Fund, 2002).

will be shared on a predetermined ratio, but the losses will be borne by the lender. For this reason, *mudharabah* is considered very risky because of the uncertain profits and the profit accuracy provided by the microentrepreneur.[38]

In the case of *musyarakah*, microfinance and microentrepreneurs both share the capital, skill and profit, and losses will be shared based on the amount of capital invested. Two or more partners can contribute to the capital and expertise of the investment. The partnership can run to completion of the project or it can be transferred to other partners. This mechanism faces many challenges since the partnership requires intensive project monitoring, which is costly and time consuming. Another challenge is a lack of book keeping and inaccurate profit reported by the borrower, which can lead to agency problems.

The voluntary charity mode is also widely implemented in microfinance. The source of funds for a non-interest loan (*Qard al-Hassan*) could come from donor funds, *zakat*, *waqf* and other forms of Islamic charity. This mode is suitable for helping the poor in improving their well-being, as well as developing a new microbusiness. The loan can be used as start-up funding and to empower the poor by providing skills and training on a subsidized basis.

3. Other microfinance services

Lease based financing (*Ijarah*) is another alternative offered by Islamic finance. Microfinance allows its clients to use the asset on its own for a rental fee. This scheme is suitable for providing the poor with equipment and physical assets to support their business, such as machinery for farming, rickshaws, boats for fishing, or shop fronts for retail business. A summary of these schemes is presented in Table 6.3.

Although, as outlined below, most Islamic finance principles are readily applicable to microfinance, the marriage of the two concepts is not easy to implement successfully. For example, in Indonesia, Islamic finance has been implemented in microfinance since the early 1990s. With two decades of experience, Islamic microfinance institutions on average have failed to prove themselves as an effective and efficient microfinance provider. The conventional form of microfinance (the rural bank) has been growing twenty times faster than the Islamic microfinance sector. Several problems have been documented by Seibel in implementing Islamic finance in Indonesia, such as the lack of expertise in this area, the lack of management and governance, the lack of supported regulation for Islamic finance cooperatives, and a general lack of awareness with regard to the availability of Islamic banking products. Therefore, it requires a major effort from many parties, including the government, Islamic organizations, donor funds, and commercial banks, and society more broadly, to support the development of Islamic microfinance in Indonesia.

---

[38] Khan, *Islamic Microfinance: Theory, Policy and Practice.*

Table 6.3 Summary of the Strengths and Weaknesses of Finance Schemes

Type of product	Islamic finance instruments	Strengths	Weakness
Microsaving	Wadiah	The amount of deposit is guaranteed by the institution	No financial return to the depositors
	Qard al- Hassan	Benevolence loan, flexible to use	No financial return to depositors
	Mudharabah	• Encourages partnership between microfinance and its clients • High returns in cases of profitable project	• No principal/ deposit amount guarantee • The depositor is responsible for all project losses
Type of product	**Islamic finance instruments**	**Strengths**	**Weakness**
Microcredit	*Murabahah* and *Bai al-Muajjal*	• Simple and easy to implement • Clear contract between microfinance and its clients • Asset backed transaction	• Similar to conventional banking interest rate, therefore, the institution has to ensure the shari'a compliance of its product • High initial cost for microfinance
	Mudharabah	• Encourages partnership between microfinance and its clients	• Lack of accurate book keeping and misreported profits from microfinance clients • Losses belong to microfinance • Agency problem
	Musyarakah	• Shares risk and return • Encourages partnership	• High monitoring cost • Misreported and inaccurate profit from the clients • Agency problem
	Qard al- Hassan	• Interest free loan • Flexible and can be utilized for many financing purposes	• Limited amount since it is purely charity and voluntary

Other microfinance services	Ijarah	• Offers alternative financing mechanism with lower risk to clients • Asset backed transaction • Easy to implement	• High initial investment cost for microfinance

Source: Compiled from Rahul Dhumale and Amela Shapcanin. 'An Application of Islamic Banking Principles to Microfinance', *Technical Note*. UNDP with the World Bank 1999; Muhammad Obaidullah, *Introduction to Islamic Microfinance*. India: IBF Net Pty Ltd, 2008.

Nevertheless, despite the problems discussed above, several success stories of these practices have been documented. The next section will describe the implementation of several Islamic finance principles in microfinance in Indonesia.

Examples of Islamic Microfinance Practices in Indonesia

Implementation of Qard al-Hassan financing in Baitul Maal Muamalat in Indonesia

Profile of the institution

Baitul Maal Muamalat is a social organization that focuses on the economic empowerment of the poor. It is a social subsidiary of Bank Muamalat Indonesia, the first Islamic Bank in Indonesia, which collects *zakat* from the stakeholders of Bank Muamalat and distributes it for social purposes. Their microfinance programme is known as *Komunitas Usaha Mikro Muamalat Berbasis Masjid* (KUMMM), or Muamalat Micro Entrepreneur Community Based on Mosque. This programme is designed to provide revolving working capital loans for low income microentrepreneurs who actively participate in mosque activities. The philosophy of this programme is to integrate economic empowerment with developing religious belief. It is implemented through developing partnerships with several mosques in Indonesia. The client's selection, mentoring and loan instalment are conducted in the mosques. By centralizing the activities in the mosque, the institution believes that they will select clients with a positive attitude and values that support the success of the programme. KUMMM is one of the largest outreach *zakat*-based microfinance institutions in Indonesia. It operates throughout Indonesia, spreading to 185 mosques in 28 cities across 21 provinces. It provides non-interest loans for 4,697 participants with total revolving funds of

$6.46 million and includes 202 mentors. The location of KUMMM is linked with the local branches of Bank Muamalat, as its affiliated institution.[39]

Products and services

KUMMM offers integrated microfinance programmes including the following activities: providing revolving working capital funds using the *Qard al-Hassan*[40] mechanism, providing training and development on business skills and providing religious mentoring. The *Qard al-Hassan* loan ranges from Rp. 500,000 to Rp. 2,000,000. The repayment of the loan is made every week over one to two years. The programme is specifically designed for street vendors, peddlers and hawkers who conduct trading activities in the districts surrounding the mosques, as well as microentrepreneurs who perform *subuh*[41] prayer in their respective mosques.

Weekly meetings are an important aspect of the programme. Every group has to attend the weekly meeting supervised by their mentors. The attendance of participants in weekly meetings is one element determining the success of the programme. The role of the mentors is to facilitate training programmes and to collect weekly loan instalments. The weekly training covers several subjects including entrepreneurship, microenterprise management, financial and marketing management, Islamic economics, leadership training and religious education. The mentors are outsourced from Microfin, an independent microfinance consultant in Indonesia and the local Islamic MFIs.

In every meeting, the participant has to pay their instalment, a compulsory group fee (Rp. 3000 / 30 US cents) and a small amount of *sadaqa* (Rp. 1000 or equal to 10 US cents. The compulsory group fee is used to cover the operational cost of the programme. Scholars have a similar opinion that an administration fee on the loan is allowable in Islam.[42] As *Qard al-Hassan* does not charge any interest return, charging administration costs on the loan can be used as the strategy to cover the costs.

KUMMM evaluates the performance of each group after the instalment period has finished. The well performing mosques will be offered a second round of financing. The performance is evaluated based on the repayment rates and the attendance of weekly meetings. It is documented that only half of the participants in the first round continue onto the second round of financing. The problem is mainly the high levels of non-repayment of the loan by the clients. The data show that only 56 per cent of the total financing given was repaid in 2009, and this dropped even more significantly to 20 per cent of the total financing being repaid in the following year.[43] This fact refutes the argument that loans that are disbursed

39 Personal interview, 12 December 2011.

40 They called this loan *pinjaman kebajikan* (benevolent loan).

41 Praying before sunrise.

42 Siddiqi, 'Potential of Islamic Microfinance in Pakistan'.

43 Unpublished report on KUMMM funding distribution 2010.

in mosques are governed by religious sanctity that encourages the loan to be repaid on time.[44]

Table 6.4 Repayment of *Qard al-Hassan* Financing KUMMM

	Total financing	**Total repayment**	**% of repayment**	**% non-performing financing**
2009	6,101,367,487.54	3,421,889,029.01	56.08%	43.92%
2011	3,309,973,000.00	689,968,425.00	20.85%	79.15%

After graduating from the second round of financing, KUMMM offers an 'exit programme' for the well performing mosques. In the exit programme, KUMMM assists the mosques in developing an Islamic financial cooperative (*Koperasi Jasa Keuangan Syariah* / KJKS). KJKS is financed from the funds collected from loan repayments. By 2011, KUMMM had initiated the development of 11 KJKS all over Indonesia with 265 members. KJKS is the continuation of the *Qard al-Hassan* programme for the community surrounding the mosques. KUMMM provides the initial capital, operating costs and standard operating procedures for the initial phase of the development. KJKS registers with the Ministry Cooperative and is regulated as a semi-formal organization under cooperative law. It offers financial services for the poor using both a profit loss sharing mechanism and sales-based transactions. KJKS is no longer voluntary microfinance; it has to cover all operational costs in order to survive. It is expected that KUMMM will be able to provide sustainable microfinance programmes for communities through the development of KJKS.

In an interview by the author with the management of KUMMM, they revealed that initiating KJKS also faces several constraints. They noted that most KJKS do not perform well. One of the important challenges is finding the right staff and management setup for the KJKS.[45] For example, in KJKS Al Falah in Jakarta, both the management and general staff have been changed several times; this is mainly due to a lack of motivation in those working in KJKS. The study by Sakai noted that a similar problem has transpired in many of the Islamic cooperatives in Indonesia. Generally, staff working in Islamic financial cooperatives have a lower salary than those in the majority of local banks.[46] This is the main reason why staff turnover in Islamic financial cooperatives is relatively high.

[44] Agus Kalifatullah, *Mitra Pengelola Zakatpada KJKS/BMT in Bimbingan Teknis Bagi KJKSDalam Rangka Optimalisasi Pendayagunaan Zakat* (Jakarta: Kementrian Koperasi, Usaha Kecil dan Menengah Republik Indonesia, 2012).

[45] Personal interview, 12 December 2011.

[46] Minako Sakai, 'Community Development Through Islamic Microfinance: Serving the Needs of the Poor in a Viable Way', in *Expressing Islam: Religious Life and Politics*

The sustainability issue

The main sources of funds to finance all the programmes are various Islamic charities including *zakat*, *sadaqa* and *awqaf*. *Zakat* is the compulsory charity that every wealthy Muslim has to pay to society, *sadaqa* is defined as giving away goods and funds for the sake of God in expression of faithfulness and in realization of the belief in resurrection and afterlife,[47] while a*wqaf* are perpetual charities, including cash and fixed assets, where the benefit can be preserved long term for society. Furthermore, others sources of funds are various organizations such as the Islamic Development Bank, the Ford Foundation and several commercial institutions, such as PT Telkom Indonesia, and Newmont Indonesia.

The management of KUMMM stated that most of the programme is funded by *zakat*, since the amount of *sadaqa* and other charity is very limited. As the subsidiary of Bank Muamalat, KUMMM has the advantage of a continual flow of *zakat* funds from the bank's stakeholders. However, the programme faces many challenges, since the *zakat* fund has strict shari'a rules in its distribution. The shari'a notes that only 12.5 per cent of the total *zakat* funds can be used to cover all management and operation costs, which is not sufficient for the implementation. To minimize the liquidity shortage, management has initiated several profit entities that can contribute to the sustainability of the programme.

In addition, the challenges to the *zakat*-based microfinance also stem from a common understanding that *zakat* is free money that is supposed to be distributed directly to the prescribed beneficiaries. When *zakat* is given as a loan people assume that this is not a loan, but charity that does not need to be repaid. This is the main reason as to why repayment rates in this organization are very low.

One major criticism of the programme is its dependency on donor funds and Islamic charity as the source of funds for microfinance. As noted in many studies, high dependency on donor funds is one of the chief obstacles to growth in the microfinance sector. Therefore, to achieve sustainability, it is suggested that the programme should mobilize commercial sources of funds through savings deposits, and implement commercial financing instruments, such as sales-based financing or profit loss sharing financing, rather than *Qard al-Hassan* alone.

Implementation of Islamic Finance Principles in BMT Al Hasan Magetan Indonesia

Profile of the institution

BMT is a unique type of Islamic microfinance in Indonesia. It was developed based on the idea of the *Bait al-Maal* in the Prophet's era. The institution was formed mainly to collect *zakat* and voluntary donations, and to distribute the

---

in Indonesia, ed. Greg Fealy and Sally White (Singapore: Institute of Southeast Asian Studies, 2008).

47 Yusuf Qaradawi, *Fiqh Al Zakah*, trans. M.D. Kahf, vol. 1 (Jeddah, Saudi Arabia: Scientific Publishing Centre, 2009).

funds for the benefit of society. The *Baitul Maal* was widely implemented during the time of the second caliph, Umar bin Khatab and was developed in each capital city to collect taxes and fees from the public. Different from the former concept, *Baitul Maal Wat Tamwil* in Indonesia includes two institutions: *Baitul Maal* for charitable purposes and Baitul Tamwil for commercial purposes. As a commercial unit, Baitul Tamwil is developed based on a similar concept to that of the financial cooperative. The capital is collected from its members and the lending and saving practices are conducted based on a profit loss sharing mechanism. As a commercial unit, *Baitul Tamwil* mainly targets the low income entrepreneurs. While *BaitulMaal* is a social unit of BMT, it usually collects donations from its members and distributes it as grant or non-interest free loans to the lowest levels of the poor.

The concept of BMT was initiated in 1992 by several Muslim scholars in Indonesia. Its development was motivated by two factors: firstly, the reluctance of Bank Muamalat as the only Islamic bank at that time to provide financial services for the poor, and the willingness of Islamic scholars to spread the concept of Islamic finance in Indonesia.[48]

The following section evaluates the implementation of the Islamic finance principle in BMT Al Hasan in Magetan East Java Indonesia. But first, a brief outline. BMT Al Hasan was developed on 17 February 1997, only five years after the development of the first BMT in Indonesia. BMT Al Hasan was developed by six founders and registered as a financial cooperative. As of 2010 BMT Al Hasan had 28 active members, 82.5 million rupiah in compulsory savings, and 531 million rupiah total assets. It is located in Magetan, a small district in East Java Province, with a total population of 699,073 people.[49]

Sources of funds

As a financial cooperative, BMT Al Hasan is funded by three major sources: the compulsory savings of its members, savings and deposit mobilization from its clients and government subsidy credit. The amount of Islamic charity collected by the institution is very limited, at only 10–15 million rupiah per year. Their operation focuses more on profit oriented activities rather than social activities.

The client profile

The majority of clients are small traders in the local market, with the total financing ranging from one million rupiah to 20 million rupiah. Financing is given on an individual basis, not based on group lending. The loan collection is carried out directly by BMT staff. They usually visit the clients and collect the loan repayments. They employ three staff to collect loan repayments. The loan collectors are remunerated based on 25 per cent of the total loan collection, and,

48 Ibid.

49 BMT Al Hasan, 'Annual Report' (2010).

as outlined in an interview with the author, this mechanism is quite successful in controlling non-performing loans, with a repayment rate of 98 per cent.[50]

Products and services

BMT Al Hasan offers both savings and financing products. The total amount of savings is 279 million rupiah and the total amount of financing is 439 million rupiah, as of 2010. The financing to deposit ratio (FDR) is 1.57, indicating a lack of liquidity in this institution. The savings products implement the *mudharabah* principle, while the financing product is given based on the concept of *murabahah*, *mudharabah* and *musyarakah*. The composition of the financing of the three schemes is described in Table 6.5.

Table 6.5 Financing Composition in BMT Al Hasan

Composition of financing	2009 (in thousand rupiah)	2010 (in thousand rupiah)
Murabahah	8746	2498
Mudharabah	260.695	357.707
Musyarakah	91.987	78.307
Total	399.025	438.512

The composition shows that the total financing provided to its clients has increased by 39.5 million rupiah in one year. The majority of financing given comes under the scheme of *mudharabah*. This is a very interesting point, since *mudharabah* is less preferable for Islamic microfinance institutions due to its complexity and its risks. The profit loss sharing scheme is a fundamental building block of the Islamic financial system that is ethically superior to its conventional counterpart.[51] As noted before, in the case of *mudharabah*, microfinance will provide total funding for microentrepreneurs, while the microentrepreneurs provide skills. The profit is to be shared at a predetermined ratio, but the losses will be the responsibility of the lenders. For this reason, as noted above, *mudharabah* is considered very risky due to the uncertainty of profits and questionable accuracy of profit information provided by microentrepreneurs.[52]

The management of BMT Al Hasan states that the main reason for selecting *mudharabah* schemes is to ensure that the shari'a concept is implemented in the institution. However, the main challenge to implementation is a lack of financial

[50] Personal interview with the manager on 13 December 2011.

[51] Muhammad Obaidullah and Salma Haji Abdul Latif, *Islamic Finance for Micro and Medium Enterprises* (Bandar Seri Begawan Brunei Darussalam: IRTI, 2008).

[52] Khan, *Islamic Microfinance: Theory, Policy and Practice.*

reporting by the clients. Most of the clients are reluctant to record their transactions because of their limited skills in book keeping and their anxiety to show that they are not making any profit in their microbusiness. Therefore, in determining the profit loss sharing, the BMT discusses with clients 'the estimation of profit', which is based on their previous profit. In some cases, BMT Al Hasan does not agree with 'the estimation of profit' proposed by the clients. Hence, there will be a negotiation between the BMT and the clients to estimate 'the shared profit'. BMT itself has determined their minimum rate of return, which is equal to 18 to 24 per cent per annum for all clients, regardless of their financial condition. In the negotiation process, BMT tries to persuade clients to achieve the minimum rate of return. The negotiation process ends when 'the shared profit' has been agreed by both parties. Then the 'shared profit' is distributed with the proportion of 30 per cent for the lender and 70 per cent for the borrower.[53] In this case, there are indications that BMT Al Hasan has simplified the rule of *mudharabah* in two respects:

1. The amount of shared profit is estimated to be 'fixed' all the time. The BMT only considers that the borrower always generates profit, but does not make any losses in their microbusiness.
2. They set the minimum rate of return equal to 18 to 24 per cent, which is similar to conventional interest rates.

Based on the description, although the reason for implementing a *mudharabah* scheme is to ensure the implementation of shari'a, it can be argued that some of the practices in the *mudharabah* scheme do not conform with Islamic finance rules as outlined in the shari'a. Unfortunately, the control mechanism of shari'a compliance for this institution has not yet been established.

The literature notes that *murabahah* is the preferred Islamic scheme available as it offers simplicity. *Murabahah* (cost plus mark-up sale) is the product offered by most of the respondents of the CGAP global survey on Islamic microfinance in 2012.[54] For example, BMT Al Hasan offers *murabahah* schemes for primary and secondary teachers in Magetan to buy notebooks as part of the government programme of 'one teacher, one laptop'.

In this scheme, the teacher will ask BMT Al Hasan to buy a laptop with certain specifications from the distributors on their behalf. BMT Al Hasan has an agreement with the local computer distributor to get a special price and with the school administration for the loan repayment. When the laptop is ready, the contract will be signed in the BMT office, to ensure that the laptop has the required specifications and that the clients agree with the mark-up fee. The mark-up fee is usually set at 30 per cent of the cost. The management reveals

[53] Personal interview, 13 December 2011.

[54] Mayada El Zoghbi, 'Islamic Microfinance: Global Supply Survey' (paper presented at the International Microfinance Conference, Yogjakarta Indonesia, 2012).

that the 30 per cent mark-up is minimal as they have to share the mark-up with the affiliated institutions: the computer distributors and the school administration. The *murabahah* loan (cost plus mark-up) will be repaid in one year by direct deductions from their monthly salary.

There are three main rules in *murabahah* schemes: firstly, the loan is given as a 'product' not as cash; secondly, the borrower knows the price and the mark-up fee of the products; lastly, the mark-up fee has been agreed upon by both the lender and the borrower. In the case of BMT Al Hasan both rules are implemented. This shows that the *murabahah* schemes in BMT Al Hasan are shari'a compliant.

Are Islamic Finance Principles Being Successfully Implemented in Microfinance?

As has been shown above, the implementation of the three transaction schemes – *Qard al-Hassan*, *Murabahah* and *Mudharabah* – face several challenges. *Qard al-Hassan* is probably the simplest shari'a-compliant method as it offers non-interest loans to beneficiaries. The issue with regard to its implementation is how the programme can be sustained if it does not generate any return. The case of KUMMM illustrated that the sustainability of such a programme is a serious concern. KUMMM has sought to rectify this problem through the development of KJKS (Islamic Financial Cooperatives), which can be seen as the continuation of the non-interest loan programme. The KJKS work on similar concepts as commercial Islamic Financial Cooperatives. If managed well, they can offer sustainable microfinance programmes for the local community. Secondly, to respond to the issue of *zakat* fund fluctuations and the limited rules on *zakat* funding, the institution has created alternative sources of funding by initiating profit entity units. These profit entity units are expected to provide financial support for the programme to ensure the sustainability of the programme.

Furthermore, the study found that the implementation of the *mudharabah* concept is often simplified by the MFIs. For example, in BMT Al Hasan, 'the profit loss sharing mechanism' has been implemented as 'profit sharing' only, without considering any losses from the borrower's business. In addition, they have also set a minimum return that is equal to 18 to 24 per cent per year. These practices are clearly prohibited by shari'a. Therefore, a crucial function needed in the implementation of Islamic microfinance is the shari'a compliance board to supervise the practice of Islamic microfinance.

Conversely, the concept of *murabahah* implemented by BMT Al Hasan complied with shari'a. However, the *murabahah* concept needs more attention when the number of transactions increases. *Murabahah* requires that the loan is given as a 'product' rather than 'cash'. This method of distribution requires high operating costs. Thus many MFIs have simplified the process by giving loans as 'cash' rather than a 'product', which also disobeys shari'a.

Conclusion

The current problems of microfinance should be taken seriously, since this will impact on the achievement of the Millennium Development Goals 2015. Financial exclusion of poor Muslims is a problem that can be solved by implementing Islamic finance principles in microfinance. For, as has been shown, Islamic finance and microfinance are ideologically and practically linked. They both have the social mission of fighting poverty, promoting entrepreneurship and risk sharing, as well as ensuring that capital is equally distributed throughout society.

Further to this, the wide variety of instruments in Islamic finance offers flexibility in designing microsaving, microcredit, and other microfinancial products. However, there are some complexities in its application. To successfully marry Islamic finance and microfinance, one has to design products that meet the needs of the market, equip staff with this new knowledge, and educate their clients about the benefits of its application.

Lastly, further study analysing the successes and failures of Islamic finance implementation are needed to help drive the design of sustainable Islamic microfinance that could potentially serve the 74 per cent of the world's Muslims that are financially excluded.

References

Abdul Rahman, Abdul Rahim. 'Islamic Microfinance: A Missing Component in Islamic Banking'. *Kyoto Bulletin of Islamic Area Studies* 1, no. 2 (2007): 38–53.

Ahmed, Habib. 'Financing Microenterprises: An Analytical Study of Islamic Microfinance Institutions'. *Islamic Economic Studies* 9, no. 2 (2002): 27–64.

Al-ZamZami, Ahmed, and Lorna Grace. 'Islamic Banking Principles Applied to Microfinance Case Study: Hodeidah Microfinance Program, Yemen'. New York: United Nations Capital Development Fund, 2002.

Armendariz, Beatriz, and Jonathan Morduch. *The Economics of Microfinance*. Cambridge, Mass.: MIT Press, 2005.

Austrade. 'Islamic Finance'. Canberra: Australian Government, 2010.

Ayub, Muhammad. *Understanding Islamic Finance*. Hoboken, NJ: John Wiley & Sons, 2007.

BMT Al Hasan. 'Annual Report'. 2010.

CGAP. 'Introducing Savings in Microcredit Institutions: When and How?', *Focus Note* April, no. 8 (1997). http://www.cgap.org/sites/default/files/CGAP-Focus-Note-Introducing-Savings-in-Microcredit-Institutions-When-and-How-Apr-1997.pdf.

Chapra, M. Umer. *Towards a Just Monetary System: A Discussion of Money, Banking, and Monetary Policy in the Light of Islamic Teachings*. Leicester, UK: Islamic Foundation, 1985.

Daley-Harris, Sam. 'State of the Microcredit Campaign Report 2009'. Washington: Microcredit Summit Campaign, 2009.

Dhumale, Rahul, and Amela Shapcanin. 'An Application of Islamic Banking Principles to Microfinance'. *Technical Note*. UNDP with the World Bank 1999.

Dusuki, Asyraf Wajdi. 'Lifting Barriers in Financing the Small and Poor Entrepreneurs: Lessons from Group-Based Lending Scheme and Ibn Khaldun's Social Solidarity'. In *Inclusive Islamic Financial Sector Development: Enhancing Islamic Financial Services for Micro and Medium Sized Enterprises (Conference Proceedings)*, edited by Muhammad Obaidullah and Hajah Salma Haji Abdul Latiff. Brunei Darussalam: Islamic Research and Training Institute, Islamic Development Bank/Centre for Islamic Banking, Finance andManagement, Universiti Brunei Darussalam 2008.

El Hawary, Dahlia A, and Wafik Grais. 'Islamic Financial Services and Microfinance'. (2005). http://siteresources.worldbank.org/EXTISLAMF/Resources/IslamicFinancialServicesandMicrofinanceJune20b.pdf.

El Zoghbi, Mayada. 'Islamic Microfinance: Global Supply Survey'. Paper presented at the International Microfinance Conference, Yogjakarta Indonesia, 2012.

Helms, Brigit. *Access for All: Building Inclusive Financial Systems*. Washington DC: Consultative Group to Assist the Poorest, The World Bank, 2006.

Kalifatullah, Agus. *Mitra Pengelola Zakatpada Kjks/Bmt in Bimbingan Teknis Bagi Kjksdalam Rangka Optimalisasi Pendayagunaan Zakat*. Jakarta: Kementrian Koperasi, Usaha Kecil dan Menengah Republik Indonesia, 2012.

Karim, Nimrah, Michael Tarazi, and Xavier Reille. 'Islamic Microfinance: An Emerging Market Niche'. *Focus Note*, August, no. 49 (2008). http://www.cgap.org/gm/document-1.9.5029/FN49.pdf.

Kettell, Brian. *Frequently Asked Questions in Islamic Finance*. United Kingdom: John Wiley and Sons, 2010.

Khan, Ajaz Ahmed. *Islamic Microfinance: Theory, Policy and Practice*. Birmingham, United Kingdom: Islamic Relief Worldwide, 2008.

Kholis, Nur. 'Murabahah Mode of Financing for Micro and Medium Sized Enterprise: A Case Study of Baitul Maal Wat Tamwil Yogjakarta'. In Muhammad Obaidullah and Salma Haji Abdul Latif, *Islamic Finance for Micro and Medium Enterprises*. Bandar Seri Begawan Brunei Darussalam: IRTI, 2008.

Ledgerwood, Joanna, and Victoria White. *Transforming Microfinance Institutions: Providing Full Financial Services to the Poor*. Washington, DC: The World Bank, 2004.

Morduch, Jonathan and Barbara Haley. 'Analysis of the Effects of Microfinance on Poverty Reduction', *NYU Wagner Working Paper* No 1014, 2002.

Obaidullah, Muhammad. *Introduction to Islamic Microfinance*. India: IBF Net Pty Ltd, 2008.

Obaidullah, Muhammad, and Salma Haji Abdul Latif. *Islamic Finance for Micro and Medium Enterprises*. Bandar Seri Begawan Brunei Darussalam: IRTI, 2008.

al-Qaradawi, Yusuf. *Fiqh Al Zakah*. Translated by M.D. Kahf, vol. 1. Jeddah, Saudi Arabia: Scientific Publishing Centre, 2009.

Robinson, Marguerite S. *The Microfinance Revolution*. Washington, D.C.: World Bank, 2001.

Rosengard, Jay K., Richard H. Patten, Don E. Johnston, and Widjojo Koesoemo. 'The Promise and the Peril of Microfinance Institutions in Indonesia'. *Bulletin of Indonesian Economic Studies* 43, no. 1 (2007): 87–112.

Rutherford, Stuart. *The Poor and Their Money*. New Delhi: The Department of International Development, 1999.

Sakai, Minako. 'Community Development through Islamic Microfinance: Serving the Needs of the Poor in a Viable Way'. In *Expressing Islam: Religious Life and Politics in Indonesia*, edited by Greg Fealy and Sally White. Singapore: Institute of Southeast Asian Studies, 2008.

Seibel, H.D. 'History Matters in Microfinance'. *Working Paper No.5*. University of Cologne, Development Research Centre, 2003.

Seibel, Hans Dieter. 'Islamic Microfinance in Indonesia: The Challenge of Institutional Diversity, Regulation, and Supervision'. *SOJOURN: Journal of Social Issues in Southeast Asia* 23, no. 1 (2008): 86–103.

Shahinpoor, Nashir. 'The Link between Islamic Banking and Microfinancing'. *International Journal of Social Economics* 36, no. 10 (2009): 996–1007.

Siddiqi, Kiran. 'Potential of Islamic Microfinance in Pakistan'. Masters Thesis, Loughborough University, 2008.

Sundaresan, Suresh M. *Microfinance: Emerging Trends and Challenges*. Cheltenham, UK; Northampton, MA: Edward Elgar, 2008.

Warsame, Muhamed Hersi. 'The Role of Islamic Finance in Tackling Financial Exclusion in the UK'. PhD Thesis, Durham University, 2009.

Wilson, Rodney. 'Why Islamic Banking Is Successful?', (n/d). http://www-stud.rbi.informatik.uni-frankfurt.de/~osman/islamic-banking.pdf.

Yunus, Muhammad, and Alan Jolis. *Banker to the Poor: Micro-Lending and the Battle against World Poverty*. 1st ed. New York: PublicAffairs, 1999.

Zeller, Manfred, and Richard L. Meyer. *The Triangle of Microfinance: Financial Sustainability, Outreach and Impact*. Johns Hopkins University Press, 2002.

Chapter 7
Mobile Phones and Religion: The Case of Women Micro-Entrepreneurs in a Religious Community in Indonesia

Misita Anwar and Graeme Johanson

Introduction

Despite the importance of religion in the political and social spheres of developing countries, it has received very little attention in mainstream discussion on development. This is partly because religion has been considered as an obstacle to the achievement of development goals. It was regarded as irrelevant because of the dedication to economic policy, where all dimensions of development and individual welfare are measured through economic indicators such as GDP and per capita income.[1] However, recent shifts in development thinking, that see factors such as values, social structures, and human capital playing more important roles in human life, have promoted a growing interest in religion as part of development studies.[2]

Deneulin, for example, discussed how a secularist framework is problematic in that it does not represent the daily reality of religion. She argued that the human development approach offers a framework to negotiate between different value systems about development and social progress across different communities.[3] In particular, she explored religion within Sen's Capability Approach (CA), because

---

[1] Carole Rakodi, 'Understanding the Roles of Religions in Development: The Approach of the Religions and Development Research Programme', *Religions and Development Working Paper 9* (International Development Department, School of Public Policy: University of Birmingham, 2009).

[2] Matthew Clarke, *Development and Religion: Theology and Practice* (Cheltenham, UK; Northampton, MA, USA: Edward Elgar, 2011); Séverine Deneulin, 'Religion in Development and the Idea of Secularism', (2007), http://www.capabilityapproach.com/pubs/Deneulin07.pdf. (accessed 27 November 2010); Filippo Osella and Caroline Osella, 'Muslim Entrepreneurs in Public Life Between India and the Gulf: Making Good and Doing Good', *Journal of the Royal Anthropological Institute* 15, no. s1 (2009): S202–S21; Rakodi, 'Understanding the Roles of Religions in Development: The Approach of the Religions and Development Research Programme'.

[3] Deneulin, 'Religion in Development and the Idea of Secularism'.

religion can determine all the 'doings' and 'beings' that people find valuable, and make it intrinsic to the freedoms that people have reason to value.[4] This chapter focuses on a nexus between the CA, Information and Communications Technologies, female micro-entrepreneurs and development in Indonesia. The connections have not been made before.

The women micro-entrepreneurs in this study belong to a religious community and manage profitable businesses as well. This account is part of a larger study about the impact of mobile phones on the well-being of micro-entrepreneurs in Indonesia. Using the CA as an evaluation framework it identifies what are the most important achievements as perceived by participants, and then reflects on how mobile phones help them to achieve these valuable capabilities. We explore the use of mobile phones in facilitating and enabling religious activities and supporting religious women in running their businesses, while adhering to their religious way of life. In the next section, we present a brief preview of mobile phones in Indonesia, and then review the CA and how Information and Communications Technologies (ICTs), such as mobile phones, are integrated within the framework. Once the broad research context of this study is outlined, and the method described, the findings show how religious and business practices in combination have been enhanced by the use of mobile phones.

Mobile Phones in Indonesia

In Indonesia, mobile phones have become an essential part of people's daily lives. Almost everywhere one sees more and more Indonesians engaging with their mobile phones – making calls, sending text messages, or simply listening to music. Mobile phones are no longer considered as a luxury item now that they are available in their cheapest form for only USD 10. With an average growth of 60 per cent per year since 2005, mobile phone penetration in Indonesia stood at 88 per cent in 2010 with more than 200 million subscribers altogether.[5]

A report published by the Nielsen Company showed that the Indonesian telecommunications market is unusual. Consumers in Indonesia have mostly headed straight to mobile phones as their communication tool and most people have never really experienced fixed lines. Also Indonesian mobile consumers are getting younger. Much of the mobile growth is being driven by teens, with more than 70 per cent having a mobile phone connection, while the number of children aged 10–14 having mobile phones increased more than five times during the five-year period of 2005 to 2010. Today's young Indonesians use mobile phones

[4] Amartya Sen, *Commodities and Capabilities* (Amsterdam: North-Holland Publishers, 1985); *Development as Freedom*, 1st ed. (New York: Knopf, 1999).

[5] International Telecommunications Union (ITU), 'Mobile Celluar Subscriptions (2000–12)', (2012), http://www.itu.int/ITU-D/ict/statistics/material/excel/Mobile-cellular 2000–2011.xls. (accessed 26 July 2012).

principally for instant messaging or chatting, preferring this functionality over voice calls.[6]

The report further stated that Indonesian mobile subscribers are spending less now than they were five years ago, with 58 per cent of consumers now spending under IDR 50,000 (USD 5) per month in 2010, compared to only 18 per cent in 2005. The service prices are down and, more importantly, new consumer segments with limited spending capacity are entering the market. Low rates remain the top factor for consumers when selecting a service provider, but most consider the reputation of networks and recommendations of friends and family, indicating that while dropping tariffs are starting to drive operator choice, consumers continue to be concerned about service quality when choosing their provider.[7]

The use of mobile phones has had many effects on the economic as well as the social fabric of communities. Mobile phones are contributing a great deal to the development of the Indonesian economy. There are several pilot projects utilizing mobile phones for development. The GSM (Group Speciale Mobile) Association Development Fund has partnered with Voxiva to develop mobile phone software that can be used in the fight against HIV/AIDS, avian flu and potential health pandemics.[8] This application will allow health workers in the field to use handheld devices to submit critical health data to authorities in real time. The Indonesian-based operator Bakrie Telecom has joined with the Bangladeshi Grameen Foundation and Qualcomm to launch the first Village Phone Program called UberASIA which will provide affordable wireless communications services for rural communities across Indonesia.[9] Most recently farmers in Indonesia have begun to reap the benefits of using their mobile phones to get agricultural services following the launch of the LISA (Farmers Information System) platform in December 2012. LISA is a mobile phone subscription service that allows farmers to interact with other corresponding community groups based on their crops and location. Within the group, users get daily SMS tips from '8Villages' and other local user-generated content. Also, they can ask their own questions and will be answered either by other farmers or by agricultural experts from 8Villages'

---

[6] Nielsen, 'Mobile Phone Penetration in Indonesia Triples in Five Years', (2011), http://www.nielsen.com/us/en/newswire/2011/mobile-phone-penetration-in-indonesia-triples-in-five-years.html. (accessed 18 July 2012).

[7] Ibid.

[8] Michael Schwartz, 'Voxiva, GSM ally against HIV/AIDS and Avian flu', *Developing Telecoms* (2006), http://www.developingtelecoms.com/tech/apps-services-devices/60-consumer-apps/629-voxiva-gsm-ally-against-hivaids-and-avian-flu.html (accessed 16 Jan 2014).

[9] Qualcomm, 'Press Release: Grameen Foundation, Bakrie Telecom and Qualcomm Join Efforts to Enable Affordable Telecommunications Access to Rural Indonesia', (2008), http://www.qualcomm.com/media/releases/2008/07/29/grameen-foundation-bakrie-telecom-and-qualcomm-join-efforts-enable-afforda.(accessed 6 July 2009).

partners. This service works without the need for an internet connection.[10] The platform was developed by '8Villages', a technology services provider to rural consumers, working closely with Mercy Corps and the Indonesian Ministry of Agriculture.

The CA and ICTs

The CA is a framework that can be used for the evaluation and assessment of individual well-being and social arrangements, or for the design of policies and proposals about social change for groups and in society. Developed by Amartya Sen,[11] and expanded upon by other authors,[12] it critiques a welfare-based approach to evaluation. Sen argued that in social evaluation and policy making, considering 'quality of life' includes consideration of the freedom of people to live the life they want, and which they find valuable. Well-being and development should be analysed from the point of view of people's capabilities to function, and the opportunities and freedoms to be and do what they want to be and do.[13]

The core ideas of the CA are *functionings* and *capabilities*. Functionings are described as the 'beings and doings' of a person, whereas capability refers to a person's or group's 'freedom to achieve' valuable functionings. Capability represents the potential sum of the actions that are open to a person from various combinations of functionings. Capability is a set of vectors of functionings (actions), demonstrating the person's freedom to lead one type of life or another.[14] In other words, the term functionings can refer to realized (actual) achievements and fulfilled expectations, whereas capabilities can refer to the effective possibilities of realizing achievements and fulfilling expectations.[15] The questions that often

---

[10] Mercy Corps, 'Farmers in Indonesia Reap the Benefits of Mobile Technology', (2013), http://www.mercycorps.org/research-resources/farmers-indonesia-reap-benefits-mobile-technology (accessed 6 May 2013).

[11] Sen, *Commodities and Capabilities*.

[12] Des Gasper, 'Sen's Capability Approach and Nussbaum's Capabilities Ethic', *Journal of International Development* 9, no. 2 (1997): 281–302; Martha Nussbaum, 'Capabilities as Fundamental Entitlement', in *Capabilities Equality: Basic Issues and Problems*, ed. Alexander Kaufman (New York ; London: Routledge, 2006); Ingrid Robeyns, 'Understanding Sen's Capability Approach', (2001), http://www.ingridrobeyns.nl/Downloads/Under_sen.pdf.(accessed 20 April 2009); Sabina Alkire, *Valuing Freedoms: Sen's Capability Approach and Poverty Reduction* (New York: Oxford University Press, 2002).

[13] Sen, *Development as Freedom*.

[14] Ibid.

[15] Yingqin Zheng, 'Exploring the Value of the Capability Approach for E-Development' (paper presented at the Proceedings of the 9th International Conference on Social Implications of Computers in Developing Countries, Sao Paulo, Brazil, May 28–30, 2007).

arise are which capabilities are the most important, and why? Sen has always refused to endorse any specific list of capabilities. He argues that to try to make one final list of capabilities should not be attempted, because such lists are used for different purposes, and each purpose might need its own list.

Having described the main concepts in the CA, it is necessary to ask: how can ICTs be integrated within this framework? Although capability theory was not explicitly applied to technological domains, a number of studies have touched on the relationship between ICTs and the CA.[16] Further, several studies have noted the expansion of capabilities for human development through the use of ICTs. Hamel focuses on the health, education, and income dimensions of human development with some notes on participation and empowerment.[17] Toboso analysed CA and its relation to ICTs in the context of people with disability,[18] while Smith et al. applied CA to existing research by categorizing functionings created by the connectedness and information-sharing characteristics of mobile phones into three networking dimensions, namely, social networks, economic networks and governance networks.[19] Using the CA as a lens, this study seeks to build on this small but growing body of literature by focusing on the potential of mobile phones to enhance and facilitate an individual's *capability* to perform religious practices, and associated values and practices.

A conceptualization of ICTs within the CA framework is proposed by Zheng[20] and refined by Heeks and Molla.[21] They place ICTs as a commodity with a value only in relation to how they help individuals to do or to be. More than has been hypothesized in the past, ICTs claim a legitimate and central place in the overall capability account. When people are able to make use of ICTs to maintain meaningful

---

[16] See Erwin Alampay, 'Beyond Access to ICTs: Measuring Capabilities in the Information Society', *International Journal of Education and Development using ICT* 2, no. 3 (2006): 4–22; Bjorn-Soren Gigler, 'Informational Capabilities – The Missing Link for the Impact of ICT on Development', *E-Transform Knowledge Platform Working Paper Series* (World Bank 2011); Zheng, 'Exploring the Value of the Capability Approach for E-Development'; Dorothea Kleine, 'The Ideology Behind the Technology – Chilean Microentrepreneurs and Public ICT policies', *Geoforum* 40, no. 2 (2009): 171–83.

[17] Jean-Yves Hamel, 'ICT4D and the Human Development and Capability Approach: The Potentials of Information and Communication Technology', *Human Development Research Paper 37* (New York: United Nations Development Programme, 2010).

[18] Mario Toboso, 'Rethinking Disability in Amartya Sen's Approach: ICT and Equality of Opportunity', *Ethics and Information Technology* 13, no. 2 (2011): 107–18.

[19] Matthew L. Smith, Randy Spence, and Ahmed T. Rashid, 'Mobile Phones and Expanding Human Capabilities', *Information Technologies & International Development* 7, no. 3 (2011): 77–88.

[20] Zheng, 'Exploring the Value of the Capability Approach for E-Development'.

[21] Richard Heeks and Alemayehu Molla, 'Impact Assessment of ICT-for-Development Projects: A Compendium of Approaches', *Development Informatics Working Paper Series 36* (University of Manchester: Development Informatics Group, Institute for Development Policy and Management, 2009).

associations with one another, or to earn a living where they could not before, or to better sustain the practice of traditional activities, we can legitimately claim an instrumental role for technology in expanding capability and achieving valued forms of functioning.[22] According to Heeks and Molla, the link between the main features of ICTs and actual CA achievements is mediated at two stages. First, conversion of ICT characteristics into capabilities for an individual is shaped by factors that may be personal or environmental. Second, conversion of ICT-based capabilities into actual functionings is shaped by individual choice (personal preferences, specific needs, and social norms). The authors further suggested that ICT can fit into four other categories. First, ICT can serve as a conversion factor, helping to convert characteristics of other commodities into capabilities. Second, as a non-conversion factor, ICT may constrain certain capabilities and choices. Third, as a conversion factor enabler, ICT can develop other conversion factors and fourth, as a choice developer, ICT can change the perception of personal preferences or needs.[23]

Research Approach

Small and medium enterprises (SMEs) in Indonesia have historically been the main players in domestic economic activities, especially as a large provider of employment opportunities, and hence a generator of primary or secondary sources of income for many households. Micro-enterprises are the smallest but most numerous businesses within the larger group of SMEs. Recent statistics show that in 2010 micro-enterprises accounted for approximately 95 per cent of all enterprises in Indonesia, absorbing 87.2 million labourers, out of the 94.3 million total labour force in Indonesia.[24]

For this project empirical data was collected in the cities of Makassar and Bandung, which represent the eastern part and the western part of the country. Using an in-depth semi-structured interview guide, 40 micro-entrepreneurs were interviewed in Bahasa Indonesia, 11 of them for the subject of this chapter. The interview guide consisted of open-ended questions about perceptions of well-being, that is, what the most important values or element for their well-being were, and how mobile phones contributed (or not) to these values.

Participants spanned a broad range of businesses within the sectors for trade, manufacturing and service industries. Their income varied from IDR 500,000 (USD 50) to IDR 6 million (USD 600) per month, with the majority of interviewees

---

22 Justine Johnstone, 'Technology as Empowerment: A Capability Approach to Computer Ethics', *Ethics and Information Technology* 9, no. 1 (2007): 73–87.

23 Heeks and Molla, 'Impact Assessment of ICT-for-Development Projects: A Compendium of Approaches'.

24 Ministry of Cooperatives and SMEs, 'SME Data', (2011), http://www.depkop.go.id/index.php?option=com_phocadownload&view=sections&Itemid=93. (accessed 28 March 2012).

earning an average of IDR 2.5 million (USD 250) per month. Eleven of these micro-entrepreneurs were self-employed with no support staff. Most enterprises used simple technology, had limited access to credit, had limited managerial skills, and operated in the informal sector. For the research, micro-enterprises were grouped according to their location (Bandung or Makassar), in product or service categories (e.g., shoe-maker, furniture-maker, blind masseur), or those belonging to the same service organization. This classification was based on the assumption (later shown to be true) that communication activities and interaction amongst similar businesses in such groupings are more likely to occur.

Subsequent discussions in this chapter are drawn from 11 interviews with women micro-entrepreneurs (of the project total of 40 interviewees) who are members of or belong to an organization affiliated with a religious *organisasi massa* (community organization) called *Wahdah Islamiyah* (WI). *Organisasi massa* is a term used in Indonesia for a community organization without any political agenda, and is often used as an opposite term for 'political party'. Such organizations are based on the common objectives and interests of their members (such as religion or education).

WI is a religious community organization. It is actively involved in education, social life, information, health and environment. It has around 15,000 members spread over 44 branches all over Indonesia and is affiliated with 26 other foundations in several districts. Practising their faith, all *Wahdah* women wear Muslim clothing such as long gowns and *jilbab* (*hijab* or female headgear that exposes the face but not ears, neck, or hair) with the majority also wearing the *niqab* (face-veil).

Because of their appearance, WI are often seen as an exclusive group. Although there are more women wearing the *niqab* in Indonesia compared to several years ago, it is still considered a rare appearance. This can lead to prejudice and discrimination towards the women of WI, as expressed by one WI member:

> It is not easy for our women to work outside the *Wahdah* circle because many places seem reluctant to accept them and it is difficult for them to interact with other people (Ira).

Women Micro-Entrepreneurs' Well-Being and Religion

Religion for these women is regarded as integral to well-being and a way of life. Religion defines how one leads his/her life and influences perceptions of a good life. So in reality, religion affects the way that development itself is conceived of within many communities. This is not the common view in the development literature. Most development studies have been conducted within a secularist framework which conceives of religion as a unique set of compartmentalized beliefs which positively or negatively affect development outcomes.[25]

[25] Deneulin, 'Religion in Development and the Idea of Secularism'.

Islamic Business Ethics

Many *Wahdah* women or those affiliated with the organization have their own businesses, work in *Wahdah* business units, or work in another member's business. *Wahdah* as an organization itself runs several businesses to support its programmes and activities. The types of businesses vary from manufacturing, retail services, to food and beverages. Unfortunately, no data can be found on the number of entrepreneurs within the group but it is clear that many of the businesses are established to meet the needs of the *Wahdah* community – like clothing suitable for shari'a or alternative medicine/therapy such as *bekam* (bloodletting) or *rukyah* (Islamic exorcism).

All participants in this group said that they are conducting their businesses in an Islamic way. They are adopting business ethics which are governed by an Islamic framework concerned with morality, making money ethically, and helping everyone to benefit. Significant practices include only selling products that are halal (food, cosmetics) and in accordance with shari'a. An entrepreneur who sells clothing explained:

> What I want is to be a *sholehah* (virtuous woman) and die as a *syahid* (martyr) so I need to conduct my business accordingly, the halal way. For example, I sell only Muslim wear prescribed by the shari'a, not following the fashion trend even though it would mean more profit. Secondly, I always try to be honest, if for example my product is faulty, I will inform my customer. That way I would feel some kind of satisfaction even if the product was not sold. After all, there is more than just our life here on earth (Jun).

Likewise, Lilis, a Bandung entrepreneur who owns a restaurant within a tourist destination area said that she would not sell harmful products such as cigarettes or alcohol even if those products are popular amongst visitors and would make more profit, because she considers her business not only as a means to earn a living, but also as being bound by Islamic values.

Businesses are not oriented towards profit alone but more to demonstrate religious adherence. Adherence to religious values defines a Muslim's objectives in life and was expressed by many participants. For them the only purpose of life is to serve *Allah*, so every action in life is focused towards this goal. They believe that it is the only way to have success in the after-life. A phone card seller in Bandung explained that

> I have many dreams, but the most important is to be a *sholehah*. It doesn't matter what I'll become, I want to have success in life and the hereafter (Tita).

Similarly, a boutique and beauty salon owner in Makassar stated:

> I want to have more peaceful time so that I can bring myself closer to *Allah* (Lina).

The Importance of Doing Dakwah

Another adherence practice by participants in this group is *dakwah* (preaching of Islam). The concept of *dakwah* consists of two elements: (1) the educational role of improving Islamic knowledge and practices; and (2) the role of certain Islamic groups to enhance Islamic practices within their community. *Dakwah* targets both individuals and the community to achieve social change by reinforcing Islamic values and practices.[26] But unlike evangelism, *dakwah* is directed more towards Muslim individuals rather than to outsiders.

Dakwah is presented in various ways by the participants in this study, not least in how they conduct business. Some reinforce it by selling products that promote Islamic teaching such as books and products and services recommended by shari'a, such as women-only beauty salons. A retailer in Makassar said:

> I hope that my business can benefit many people. So, beside Muslim wear, I am also selling other products that I think are beneficial to my customers, such as health products and Islamic books, because my business is not only for the money but also for *dakwah* (Juniati).

Another explained:

> my beauty salon is for women only; we accept wedding make-ups but only those recommended by shari'a. In fact, I could have more customers if I'd waive those restrictions but I don't want to, as I know that my fortune comes from *Allah* (Lina).

Others choose to provide specific services that can be directed towards progressing *dakwah*, such as health services and education. As one clinic owner explained:

> I want to achieve the financial freedom so that someday I don't have to work and can spend all my time to worship Allah. I know the purpose of my life. Even my occupation as a doctor was purposely chosen to give *dakwah*, because patients usually listen to their doctor. I hope I can give *dakwah* through my profession (Ira).

Dakwah is also emphasized through social networks of friends and acquaintances. They use various form of preaching. Some go to meetings and gatherings and talk directly about Islam. Others send hadith[27] and *ayat* (verses of

[26] A. Pratiwi, 'Sustaining Dakwah Movement: A Study of Kammi Alumni Role in the Democratic Era of Indonesia' (paper presented at the Social Causes Private Lives TASA Conference, Sydney, Macquarie University, 6–9 December 2010).

[27] Hadith refers to reports of statements or actions of the Prophet Muhammad, or of his tacit approval of something said or done in his presence.

the Qur'an) to their networks through social networking sites and mobile phones. As a restaurant owner in Bandung explained:

> I send hadith and *ayat* to my friends in Facebook, my husband sends hadith to 120 of his friends and acquaintances every day (Lilis).

Mobile Phones, Business and Religious Practices

Further discussion with the 11 participants revealed that the use of mobile phones is significant for facilitating, enhancing and enabling religious activities while at the same time running their business. Although limited in scope, some studies have identified the use of technology for religious purposes.[28] The previous section has shown that participants are conducting their business according to Islamic ethics and following the shari'a. Mobile phones have been beneficial for this purpose, particularly in their capacity to replace face-to-face communication (with the opposite sex) and to avoid *ikhtilath*. Therefore, *Wahdah* women tend to avoid face-to-face conversations with the opposite sex or going to crowded places where *ikhtilath* are likely to be compromised, such as in markets. A beauty salon owner said:

> I used to run a mini-market but it was difficult because there were many male distributors who just walk into the store. I replaced it with my boutique and

[28] Woodruff et.al, explored religious practice of Jewish people who improve observing the Sabbath by means of automation of household activities. See A. Woodruff, S. Augustin, and B. Faucault, 'Sabbath Day Home Automation: "It's Like Mixing Technology and Religion"' (paper presented at the Conference on Human Factors in Computing Systems, San Jose, California, USA, 28 April–3 May, 2007). Georgia Tech students have developed a series of concepts that support the prayer practice of Islamic students. They identified prayer as an activity that can be supported with technology then developed an application prototype to assist this activity. See S. Wyche, K. E. Caine, and B. Davison, 'Sun Dial: Exploring Techno-Spiritual Design through a Mobile Islamic Call to Prayer Application' (paper presented at the Conference on Human Factors in Computing Systems, Florence, Italy, April 5–10, 2008). Current uses of mobile phones have been reported on everything from text message services from the Pope to accounts of a Mobile Rosary. See James Everett Katz and Mark A. Aakhus, 'Conclusion: Making Meanings of Mobiles – A Theory of Apparatgeist', in *Perpetual Contact: Mobile Communication, Private Talk, Public Performance* ed. James Everett Katz and Mark A. Aakhus (Cambridge, UK ; New York: Cambridge University Press, 2006). Also, in a study about the role of mobile phones in religious practice of the Zen Buddhist community, Sterling and Zimmerman found that there are many opportunities for the phone to help maintain and enhance the bonds between members of religious congregations, helping them to feel a stronger sense of religious connection. See R. Sterling and J. Zimmerman, 'Shared Moments: Opportunities for Mobile Phones in Religious Participation' (paper presented at the Conference on Designing Pleasurable Products and Interfaces, 22–25 August, Helsinki, Finland, 2007).

> female-only beauty salon. That way I don't have to deal with male customers and distributors (Lina).

They also are aware of their very responsibility to take care of children and household matters. Thus, for these micro-entrepreneurs, the fact that ordering supplies can be done while at home minding their young children has been very beneficial to their businesses. Mobile phones have provided ways of overcoming this limitation. They might not be able to work otherwise.

> My children are young so I can't go out very often, so mostly everything is done via mobile phone. *Alhamdulillah*, I haven't had any problem ordering products. Sometimes my supplier will send the goods even before I paid, that is because they trust me, that I would pay when I place an order (Jun).

Another example was given by a catering owner in Makassar. She specifically chooses and only deals with suppliers and distributors that allow phone orders to ensure that she does not have to go out a lot or meet the supplier (who might be male):

> Yeah, I've done most business affairs with phones, before with home phones, but now its mobile phones. The first time we started this catering business, my husband had designed the business so that I don't have to go the market. He'd looked for distributors that offer phone orders, so that as a woman I don't have to go out a lot. That way, I can keep doing business but stay at home (Yani).

Mobile phones facilitate participants in conducting religious rituals. There are various daily rituals to be performed by Muslim people. Participants described how they use many mobile features to assist in this. Mobiles are used as a reminder for prayer time. Muslims must pray five times at a certain time every day. In Indonesia, every mosque will sound an *athan* (call to prayer). Many participants have also stored *athan* sound files in their mobile and use them as a prayer reminder. When they are travelling they may not hear the sound from the mosque. Participants use mobiles to listen to the Qur'an being read by their favourite reader, whereas some others read the Qur'an text from an application on the mobile phone. Some participants listen regularly to Islamic lectures to enhance their religious knowledge and there are those who listen to Muslim radio on the mobile.

For many participants in the *Wahdah* group, *dakwah* is the main religious activity. *Dakwah* can be done in many ways, through *pengajian* (Qur'an recitation),[29] distributing *ayat* (Qur'an passages) and hadith, or providing other services that are considered as *dakwah*. *Pengajian* can be done for many occasions

[29] *Pengajian* or Qur'an recitation is a common activity within the Indonesian Muslim community. In a *pengajian*, the Qur'an is not only recited but also analysed by a scholar for the explanation or interpretation of its texts. Individual Muslims also recite the Qur'an, for religious merit, for reflection on its meaning, and for spiritual refreshment. See Frederick

such as weddings, funerals, Islamic celebration days, or at other times. These are usually occasional and a one-off activity. *Pengajian* is arranged by a group of people, usually those who are related through neighbourhood, work, organization, college, or other common interest. For those willing to learn more about the Qur'an, regular meetings for *pengajian* can be arranged. These are mostly gender-specific, for men only or women only. *Wahdah* members see these *pengajian* as a way to spread *dakwah*. Therefore, many members are trained to be *uztad/uztadzah* (Islamic scholar/s) to give lectures in such *pengajian*. They also arrange *pengajian* within their organization called *tarbiyah*,[30] which is a more advanced Qur'an recitation and analysis, compared to the basic preaching done in public.

The mobile phone is used to arrange activities like *pengajian*. It is used for inviting guests and speakers, providing information on the topic of a *pengajian*, and to deal with other matters of an event such as a venue or logistics. Mobile phones provide a more efficient way of sending out invitations. A participant sent an invitation letter to each guest. With mobile phones, the invitation can be formatted in an SMS then sent to multiple guests, and the same SMS can be re-used as a reminder for the event. Furthermore, SMS messages can be devised as a chain message, where anyone who receives the message can forward it to relevant contacts. A veterinary drugs producer took advantage of this communication tool:

> We are doing a lot of *pengajian*. For those events, we use mobile phones to invite people as it is easier. We do not need invitation cards or to deliver them to each person. Plus, with SMS, you don't even have to send it to everyone because when you say, 'please forward this to others', people will forward the message to relevant persons in their contact lists (Wiwik).

Another form of *dakwah* that was assisted by the use of mobile phones is the *Tahajjud Call*. Although not compulsory, getting up in the middle of the night to pray (*Tahajjud*) is considered one of the main occasions for worship that is widely practised. It can be quite daunting for those who are not accustomed to this task. Some use alarm clocks but it is very easy to turn them off and go back to sleep. A *Tahajjud Call* can be provided by another person or an organization. It is free of charge and is not compulsory. When a mobile user subscribes to this service, someone will call to remind them of the *Tahajjud* time to pray. Wiwik, a participant who recently established this service, argued that this is seen as a more successful approach because people can listen to a short lecture on praying provided by the caller, and thus will be reluctant to go back to sleep.

M. Denny, 'Qur'ān Recitation: A Tradition of Oral Performance and Transmission', *Oral Tradition* 4, no. 1–2 (1989): 5–26.

[30] *Tarbiyah* refers to an in-depth study of the Qur'an and hadith within a group of people. The group is usually small and caters for those who want to become an Islamic scholar. The schedule for this training is regular with the same teacher, so there is a good attachment between students and teacher.

A popular service provided by and subscribed to by *Wahdah* members are *tausiah* SMS. *Tausiah* means advice, how to lead one's life according to Islamic values. In many *pengajian*, the speaker would often give *tausiah* as part of his or her preaching. *Tausiah* can be provided and funded by anyone, but usually by an *uztad* and it is mostly free of charge. People can subscribe to this service by sending a register message. Periodically (daily or weekly), the service will send an SMS to the subscribers containing short advice on a particular topic together with the relevant *ayat* or hadith.

Funding a *Tausiah* SMS service is mostly by individuals, and it is considered as a donation by individuals. Those who register for a *Tausiah* SMS can forward it to anyone they wish, thus giving *dakwah* themselves. The regular service is described by a retailer in Bandung:

> Now, I subscribe to a free *tausiah* SMS. With this service, I can receive *ayat* and hadith periodically and we can distribute those SMSs to anyone we want. I would forward those SMSs to my friends and family (Ety).

Many *Wahdah* members and participants are located in suburban and rural areas, where means of transportation can be costly or not always available, and travelling can take time. It is important for these members and participants to keep having regular *pengajian* and *tarbiyah*. This can be quite challenging, especially for a female presenter who is restricted by shari'a requirements to be accompanied by her husband or *mahram*[31] when travelling. For these women, mobile phones have been very beneficial as they can arrange to have a teleconference for those events which the presenter cannot attend. The presenter will give her speech through the mobile, and at the other end another mobile is attached to a loud-speaker for the participants to listen to. One member in Makassar pointed to the necessity of mobiles for smooth dissemination of the faith:

> The mobile phone has become a necessity. In our organization, we often use mobile phones and the internet for teleconferences. Teleconferencing might not be very effective but it saves a lot of time and cost. It is also very useful when the *uztad* is a woman, who might not be able to travel because of shari'a requirements (Ira).

Another innovative use of mobile phones was described by *Wahdah* participants in the way that they use the technology for a mass gathering. Mobiles are linked to a communication network. This network is designed according to a hierarchy within the organization structure. The messages are sent using SMS and travel down through the network by means of SMS forwarding. The phone

---

[31] A Muslim woman who needs to travel must be accompanied by her husband or *mahram*. *Mahram* is Islamic *Shari'a* legal terminology, referring to an unmarriageable kin with whom sexual intercourse would be considered incestuous.

tree is very effective in gathering mass as messages spread very fast to a large number of people. A *Wahdah* member who owns a beauty salon can collect 2,000 people immediately:

> I think the mobile phone is very helpful for me in dealing with many things. Sometimes when there is a big event or a visit by an overseas scholar, we need to gather many people in a very short time. For that we use a communication network using mobile phones, designed like a tree according to the level within our organization structure. Using this technique we can gather as many as 2,000 people in one day which would not be possible if it was not for mobile phones (Lina).

The mobile phone can also be very useful in avoiding *ikhtilath* (mixing of the sexes). Muslims believe that *ikhtilath* might create a situation which might lend itself to sinful acts such as having sex before marriage, or other sexual misdemeanours. Therefore, Muslim men and women (who are not related by marriage or kin) do not mingle in public or private spaces. To some extent, those who are being very careful with this rule will make an effort not to meet or speak with the other sex except when there is a *hijab* (separator) between them, or it is in some unavoidable circumstances, such as in a crowded market. In a situation where speaking is unavoidable, there are certain rules that must be followed – such as speaking with a flat, superficial tone without any sound that could be interpreted as in any way flirtatious.

The mobile phone can be used to contact other people without physically meeting them and thus the *hijab* is maintained. The mobile phone also provides a way of avoiding speaking to the other sex if the conversation is via SMS messaging. A *Wahdah* member (who is also a clothing retail owner) felt more comfortable messaging than speaking:

> I think mobile phone can be very significant for my goal, to be a *sholehah* (virtuous woman). For example, in Islam, we are advised to avoid *ikhtilath*. Avoiding *Ikhtilath* will prevent social deviancy such as [having] an affair. With a mobile phone, I can fortify my faith by not having direct contact with the opposite sex. I can just send an SMS to make sure that my voice is not heard by him (Tita).

Further, this participant explained that she used a mobile phone to facilitate match-making between the members of *Wahdah*. Members were accustomed to a match-making tradition because the concept of dating is not supported in Islam. In *Wahdah* a special committee is formed to help members to find a suitable partner. These people make their contact available through the organization's formal and other publications. Those who need to find a partner are encouraged to contact a member of this committee. She described how versatile and ubiquitous mobile use was:

> I give out my mobile number as a match-maker and even put it on Facebook. Those who need my help can call me and I will call those who I think might be suitable and perhaps arrange a supervised meeting when necessary. I had a lot of success just by using mobile phone (Tati).

Mobile Phones and the Well-Being of Women Micro-Entrepreneurs

We have shown in the two previous sections that participants regarded religion and religious values as the most important elements in their lives. From a CA perspective, the value of mobile phones as a tool and commodity is seen in relation to how it helps individuals to do or to be. Mobile phones were used in many religious activities. Mobile phones have expanded several capabilities deemed important by our participants by enhancing existing functionings and creating new ones in three distinct ways.

First, mobile phones enhanced how participants perform daily rituals. Functionings enhanced by mobile phone include a reminder for prayer time, being able to read or listen to the Qur'an, and listen to Islamic lectures. Without the mobile phone these functionings can be achieved by means of other devices, reading the Qur'an in print or physically attending the lecture, but a mobile phone with its personal, multi-features and mobility was more efficient. Mobiles also added more religious experiences, e.g., its ability to record the *athan* sound.

Secondly, mobile phones facilitated and enhanced participants' capability of being able to do *dakwah*. Mobiles assisted in giving and arranging *pengajian*, distributing *tausiah*, conducting the *tahajjud call*, distributing information, and arranging a mass gathering. Some of these functionings were newly-created by the mobile phone, such as giving long-distance *pengajian* using teleconferences. Another new functioning created by the use of mobile phone was sending *tausiah* using SMS, which was a simpler and more personal way of doing *dakwah*. Thirdly, mobile phones have assisted participants in avoiding *ikhtilath*, by being used to avoid direct conversation with the opposite sex. Functionings created from this perspective are avoidance rather than enforcement. These functionings, coupled with the ease of access afforded by mobile phones, have facilitated yet another functioning, namely that of match-making. For individuals such as our participants, who regard their religious guidance very seriously, these capabilities are very significant.

Conclusion

Our preliminary findings confirm that well-being not only relates to material sufficiency but also to the important role of religion. It adds to the current discourse in development studies where economic indicators such as GDP and income are no longer the only concern. Human development is now seen as the expansion of people's choices to be able to do and to be, and in this study information and communications technologies (ICTs) in the form of mobile phones support these choices in a variety of ways. We have shown that for the participants, religion defines how they live, and what life means to them. Being able to conduct religious practice is essential to well-being. We described how religious women micro-entrepreneurs use mobile phones in everyday life, and how this utilization enhanced their capabilities in practising religious commitment, creating business opportunities, consolidating their business networks, enhancing their spiritual experience, and investing for their futures. In their own minds they do not separate these capabilities, and there is little reason for development analysts to do so.

References

Alampay, Erwin. 'Beyond Access to ICTs: Measuring Capabilities in the Information Society'. *International Journal of Education and Development using ICT* 2, no. 3 (2006): 4–22.

Alkire, Sabina. *Valuing Freedoms: Sen's Capability Approach and Poverty Reduction*. New York: Oxford University Press, 2002.

Clarke, Matthew. *Development and Religion: Theology and Practice*. Cheltenham, UK; Northampton, MA, USA: Edward Elgar, 2011.

Deneulin, Séverine. 'Religion in Development and the Idea of Secularism'. (2007). http://www.capabilityapproach.com/pubs/Deneulin07.pdf.

Denny, Frederick M. 'Qur'ān Recitation: A Tradition of Oral Performance and Transmission'. *Oral Tradition* 4, no. 1–2 (1989): 5–26.

Gasper, Des. 'Sen's Capability Approach and Nussbaum's Capabilities Ethic'. *Journal of International Development* 9, no. 2 (1997): 281–302.

Gigler, Bjorn-Soren. 'Informational Capabilities – the Missing Link for the Impact of ICT on Development'. *E-Transform Knowledge Platform Working Paper Series*: World Bank 2011.

Hamel, Jean-Yves 'ICT4D and the Human Development and Capability Approach: The Potentials of Information and Communication Technology'. *Human Development Research Paper 37*. New York: United Nations Development Programme, 2010.

Heeks, Richard, and Alemayehu Molla. 'Impact Assessment of ICT-for-Development Projects: A Compendium of Approaches'. *Development Informatics Working Paper Series 36*. University of Manchester: Development Informatics Group, Institute for Development Policy and Management, 2009.

International Telecommunications Union (ITU). 'Mobile Celluar Subscriptions (2000–12)'(2012).http://www.itu.int/ITU-D/ict/statistics/material/excel/Mobile-cellular2000–2011.xls.

Johnstone, Justine. 'Technology as Empowerment: A Capability Approach to Computer Ethics'. *Ethics and Information Technology* 9, no. 1 (2007): 73–87.

Katz, James Everett, and Mark A. Aakhus. 'Conclusion: Making Meanings of Mobiles – a Theory of Apparatgeist'. In *Perpetual Contact: Mobile Communication, Private Talk, Public Performance* edited by James Everett Katz and Mark A. Aakhus. Cambridge, UK ; New York: Cambridge University Press, 2006.

Kleine, Dorothea. 'The Ideology Behind the Technology – Chilean Microentrepreneurs and Public ICT Policies'. *Geoforum* 40, no. 2 (2009): 171–83.

Mercy Corps. 'Farmers in Indonesia Reap the Benefits of Mobile Technology' (2013). Published electronically 16 April. http://www.mercycorps.org/research-resources/farmers-indonesia-reap-benefits-mobile-technology.

Ministry of Cooperatives and SMEs. 'SME Data' (2011). http://www.depkop.go.id/index.php?option=com_phocadownload&view=sections&Itemid=93.

Nielsen. 'Mobile Phone Penetration in Indonesia Triples in Five Years' (2011). Published electronically 23 February. http://www.nielsen.com/us/en/newswire/2011/mobile-phone-penetration-in-indonesia-triples-in-five-years.html.

Nussbaum, Martha. 'Capabilities as Fundamental Entitlement'. In *Capabilities Equality: Basic Issues and Problems*, edited by Alexander Kaufman. New York; London: Routledge, 2006.

Osella, Filippo, and Caroline Osella. 'Muslim Entrepreneurs in Public Life between India and the Gulf: Making Good and Doing Good'. *Journal of the Royal Anthropological Institute* 15, no. s1 (2009): S202-S21.

Pratiwi, A. 'Sustaining Dakwah Movement: A Study of Kammi Alumni Role in the Democratic Era of Indonesia'. Paper presented at the Social Causes Private Lives TASA Conference, Sydney, Macquarie University, 6–9 December 2010.

Qualcomm. 'Press Release: Grameen Foundation, Bakrie Telecom and Qualcomm Join Efforts to Enable Affordable Telecommunications Access to Rural Indonesia'. (2008). http://www.qualcomm.com/media/releases/2008/07/29/grameen-foundation-bakrie-telecom-and-qualcomm-join-efforts-enable-afforda.

Rakodi, Carole. 'Understanding the Roles of Religions in Development: The Approach of the Religions and Development Research Programme'. *Religions and Development Working Paper 9*. International Development Department, School of Public Policy: University of Birmingham, 2009.

Robeyns, Ingrid. 'Understanding Sen's Capability Approach'. (2001). http://www.ingridrobeyns.nl/Downloads/Under_sen.pdf.

Schwartz, Michael. 'Voxiva, GSM Ally against HIV/AIDS and Avian Flu'. *Developing Telecoms* (2006). Published electronically 30 October http://www.developingtelecoms.com/tech/apps-services-devices/60-consumer-apps/629-voxiva-gsm-ally-against-hivaids-and-avian-flu.html.

Sen, Amartya. *Commodities and Capabilities*. Amsterdam: North-Holland Publishers, 1985.

———. *Development as Freedom*. 1st ed. New York: Knopf, 1999.

Smith, Matthew L., Randy Spence, and Ahmed T. Rashid. 'Mobile Phones and Expanding Human Capabilities'. *Information Technologies & International Development* 7, no. 3 (2011): 77–88.

Sterling, R., and J. Zimmerman. 'Shared Moments: Opportunities for Mobile Phones in Religious Participation'. Paper presented at the 2007 Conference on Designing Pleasurable Products and Interfaces, 22–25 August, Helsinki, Finland, 2007.

Toboso, Mario. 'Rethinking Disability in Amartya Sen's Approach: ICT and Equality of Opportunity'. *Ethics and Information Technology* 13, no. 2 (2011): 107–18.

Woodruff, A., S. Augustin, and B. Faucault. 'Sabbath Day Home Automation: "It's Like Mixing Technology and Religion"'. Paper presented at the Conference on Human Factors in Computing Systems, San Jose, California, USA, 28 April–3 May, 2007.

Wyche, S., K. E. Caine, and B. Davison. 'Sun Dial: Exploring Techno-Spiritual Design through a Mobile Islamic Call to Prayer Application'. Paper presented at the Conference on Human Factors in Computing Systems, Florence, Italy, April 5–10, 2008.

Zheng, Yingqin. 'Exploring the Value of the Capability Approach for E-Developmen'. Paper presented at the Proceedings of the 9th International Conference on Social Implications of Computers in Developing Countries, Sao Paulo, Brazil, May 28–30, 2007.

Chapter 8
Religion and Post-Disaster Development[1]

Ismet Fanany and Rebecca Fanany

Introduction

This chapter explores the role religion and religious organizations can play in development in a post disaster context. Special attention will be given to the development efforts in Aceh, Indonesia, following the 2004 Indian Ocean tsunami. This province of Indonesia was disproportionately affected by the disaster, both in terms of loss of life and physical destruction. This chapter begins with an overview of the place of religion in development and how scholars and practitioners view it. Development and the Islamic world specifically and the way religion is currently seen in the context of post-disaster aid will also be discussed. An overview of Acehnese society around the time the tsunami occurred is provided as background for a consideration of religion and development post-tsunami. How the Acehnese view the disaster and the role of the religious faith in shaping their perceptions of the event and post-tsunami development efforts is described with the chapter closing with a discussion of what this might mean for future development efforts, especially in the context of natural disaster.

Religion and Development

The aim of international development is to foster economic growth and reduce poverty. In this context, the importance of culture has long been acknowledged in producing the desired results, but religion, which is a central aspect of culture, is often overlooked or avoided.[2] Ver Beek, for example, suggests that religion is consciously avoided by development agencies and scholars of development studies.[3] Selinger reached a similar conclusion based on the online articles and

[1] The data in this chapter come from the field work in Aceh conducted by I. Fanany in the second half of 2010. The author wishes to acknowledge the time and funding provided by Deakin University through its Outside Study Program scheme that made this field work possible.

[2] Katherine Marshall, 'Development and Religion: A Different Lens on Development Debates', *Peabody Journal of Education* 76, no. 3–4 (2001): 339–75.

[3] Kurt Alan Ver Beek, 'Spirituality: A Development Taboo', *Development in Practice* 10, no. 1 (2000): 31–43.

materials made available by the United Nations, World Bank, and other major development organizations.[4] When religion does figure in the development discourse, it is usually not applied to the development of strategies or programmes.

Religion is generally conceptualized in one of three ways by development scholars. It may be seen as a societal structure or institution that might be used to support the aims of a development programme. Alternatively, religion is sometimes seen as an aspect of culture that is viewed as impeding development efforts. Finally, religion may be seen as a form of personal motivation that is a means to support the ideological aims of a development programme.[5] Religion is not generally viewed as a positive structural factor that might be useful in the implementation of development programmes or strategies or in development theory. The reasons for this have been suggested to be fear of imposing an outside perspective, fear of creating conflict, lack of precedent relating to the issue in question, and the separation of religion from science that dominates Western sociological and political approaches.[6] Marshall proposes similar reasons and suggests that the separation of religion and state, where religion addresses spiritual issues and the state material ones, has institutionalized the gap between religion and development.[7]

If religion has been missing from the development activities of governments and international aid organizations, it has been significantly more important in the practical activities of some religious NGOs, even though recent literature on development has tended to overlook the specifically religious organizations operating in this field.[8] The term 'faith based organization' has come into use to distinguish these religiously based NGOs from others with a different orientation.[9] In fact, religious organizations have a long history of participation in charity activities. Religious organizations have a number of strengths relevant to the development field as well as weaknesses. The fact that they tend to work at every level of society and exist in every community has given them a very significant ability to reach rural areas and even those experiencing conflict or social upheaval. This has meant they have been very effective in distributing aid, especially in the context of emergencies or disasters.[10] Further, religious organizations often exhibit a high level of motivation and are seen as working for the public good to

[4] Leah Selinger, 'The Forgotten Factor: The Uneasy Relationship Between Religion and Development', *Social Compass* 51, no. 4 (2004): 523–43.

[5] Ibid.

[6] Ver Beek, 'Spirituality: A Development Taboo'.

[7] Marshall, 'Development and Religion: A Different Lens on Development Debates'.

[8] Jenny Lunn, 'The Role of Religion, Spirituality and Faith in Development: A Critical Theory Approach', *Third World Quarterly* 30, no. 5 (2009): 937–51.

[9] Gerard Clarke, 'Faith Matters: Faith-Based Organisations, Civil Society and International Development', *Journal of International Development* 18, no. 6 (2006): 835–48.

[10] Judith A. Mayotte, 'Religion and Global Affairs: The Role of Religion in Development', *SAIS Review* 18, no. 2 (1998): 65–9; Emma Tomalin, 'Religion and a Rights-based Approach to Development', *Progress in Development Studies* 6, no. 2 (2006): 93–108.

a greater extent than government agencies. They also tend to be more sensitive to local need and more flexible in their programmes and initiatives.[11] However, religious organizations are often viewed more warily because humanitarian aid and development activities have been used to legitimize evangelism and conversion.[12] Examples of this are presented in the literature, such as when the real aim of literacy programmes is to allow participants to read scripture.[13]

It has been noted, however, that there seems to be a growing interest in religion in the context of development. This recognizes the central role faith plays in the lives of many individuals as well as in structuring the group dynamic and communal life of many societies.[14] Interestingly, this rediscovery of religion as a motivating factor in a whole range of human behaviours is also observable in other fields, such as psychology,[15] health,[16] and social behaviour.[17] It is not coincidental that these aspects of the human experience are also significant in influencing the outcomes of development programmes, suggesting that religion cannot be ignored as an important force in understanding how people see themselves, interact with others, and create the social structures in which their lived experiences occur.

Development and the Islamic World

As described above, religion has not been a major factor in development studies, which, like many other fields, has been strongly influenced by what has been

---

[11] Mayotte, 'Religion and Global Affairs: The Role of Religion in Development'; Steven Rathgeb Smith and Michael R. Sosin, 'The Varieties of Faith-Related Agencies', *Public Administration Review* 61, no. 6 (2001): 651–70; Jack R. Goody, 'Religion and Development: Some Comparative Considerations', *Development* 46, no. 4 (2003): 64–7.

[12] Lunn, 'The Role of Religion, Spirituality and Faith in Development: A Critical Theory Approach'.

[13] Goody, 'Religion and Development: Some comparative considerations'; O. Salemink, 'Development Cooperation as Quasi-Religious Conversion', in *The Development of Religion, The Religion of Development*, ed. Ananta Kumar Giri, Anton van Harskamp, and Oscar Salemink (Delft: Eburon, 2004).

[14] Matthew Clarke, *Development and Religion: Theology and Practice* (Cheltenham, UK; Northampton, MA, USA: Edward Elgar, 2011).

[15] See for example Helen Lavretsky, 'Spirituality and Aging', *Aging Health* 6, no. 6 (2010): 749–69.

[16] See Kevin S. Seybold and Peter C. Hill, 'The Role of Religion and Spirituality in Mental and Physical Health', *Current Directions in Psychological Science* 10, no. 1 (2001): 21–4.

[17] See Pamela Ebstyne King and James L. Furrow, 'Religion as a Resource for Positive Youth Development: Religion, Social Capital, and Moral Outcomes', *Psychology of Religion and Spirituality* S, no. 1 (2008): 34–49; Chaeyoon Lim and Robert D. Putnam, 'Religion, Social Networks, and Life Satisfaction', *American Sociological Review* 75, no. 6 (2010): 914–33.

called 'secular reductionism';[18] this has led to a great deal of attention being paid to sociological characteristics (ethnicity, class, gender, etc.) and little to religious issues. This has gradually begun to change with a 'deprivatization' of religion,[19] which has coincided with the emergence of religious nationalism in several parts of the world.[20] At the same time, a polarization between the West and Islamic world has emerged that is deeper than immediate development concerns, and relates as well to a conflict between cultures that have and have not benefitted to the same degree from the current state of globalization.[21]

This issue is of particular importance in light of the fact that countries with a large Muslim population have historically been underdeveloped compared to the West and have earned a significantly lower share of world income than their population would indicate.[22] Further, high population density and geographic location have made many of these nations particularly susceptible to natural disaster which often occasions relief efforts and aid programmes, frequently from the West. For example, of the 55 members of the Islamic Development Bank, 27 are categorized as low income countries.[23] The UN Office for Humanitarian Affairs has disbursed 27 per cent of funds raised in various humanitarian appeals in countries where most of the population is Muslim.[24] Similarly, about 48.5 per cent of persons registered by the UN High Commissioner for Refugees are Muslim.[25] This is not to say, however, that Muslim countries are always the recipients of aid programmes or are the only regions of the world that experience poverty and social upheaval. Nonetheless, the significant level of need, coupled with the dominance of Western organizations and donors in the aid sector, makes for a special situation.

Part of the problem seems to stem from a perceived failure of Western approaches to social development to create lasting change in many Islamic (as well as non-Islamic) societies. A particularly problematic aspect of such approaches

---

18 Clarke, 'Faith Matters: Faith-Based Organisations, Civil Society and International Development'.

19 José Casanova, *Public Religions in The Modern World* (Chicago: University of Chicago Press, 1994).

20 Mark Juergensmeyer, *The New Cold War? Religious Nationalism Confronts the Secular State* (Berkeley: University of California Press, 1994).

21 Bruno De Cordier, 'The "Humanitarian Frontline", Development and Relief, and Religion: What Context, Which Threats and Which Opportunities?', *Third World Quarterly* 30, no. 4 (2009): 663–84.

22 Timur Kuran, 'Islam and Underdevelopment: An Old Puzzle Revisited', *Journal of Institutional and Theoretical Economics* (1997): 41–71.

23 Islamic Development Bank, 'Annual Report 29 1424H (2003–2004)', (Jeddah: IDB, 2004).

24 IRIN, '"A clash of ignorances" – Relief Aid and the Arab and Islamic World', (2007), http://www.irinnews.org/fr/reportfrench.aspx?reportid=70771.

25 United Nations High Commissioner on Refugees, 'The State of the World's Refugees: Human Displacement in the New Millennium', (Geneva: UNHCR, 2006).

has been the trend towards secularism inherent in most Western development initiatives.[26] This has been associated with religious resurgence in the Muslim world that has a number of separate components. The first of these is a change in the nature of Western influence from a physical presence (through colonialism) to cultural domination. A second is a selective desire for Western products and technologies with a concurrent rejection of things viewed as culturally 'Western'. Finally, a third force is the re-emergence of traditional, cultural practices resulting from the long process of decolonization.[27] At the same time, both Islamic and non-Islamic nations are experiencing rapid social change, urbanization, modernization, conflict, spread of technology, collapse of traditional cultural identities, and the emergence of new identities along religious lines.

Disaster relief takes place in contexts of high stress in which those affected may turn strongly to traditional and cultural means of adapting in which religion often figures significantly. Religious organizations and faith based aid agencies have long been involved in disaster relief, among their other activities. It happens that many of these groups have worked in regions vulnerable to natural disaster and hence have been well placed to respond when unusual events occur. Further, it is likely that, in some situations at least, the spiritual principles on which these organizations were founded provide a philosophical basis from which to approach the problem as well as to provide insight into a conceptualization of the suffering of those affected.

Aceh and the 2004 Tsunami

At the time of the tsunami, Aceh had a population of about 4 million, consisting of members of a number of Indonesian ethnic groups, and was almost entirely Muslim. Sometimes referred to as 'The Veranda of Mecca', the province is religiously conservative and fundamentalist and, when the tsunami occurred, had already begun to express these views in its local laws. Regional Autonomy became law in Indonesia in 2001[28] and led to a large-scale programme of government

[26] Andreas Wigger, 'Encountering Perceptions in Parts of The Muslim World and their Impact on the ICRC's Ability to be Effective', *International Review of the Red Cross* 87, no. 858 (2005): 343–65.

[27] De Cordier, 'The "Humanitarian Frontline", Development and Relief, and Religion: What Context, Which Threats and Which Opportunities?'.

[28] Regional Autonomy, as defined by the 1999 and 2000 laws concerning the nature of the resulting decentralization, changed the structure of government administration from a highly centralized system under the New Order government (which ended in 1997) to one where county-like divisions of provinces and municipal governments (*kabupaten* and *kotamadya*, respectively) became the main administrative centres. This change removed the provincial governments from the decision-making process, except at the highest policy level, as most services, including health, education, and commerce, were now run in the regions.

decentralization which resulted in devolution of responsibility for a wide range of public services to the regions. Regional Autonomy also gave new momentum to the *Gerakan Aceh Merdeka* (GAM) [Free Aceh Movement] which had been in a state of rebellion against the government of Indonesia since the 1970s. This movement, which demanded independence for Aceh, was widely supported by the public through the 1990s. Following the tsunami, however, a ceasefire was declared, and the parties resolved to end the conflict. A peace agreement was signed in 2005, giving Aceh special autonomy status and mandating the withdrawal of a majority of Indonesian troops in exchange for the disarmament of GAM. Former GAM members remain active in regional politics and administration, however, along with representatives of various national parties from other backgrounds.

The armed conflict with the government of Indonesia contributed in some ways to how the Acehnese viewed the tsunami. Many Acehnese, especially in the areas around the provincial capital Banda Aceh, blamed what they perceived as decadent, non-Islamic behaviour of government forces in Aceh as one of the factors that prompted God to send the tsunami to their region. During the early stages of the recovery period, stories circulated among the Acehnese in this part of the province of how, on the evening before the disaster, members of the military were celebrating in their barracks, drinking and engaging in inappropriate acts with women who were not their wives. Rumour held that not only were they all killed in the disaster, but that they and their barracks were swallowed up by the earth. In fact, the location of their former post became part of the ocean floor that ended up underwater following subsidence of the coastline. Whether the party in question really occurred is not clear, but the Acehnese still express their moral interpretation of the disaster and the religious overtones they ascribe to the event in stories of this kind, which have become a kind of oral history of the tsunami.

The people of Aceh are almost entirely Muslim. As is the case throughout the Malay world, of which Aceh is a part, adherence to Islam is a characteristic element of identity and is required of anyone who is a member of the Acehnese ethnic group. The Acehnese people are native to the northernmost part of the island of Sumatra and speak a local language that is linguistically related to Malay. They make up approximately 50 per cent of the province's population, with the rest being drawn from the Javanese, Gayo, Alas, and other ethnic groups, who are also almost entirely Muslim. In total, about 99 per cent of the province's population is thought to be Muslim.[29] The province's full name, *Nanggroe Aceh Darussalam*, reflects both Acehnese culture and Islamic influence, and local scenery is characterized by the presence of mosques in every occupied location. Other manifestations of Islamic culture and society are easily observable and include the widespread wearing of Islamic dress, the use of Arabic script on buildings and in political and public information campaign slogans, decorative arts reminiscent of those of the Middle East, and more recently the implementation of shari'a (Islamic) law at the local level.

---

[29] Badan Pusat Statistik, 'Statistik Nanggroe Aceh Darussalam', (2009), http://aceh.bps.go.id/ (accessed 3 July 2013).

Islam in Indonesia is usually described as syncretic, drawing on a range of sources including older, pre-Islamic religious beliefs.[30] In some parts of the nation, this aspect of the religion is taken to be a moderating influence, and religious expression in certain areas, such as in Java, is viewed as considerably less orthodox than in other parts of the world and often includes a strong element of pre-Islamic belief.[31] In Sumatra, however, there are several areas that are seen as religiously conservative and more fundamentalist in their views of Islam. These include the province of West Sumatra, inhabited almost entirely by members of the Minangkabau ethnic group; some parts of eastern and southern Sumatra, including the province of Riau, inhabited largely by Malay; and of course Aceh, at the northern tip of the island. Islam seems to have come to this region with traders, was adopted by choice, rather than imposed by force, and incorporates many elements of Sufi beliefs.[32] Sufism (or *tasawwuf*) represents the inner, mystic dimension of the religion and places strong emphasis on hospitality (*zihkr*), ritualized acknowledgement of God (*ziarah*), and divine determinism (*takdir*).[33] In Aceh, these elements of belief lie at the core of individual and group response to disaster and tragedy. An Acehnese proverbial saying derived from the Qur'an states that, in times of trouble, people should 'hold fast to the rope of God'.

The Acehnese View and Understanding of the Tsunami

Almost without exception, the Acehnese public ascribed the undersea earthquake and resulting tsunami to an act of God. In the West, this expression is usually used to refer to a natural event which is outside of people's control and often carries the connotation that no blame can be laid on human agents for any resulting damage. To the people of Aceh, however, an act of God means something quite different, for they do not perceive acts of God to be random, and such events are believed to occur deliberately for a purpose known only to God, but may be deduced by human beings. This means that it is not possible for human beings to understand or know God's plan for them, but it may be possible to discern certain aspects of God's intent and to respond to them through religious and moral actions.

Following the tsunami, it was obvious to many people in Aceh that the disaster resulted from laxity in their own moral and religious attitudes as well as to un-Islamic activities that occurred in their area, regardless of who was involved.

---

[30] See S. Cederroth, 'Indonesia and Malaysia', in *Islam Outside the Arab World*, ed. David Westerlund and Ingvar Svanberg (New York: St. Martin's Press, 1999).

[31] See for example Andrew Beatty, 'Adam and Eve and Vishnu: Syncretism in the Javanese Slametan', *Journal of the Royal Anthropological Institute* (1996): 271–88.

[32] Robert Day McAmis, *Malay Muslims: the History and Challenge of Resurgent Islam in Southeast Asia* (Grand Rapids, Mich.: W.B. Eerdmans Pub., 2002).

[33] Julia Day Howell, 'Sufism and the Indonesian Islamic Revival', *The Journal of Asian Studies* 60, no. 03 (2001): 701–29.

To many, the evidence suggesting this was overwhelming and was easily visible in many locations where mosques had been spared when every other building around them was destroyed by the tidal wave. This occurred in Banda Aceh, Lampuuk, Baet, Kaju, Meulaboh, and many others and was reported by the media across the region.[34] Many residents who sought refuge in mosques survived, further strengthening the idea that the disaster was a form of divine commentary on the community's religious behaviour. A number of observers, including several from international aid agencies, saw a more prosaic explanation for this phenomenon, ascribing it to the fact that mosques were more strongly built because of their social importance, and were frequently located at the highest point available as a sign of reverence. Survivors often accepted this judgement, saying that this was equally a sign of God's participation in the affairs of humans, as surely it was He who caused people to build their mosques in this way and in these locations.

To many people in Aceh, the need for a divine warning in the form of a tsunami was a result of a perceived slackening of religious observance and declining moral standards that resulted from a number of social factors. These included the long period of conflict between the Acehnese and the government of Indonesia which distracted the public from its religious life; a growing interest in material objects and a corresponding weakening of traditional communal institutions; and the increasingly secular nature of the public sphere, possibly as a result of integration into Indonesian national culture. To many Acehnese, the tsunami was viewed as a divine pronouncement about the social change that many people had observed for some time and that had accelerated in recent years. The verdict seemed to be overwhelmingly negative to the majority of those affected.

One woman with a university degree, who served as chair of the provincial branch of a national Islamic women's organization, expressed this general idea in a very personal and vehement manner. She recounts watching television at her home in Banda Aceh on Christmas Eve 2004 and being shocked to find a national Christmas variety programme was being broadcast by the Aceh affiliate of TVRI, the Indonesian national television station. She was affronted, as this programme contained references to the religious nature of the holiday even though it also featured entertainment acts of a secular nature. She says that, on seeing the programme, she prayed to God, asking that He destroy the world if even Aceh was now showing Christmas programming to its Muslim population. The next day, the tsunami struck; this woman and two of her daughters took refuge on the second floor of the house. As the building began to fill with water and she realized they were going to die, she changed her mind and began to pray that God would save them. The water receded after a time, sparing the woman and one of the daughters but killing the other as well as many friends, relatives, and colleagues. When interviewed after the disaster, this survivor was convinced both her prayers had been answered and was proud to

[34] See for example ChannelNewsAsia, '"Miracle" Mosques Defy Tsunami Onslaught', (2005), http://www.channelnewsasia.com/stories/afp_asiapacific/view/125438/1/.htm. (accessed 3 July 2013).

relate this story of what she believes is God's direct response to her prayers. She seems to feel no internal conflict at the idea that, if she is correct, her prayers were directly responsible for the deaths of hundreds of thousands of people in her town and elsewhere, as well as widespread destruction across South and Southeast Asia.

While extreme in nature and intensely personal, this survivor's perception of the disaster is by no means unique in Aceh. A majority of survivors have the same kind of view about their importance to God and see the tsunami as a reasonable warning about their behaviour. While they, of course, feel the loss of loved ones, property, livelihood, and cultural institutions, they believe that this was their fate (*takdir*) and there is no point fighting God's will. It is worth noting that a similar response is often seen in religious Muslims elsewhere in Indonesia as a response to natural disasters. Some observers outside of Aceh placed a different kind of religious interpretation on the event, however. They noted that the Acehnese were extremely arrogant about the quality of their religious observance and piety, and the tsunami had been intended as a warning from God to be more humble and stop placing themselves above the rest of the Indonesian Muslim community.[35] Some Indonesian bloggers even suggested the reason so many young people were killed by the tsunami was because their excessive religious zeal would lead them to become terrorists in the future, and God wished to prevent this before it happened.[36]

Generally, however, there was wide agreement among the public in Aceh that the tsunami had been a warning sent by God and that the appropriate response required not only rebuilding and re-establishing their culture and society, but also a re-evaluation of their own behaviour and attitudes in the context of Islamic law and theology. It was this understanding that led to the rejection of foreign aid that came from organizations thought to have a 'Christianizing' mission or that seemed to impose requirements that were incompatible with traditional social patterns and lifestyle. The issue of missionary activity (*Kristenisasi*) in Aceh has been widely discussed in Indonesia and led directly to demands by the Acehnese public that certain aid agencies be expelled from the region.[37]

Islam and Post-Tsunami Development in Aceh

Post-disaster development is different from other types of development in at least one important respect: it is preceded by an unanticipated event that leads

---

[35] See for example A. Miftach, 'Pengajian Tauhid Wahdatul Ummah', *Front Persatuan Nasional* (2004), http://persatuan.web.id/?p=127.(accessed 3 July 2013).

[36] See for example JockoThinker, 'Re: Tahukah Anda…? Ada apa dengan Obama…?' (BlogPosting)',(2009),http://newsgroups.derkeiler.com/Archive/Soc/soc.culture.indonesia /2009–01/msg01587.html (accessed 3 July 2013).

[37] For complete documentation of this issue as discussed in the Indonesian media see Artawijaya, H.A. Bastoni, and E. Mulyatman, *Serambi Mekkah Dihempas Tsunamai, Diterjang Kristenisasi: Liputan Langsung Wartawan Sabili* (Jakarta: Qalammas, 2006).

to destruction. The people for whom the development is intended, therefore, are already disadvantaged in terms of their emotional state and available resources during the planning and implementation of the development programme. The worse the disaster, the more disadvantaged they may be, relative to their pre-disaster state. The 2004 tsunami, for example, was one of the worst natural disasters in modern history. Hundreds of thousands of people were killed, communities were completely destroyed, and material loss and destruction were enormous.

In the case of the Aceh, the destruction caused by the disaster can be grouped into two categories: 1) destruction to the visible landscape and 2) destruction to the invisible landscape. The first type includes the loss of houses, schools, hospitals, mosques, and other buildings; roads, bridges, power generators, and other infrastructure; and loss of life. These are easy to quantify. Some of the physical elements of society, like buildings and infrastructure, can be replaced even though the experience in Aceh has shown that more is involved in replacing schools than simply rebuilding. Loss of human capital – teachers and students – has been much more difficult to replace, as human beings are not interchangeable and there are strong affective elements associated with missing individuals. The destruction to the invisible landscape is much harder to assess and even harder to repair. In the case of Aceh, this has been equally serious and relates to the loss of community and the accumulated knowledge it contained. The survivors of the disaster experienced personal loss taking a range of forms and also had to reorient themselves in a post-disaster landscape that lacked, not just their own loved ones, but also a significant portion of the pre-disaster community whose skills and abilities were instrumental in the functioning of society. In other words, the social structures that formed a backdrop for their pre-disaster experience, and that provided the affective context in which they lived, had been altered so as to be almost unrecognizable.

How survivors view and understand the effects of natural disaster will have a significant impact on their perceptions about appropriate reconstruction. Their acceptance of development efforts will also be determined to a significant degree by this view and understanding. For example, as described above, the Acehnese saw the tsunami as an undeniable message from God, as a warning or punishment or both. They have no doubt that God will send a similar or worse disaster in the future if they do not heed this warning.

The role religion plays in post-disaster development, then, depends on the extent to which it plays a role in the way people view and understand natural disaster. In the case of Aceh religion provides a complete aetiology of disaster. To many Acehnese, faith is, in fact, the only explanation. This religious conviction has played a much greater role in the development of the invisible landscape than of the visible one. The influence of religion in physical development can be seen, for example, in the insistence of survivors that aid donors who proposed to rebuild their houses should also rebuild their mosque or repair it if it was not destroyed. There was no opposition to non-Muslim organizations constructing houses and mosques until when rumours began to spread, that Christian organizations might be in Aceh, not just to help, but also to proselytise. This generated strong reactions from the community, leading to certain groups being asked to leave, even though this was never enforced.[38]

The religious views of the Acehnese and their understanding of the disaster had two main effects in the impact of the disaster on the invisible landscape in Aceh. First there is evidence to suggest that their religious faith lessened the impact of the disaster. Members of the public almost invariably state that they accept the tsunami and its aftermath. Some have noted that, despite the loss, pain and suffering it caused, the disaster had an important and beneficial result, in that it showed that God still loves them and cared enough to warn them that they had strayed too far from their religion. This may explain, at least partly, the conclusion of the WHO, in its recommendations about mental health services in Aceh, that Western constructs of community development were misguided and unwelcome.[39]

The second role of religious views and understanding of the disaster among the Acehnese lies in the development and reconstruction of their invisible landscape. To the extent that this landscape was damaged by the disaster, its reconstruction has been shaped much more by faith than by the restoration of buildings and infrastructure. The precepts of Islam, as understood and applied by the Acehnese public, provided a source of resilience and also dictated a socially acceptable response that included, as noted, a strengthening of religious institutions and practices in the public sphere.

Survivors of the tsunami overwhelmingly did not experience the emotional distress and trauma reaction that would have been expected in a Western setting and which relief agencies had prepared for. In fact, survivors were observed to be surprisingly resilient given the scope of the disaster and level of loss and did not themselves feel in need of any kind of psychological support. Perceptions of need centred on housing, the means of making a living, and being reunited with friends and family members in an attempt to return to a normal life. This is not to suggest that individual survivors were not distressed at all, but the level of emotional disturbance seemed to be well within the capacity of sufferers, as

---

[38] For examples of this problem see S. Behn, 'Indonesia Ousts Christian Groups', *The Washington Times*, 17 March 2005; Nadhatul Ulama. 'Tokoh Agama Kecam LSM Asing Bawa Anak Korban Tsunami'. (2005) http://www.nu.or.id/a,public-m,dinamic-s,detail-ids,1-id,2643-lang,id-c,warta-t,Tokoh+Agama+Kecam+LSM+Asing+Bawa+Anak+Korban+Tsunami-.phpx; M. Gartland, 'Banda Aceh Invites Christians' Aid, But Not Their Proselytizing', *The Post and Courier*, 26 December 2005; S. Powell, 'Christian Groups "Proselytizing" Muslims', *The Australian* 24 December 2005; Drew Warne-Smith, 'Aid Groups Warned Against Preaching', *The Australian* 11 January 2005; A. Cooperman, 'Tsunami Orphans Will Not Be Sent to a Christian Home', *The Washington Post*, 14 January 2005.

[39] World Health Organization, 'Manual for Community-Level Workers: Psychosocial Care of Tsunami-Affected Populations', (New Delhi: WHO, Regional Office for South East Asia, 2005); 'WHO Recommendations for Mental Health in Aceh', (2005), http://www.who.or.id/eng/contents/aceh/WHO_Recommendations_Mental_Health_Aceh.pdf. (accessed 3 July 2013).

well as the community, to absorb. Their faith provided a meaning for the disaster and this meaning was viewed as applying to everyone in the community. This perception of a shared lot grounded in religious aetiology came to be a source of strength in adapting to loss.

In this context, it is worth considering how some affected individuals compared the emotional and psychological impact of the devastation caused by the tsunami with that resulting from armed conflict with the Indonesian army. Unlike the tsunami, this conflict was seen as a worldly problem without religious connotations. A high ranking provincial government official with an overseas postgraduate degree, for example, noted that, while the severity of the tsunami was many times greater than the conflict in terms of loss of life and material damage, the trauma and emotional impact of the conflict was much greater. He could accept what he saw as the wrath of God, but not the cruelty of other human beings. He also found he could easily understand that God might warn or even punish the Acehnese with a natural disaster and believed that God always acted in their best interest. The Indonesian army, however, clearly did not have the interests of the Acehnese at heart. He wondered why there had been no counselling available during the conflict when some Acehnese might have needed it and did not comprehend why foreign aid providers, in particular, insisted on offering this service when the Acehnese felt quite relaxed and accepting about the tsunami. Similar views were expressed repeatedly by many individuals and illustrate the depth of the Acehnese belief in God's will and their acceptance of even extremely severe events that they attribute to this cause.

The importance of community in the emotional response and ability of survivors to adapt and to develop the post-tsunami invisible landscape cannot be ignored. Malay culture tends to be highly sensitive to social norms; a very high premium is placed on consensus and conformity, and it is generally not considered desirable to stand out or go against the group. There is a religious basis for this cultural feature. In Islam, people are seen as all the same to God, and the only thing that allows one individual to stand out from others to God is *taqwa* (obedience to God's will). An example of this attitude was observed in the town of Lampuuk, which was almost totally destroyed (except for its mosque) by the tidal wave. One of the most pressing needs of survivors in this area following the disaster was housing, as most of the village had been destroyed. They quickly formed a group to represent their joint interests and began negotiating with aid agencies for assistance in replacing their lost dwellings. Eventually, the residents' committee decided to accept aid from the Turkish Red Crescent. After many delays during which survivors had to live in emergency accommodation, all 700 promised dwellings were ready for them to move into in April 2007. Even though many houses had been available long before this, and there had been serious disagreements about how these houses should be allotted, the Lampuuk survivors all waited to move in until everyone could be accommodated because of their desire to preserve their community structure and maintain the traditional orientation of their village. Many new houses remained empty, however, as the residents preferred to live in groups and chose to occupy only certain buildings. Many of them had lost all or most of their family members and did not want to live in relatively empty houses or by themselves. This reaction is typical in the Malay world where support networks, based first on extended family ties and then on community or group affiliation, are the main social structures in coping with adverse situations. In better times when more opportunities are available, this behaviour is not usually seen, with individuals generally acting in their own interest. The reversion to a group mentality fostering mutual dependence among individuals who are related through family or geographical ties is an important emotional strategy among the Malay that serves to promote emotional resilience and support a return to normal life that maintains social norms, including religious behaviour.

This group mentality has a strong religious aspect as well. Many required observances in Islam are best performed in a group. The most important of these observances is *shalat*, the five daily prayers that have a specific form and timing. Islam in Indonesia holds that it is best, in terms of religious virtue, if prayers are carried out communally, with family members when performed at home or with other people when performed at mosques or community prayer houses. Fasting during the month of Ramadan, another pillar of Islam, also has a strong communal element. Breaking the fast in a group at sunset is an important ritual, and fast breaking is an opportunity to entertain at home as well as to be a guest in other people's homes. In Aceh, as well as elsewhere in Indonesia, the group orientation of these religious rituals serves to strengthen a communal mentality and foster a strong sense of belonging to the group. Shared religious faith forms the basis for social groupings at various levels, from the family at the lowest and expanding to include the whole Muslim population of Indonesia or the world.

To survivors, there was no reason to be upset about the tsunami and its results. In fact, they tended to be completely calm and matter of fact in discussing what had happened in general, as well as what they had personally experienced. Their belief in the infallibility of God's decisions seems to underpin this reaction, and, in this sense, even the most extreme loss of life and possessions seemed reasonable and acceptable as survivors believed that God must have had a good reason for His actions. For this reason, there was no sense that the disaster was unfair, represented an insurmountable burden, or should result in inconsolable grief. The fact that God permitted something of this magnitude to occur seemed to offset any personal emotional trauma that might be expected to result from such a loss, as the whole experience was rooted in deeply held religious convictions.

For this reason, for survivors of the tsunami, the experience often served to renew their interest in religious practice and identification. It is important to note, however, that outward expressions of faith – such as attendance at religious services and events, modes of dress, fasting at appropriate times, and so on – are not necessarily an indication of personal feelings or belief, but these visible aspects of religion were considered extremely important following the tsunami as part of the new, reconstructed society in Aceh. In other words, the visible manifestation of religious observance took on even greater importance as part of a newly re-established social norm. The widely held view that it was necessary to restore Islamic culture and institutions in the region meant for many people that this would have to include conformity to certain aspects of religious practice in daily life. If people were not inclined to conform to more rigorous social norms, many survivors felt it would be appropriate to require such behaviour by law.

Additionally, while there is a strong evidence to suggest that religion is most influential in the way the Acehnese view the tsunami and the devastation it caused and that religion has had an equally strong impact on post-disaster development in the region, there are equally strong reasons to suggest that the influence of religion in Aceh has significant limitations. For example, one of the most common complaints among members of the community is that corruption in the context of post-disaster development has been a serious problem. It was well-known, for example, that officials and other well-connected individuals were able to obtain new houses built for tsunami survivors, even though they themselves did not experience any loss as a result of the event. Similarly, roads and other infrastructures built to replace those destroyed by the tsunami did not always conform to specifications, with contractors cutting corners and using inferior materials. At the same time, every Acehnese agrees that corruption is prohibited by their religion and those in positions of authority, in particular, should act for the best interests of the community. They have no answer to the question of why their strong religious faith has failed to check corruption of this kind. Some feel that only God can devise a punishment sufficient to end corruption in Aceh. As corruption is endemic in Indonesia and is an inevitable part of doing business of any kind, it may be worth investigating further the relationship of this practice to religious belief in Aceh and elsewhere in the country.

Religion and Development in Future Disasters

The experience in Aceh following the 2004 Indian Ocean tsunami provides ample evidence of the importance of religion in the understanding and interpretation of such events by the people who experience them. It is difficult, however, to predict in advance exactly how the religious views of any given population might shape their response to disaster and even more difficult to apply such knowledge in designing development programmes intended to address their needs. Disaster, by its nature, generally cannot be anticipated, even in parts of the world prone to natural events like floods or earthquakes. It is for this reason that the need for more in depth cultural, including religious, knowledge of groups who are to be the recipients of development aid is frequently noted in the literature.[40]

[40] See for example Powell, 'Christian Groups "Proselytizing" Muslims'; Sheila Miyoshi Jager, *On the Uses of Cultural Knowledge* (Carlisle, PA: Strategic Studies Institute, U.S. Army War College, 2007); Lunn, 'The Role of Religion, Spirituality and Faith in Development: A Critical Theory Approach'.

Because a large portion of development aid for disaster relief is provided by Western agencies whose guiding principles derive from the philosophical views of their societies of origin, it is likely, if not inevitable, that there will exist fundamental differences of perception between them and the communities in which they wish to operate. In particular, the Western social/political paradigm separates religion from the public sphere; when religious organizations provide social services, they tend to model their activities after secular agencies working in the same field. That is, in the West, the religious orientation of an aid-providing organization generally remains far in the background and often is only evident in the stated basis of the group in question. This has been noted in the context of religious or faith based organizations providing disaster relief in Western countries, such as following Hurricane Katrina in the US.[41] In many non-Western countries, however, religious expression is considered appropriate and expected in the public sphere, as in the case of Aceh above and in Indonesia in general. In the Islamic world, this may be a special problem, exacerbated perhaps by events in the political arena that suggest a natural opposition between the West (and its assumed Christian orientation) and Islam.

For this reason, disaster aid, whether from an international organization or from within the country itself, must be seen as according with local interpretation and local expectations. Following the tsunami in Aceh, for example, aid that was clearly associated with the dominant religion of the area, in this case Islam, was clearly preferable to that from sources that were locally associated with other religions (even if religion played no part in the proffered aid). It was for this reason that the development efforts of the Turkish Red Crescent were greatly preferred to those of other secular groups, and especially to those of groups believed to be Christian in orientation. In this case, it was the perception of religious orientation that seemed to be more significant than any actual religious principles that may have directed the activities of the organizations in question. The Acehnese, for example, had no particular knowledge of the nature of Islam in Turkey or any specific information about the Red Crescent itself. Rather, they were reacting to a perception that any group affiliated with their own religion was preferable to one of unknown, potentially conflicting, origin. This highlights the observation that response to disaster may include an intensification of identity issues and distinctions between those within and outside of the group.[42] Religion, then, may

[41] See for example Daphne S. Cain and Juan Barthelemy, ‘Tangible and spiritual relief after the storm: The religious community responds to Katrina’, *Journal of Social Service Research* 34, no. 3 (2008): 29–42.

[42] See Pat Deeny and Brian McFetridge, ‘The Impact of Disaster on Culture, Self, and Identity: Increased Awareness by Health Care Professionals is Needed’, *Nursing Clinics of North America* 40, no. 3 (2005): 431–40; Bridget Dugan, ‘Loss of Identity in Disaster: How Do You Say Goodbye to Home?’, *Perspectives in Psychiatric Care* 43, no. 1 (2007): 41–6; Francis X. Gunn, ‘Spiritual Issues in the Aftermath of Disaster’, *Southern Medical Journal* 100, no. 9 (2007): 936–37.

colour aid recipients' perception of the value and appropriateness of development programmes in a manner that has little relationship to the content of that aid, which, in most cases, is in fact neutral and consists of the physical necessities required for survival.

Concluding Thoughts

Thus, the religious beliefs of the target population also relate closely to their perception of what aid is required and the direction development should take. In Aceh, for example, tsunami survivors felt little need for psychological counselling and support. Their requirements centred on housing, food, and medical aid immediately following the disaster and restoration of infrastructure and community structures in the longer term. They felt capable of providing for their own emotional recovery and demonstrated a notable level of long term community and individual resilience. As described above, this resilience seemed to derive almost wholly from their religious faith and the interpretation and meaning of the event their beliefs ascribed to it. This meaning-related resilience has been shown to be extremely important in coping with adverse events and is one of the major benefits religious faith may provide, regardless of the specific religion or the location and population of interest.[43] In practical terms, development programmes that do not fit with this perception of need are likely to be viewed as irrelevant by potential recipients, pointing up the dilemma of Western paradigms that have largely excluded the role of religious faith and may fail to take it into account in other cultural contexts. In fact, Western models of human response to disaster and other kinds of adversity that are deeply rooted in enlightenment philosophy are increasingly seen as culture bound and unable to address the cognitive and affective needs of people in non-Western cultures.[44]

Finally, and perhaps most importantly, the religious beliefs of a community may define the meaning they give to a natural disaster, as in the case of Aceh. This, in turn, may have important implications for what is seen as acceptable and desirable. In practice, it may be difficult to determine in advance what specific elements of assistance are seen locally as being of first priority and, conversely, which are seen as expendable or have not even been thought of. The desire of the public in Aceh to have mosques rebuilt or repaired first is an example of the former, while the perceived lack of need for counselling services is an example of the latter. The

---

43 See K.I. Pargament and J. Cummings, 'Anchored by Faith: Religion as a Resilience Factor', in *Handbook of Adult Resilience*, ed. John W. Reich, Alex Zautra, and John Stuart Hall (New York: Guilford Press, 2010).

44 See for example Sebastian Von Peter, 'The Experience of Mental Trauma and its Transcultural Application', *Transcultural Psychiatry* 45, no. 4 (2008): 639–51; Frank Kortmann, 'Transcultural Psychiatry: From Practice to Theory', *Transcultural Psychiatry* 47, no. 2 (2010): 203–23.

ability of aid providers to accommodate these perceptions in their programmes may mean the difference between being seen as welcome assistance or an unwanted intruder. The problem, of course, is how to identify such perceptions and respond to them in the short timeframe available following natural disaster, a situation complicated by the fact that many donor organizations operate around the world based on need and do not necessarily have a great deal of insight into local culture. Again, using Aceh as an example, the prolonged period of conflict preceding the tsunami combined with the comparatively closed nature of the community meant that potential aid providers knew little about the pre-disaster situation. This all points to a growing need for greater insight into religion and cultures around the world where development activities of all kinds take place and suggests there may be great value in incorporating some of the knowledge base available in other disciplines, such as anthropology, sociology, psychology, and other related fields, into the planning of development programmes, especially in the special context of post-disaster aid where more appropriate efforts are of even greater significance.

References

Artawijaya, H.A. Bastoni, and E. Mulyatman. *Serambi Mekkah Dihempas Tsunamai, Diterjang Kristenisasi: Liputan Langsung Wartawan Sabili*. Jakarta: Qalammas, 2006.

Badan Pusat Statistik. 'Statistik Nanggroe Aceh Darussalam'. (2009). http://aceh.bps.go.id/.

Beatty, Andrew. 'Adam and Eve and Vishnu: Syncretism in the Javanese Slametan'. *Journal of the Royal Anthropological Institute* (1996): 271–88.

Behn, S. 'Indonesia Ousts Christian Groups'. *The Washington Times*, 17 March 2005.

Cain, Daphne S., and Juan Barthelemy. 'Tangible and Spiritual Relief after the Storm: The Religious Community Responds to Katrina'. *Journal of Social Service Research* 34, no. 3 (2008): 29–42.

Casanova, José. *Public Religions in the Modern World*. Chicago: University of Chicago Press, 1994.

Cederroth, S. 'Indonesia and Malaysia'. In *Islam Outside the Arab World*, edited by David Westerlund and Ingvar Svanberg. New York: St. Martin's Press, 1999.

ChannelNewsAsia. '"Miracle" Mosques Defy Tsunami Onslaught'. (2005). http://www.channelnewsasia.com/stories/afp_asiapacific/view/125438/1/.htm.

Clarke, Gerard. 'Faith Matters: Faith-Based Organisations, Civil Society and International Development'. *Journal of International Development* 18, no. 6 (2006): 835–48.

Clarke, Matthew. *Development and Religion: Theology and Practice*. Cheltenham, UK; Northampton, MA, USA: Edward Elgar, 2011.

Cooperman, A. 'Tsunami Orphans Will Not Be Sent to a Christian Home'. *The Washington Post*, 14 January 2005.

De Cordier, Bruno. 'The "Humanitarian Frontline", Development and Relief, and Religion: What Context, Which Threats and Which Opportunities?'. *Third World Quarterly* 30, no. 4 (2009): 663–84.

Deeny, Pat, and Brian McFetridge. 'The Impact of Disaster on Culture, Self, and Identity: Increased Awareness by Health Care Professionals Is Needed'. *Nursing Clinics of North America* 40, no. 3 (2005): 431–40.

Dugan, Bridget. 'Loss of Identity in Disaster: How Do You Say Goodbye to Home?'. *Perspectives in Psychiatric Care* 43, no. 1 (2007): 41–6.

Ebstyne King, Pamela, and James L. Furrow. 'Religion as a Resource for Positive Youth Development: Religion, Social Capital, and Moral Outcomes'. *Psychology of Religion and Spirituality* Vol. S, no. 1 (2008): 34–49.

Gartland, M. 'Banda Aceh Invites Christians' Aid, but Not Their Proselytizing'. *The Post and Courier*, 26 December 2005.

Goody, Jack R. 'Religion and Development: Some Comparative Considerations'. *Development* 46, no. 4 (2003): 64–7.

Gunn, Francis X. 'Spiritual Issues in the Aftermath of Disaster'. *Southern Medical Journal* 100, no. 9 (2007): 936–7.

Howell, Julia Day. 'Sufism and the Indonesian Islamic Revival'. *The Journal of Asian Studies* 60, no. 03 (2001): 701–29.

IRIN. '"A Clash of Ignorances" – Relief Aid and the Arab and Islamic World'. (2007). http://www.irinnews.org/fr/reportfrench.aspx?reportid=70771.

Islamic Development Bank. 'Annual Report 29 1424H (2003–2004)'. Jeddah: IDB, 2004.

Jager, Sheila Miyoshi. *On the Uses of Cultural Knowledge*. Carlisle, PA: Strategic Studies Institute, U.S. Army War College, 2007.

JockoThinker. 'Re: Tahukah Anda…? Ada Apa Dengan Obama…?' (Blog Posting)'. (2009). http://newsgroups.derkeiler.com/Archive/Soc/soc.culture.indonesia/2009–01/msg01587.html.

Juergensmeyer, Mark. *The New Cold War? Religious Nationalism Confronts the Secular State*. Berkeley: University of California Press, 1994.

Kortmann, Frank. 'Transcultural Psychiatry: From Practice to Theory'. *Transcultural Psychiatry* 47, no. 2 (2010): 203–23.

Kuran, Timur. 'Islam and Underdevelopment: An Old Puzzle Revisited'. *Journal of Institutional and Theoretical Economics* (1997): 41–71.

Lavretsky, Helen. 'Spirituality and Aging'. *Aging Health* 6, no. 6 (2010): 749–69.

Lim, Chaeyoon, and Robert D. Putnam. 'Religion, Social Networks, and Life Satisfaction'. *American Sociological Review* 75, no. 6 (2010): 914–33.

Lunn, Jenny. 'The Role of Religion, Spirituality and Faith in Development: A Critical Theory Approach'. *Third World Quarterly* 30, no. 5 (2009): 937–51.

Marshall, Katherine. 'Development and Religion: A Different Lens on Development Debates'. *Peabody Journal of Education* 76, no. 3–4 (2001): 339–75.

Mayotte, Judith A. 'Religion and Global Affairs: The Role of Religion in Development'. *SAIS Review* 18, no. 2 (1998): 65–9.

McAmis, Robert Day. *Malay Muslims: The History and Challenge of Resurgent Islam in Southeast Asia*. Grand Rapids, Mich.: W.B. Eerdmans Pub., 2002.

Miftach, A. 'Pengajian Tauhid Wahdatul Ummah'. *Front Persatuan Nasional* (2004). Published electronically 31 December. http://persatuan.web.id/?p=127.

Nadhatul Ulama. 'Tokoh Agama Kecam LSM Asing Bawa Anak Korban Tsunami'. (2005) http://www.nu.or.id/a,public-m,dinamic-s,detail-ids,1-id,2643-lang,id-c,warta-t,Tokoh+Agama+Kecam+LSM+Asing+Bawa+Anak+Korban+Tsunami-.phpx.

Pargament, K.I., and J. Cummings. 'Anchored by Faith: Religion as a Resilience Factor'. In *Handbook of Adult Resilience*, edited by John W. Reich, Alex Zautra and John Stuart Hall. New York: Guilford Press, 2010.

Powell, S. 'Christian Groups "Proselytizing" Muslims'. *The Australian* 24 December 2005.

Salemink, O. 'Development Cooperation as Quasi-Religious Conversion'. In *The Development of Religion, the Religion of Development*, edited by Ananta Kumar Giri, Anton van Harskamp and Oscar Salemink. Delft: Eburon, 2004.

Selinger, Leah. 'The Forgotten Factor: The Uneasy Relationship between Religion and Development'. *Social Compass* 51, no. 4 (2004): 523–43.

Seybold, Kevin S., and Peter C. Hill. 'The Role of Religion and Spirituality in Mental and Physical Health'. *Current Directions in Psychological Science* 10, no. 1 (2001): 21–4.

Smith, Steven Rathgeb, and Michael R. Sosin. 'The Varieties of Faith-Related Agencies'. *Public Administration Review* 61, no. 6 (2001): 651–70.

Tomalin, Emma. 'Religion and a Rights-Based Approach to Development'. *Progress in Development Studies* 6, no. 2 (2006): 93–108.

United Nations High Commissioner on Refugees. 'The State of the World's Refugees: Human Displacement in the New Millennium'. Geneva: UNHCR, 2006.

Ver Beek, Kurt Alan. 'Spirituality: A Development Taboo'. *Development in Practice* 10, no. 1 (2000): 31–43.

Von Peter, Sebastian. 'The Experience of Mental Trauma and Its Transcultural Application'. *Transcultural Psychiatry* 45, no. 4 (2008): 639–51.

Warne-Smith, Drew 'Aid Groups Warned against Preaching'. *The Australian* 11 January 2005.

Wigger, Andreas. 'Encountering Perceptions in Parts of the Muslim World and Their Impact on the ICRC's Ability to Be Effective'. *International Review of the Red Cross* 87, no. 858 (2005): 343–65.

World Health Organization. 'Manual for Community-Level Workers: Psychosocial Care of Tsunami-Affected Populations'. New Delhi: WHO, Regional Office for South East Asia, 2005.

———. 'Who Recommendations for Mental Health in Aceh'. (2005). http://www.who.or.id/eng/contents/aceh/WHO_Recommendations_Mental_Health_Aceh.pdf.

Chapter 9
Piety, Gender Relations and Muslim Women's Empowerment: The Case of Islamic NGOs in Bangladesh

Mohammad Musfequs Salehin[1]

Introduction

This chapter deals with the constructions of gender by Bangladeshi Islamic NGOs through an analysis of discourse. Gender issues in general and promotion of women rights in particular have long been considered as a 'secular enterprise' in the development practices of western NGOs and their counterparts in the global south.[2] However, with the return of religion in development practices in the 1990s and the increased presence of faith-based organizations (FBOs), particularly Islamic NGOs in the Muslim world, academics and researchers have reconceptualized the perceived antagonism between religion and feminism. While research shows that the Islamic NGOs typically advocate a return to more conservative gender roles,[3] some Muslim FBOs argue for more liberal rights in their practice. Therefore, the emergence of Islamic NGOs and the rise of 'Islamic Feminism' in many parts of the Muslim world require urgent attention to critically explore the specificity, as well as the complexity, of such frameworks to promote gender issues within Muslim societies like Bangladesh.

Islamic NGOs in Bangladesh entered into the development discourse in the 1990s after a devastating cyclone in the coastal areas of Bangladesh. In the beginning, most of the Islamic NGOs in Bangladesh were involved in relief

[1] I am grateful to Stephen Castles, Laura Beth Bugg, Rebecca Williamson, and anonymous reviewers for their comments on an earlier version of this chapter, which was presented at the Australian Sociological Association (TASA) Annual Conference held in Newcastle, Australia from November 28 to December 1, 2011. I also gratefully acknowledge the Australia Awards, DIISRTE, and the Government of Australia for granting me an Endeavour Award to conduct this research.

[2] Nida Kirmani and Isabel Phillips, 'Engaging with Islam to Promote Women's Rights', *Progress in Development Studies* 11, no. 2 (2011): 87–99.

[3] For example see Kristen Ghodsee, 'Religious Freedoms versus Gender Equality: Faith-Based Organizations, Muslim Minorities, and Islamic Headscarves in the New Europe', *Social Politics: International Studies in Gender, State & Society* 14, no. 4 (2007): 526–61.

and humanitarian activities, and assumed a service delivery role, for example, providing microcredit and education after the disaster. While the use of the terms 'religious' or 'faith-based' as a prefix to any NGO is contested,[4] this research has defined as Islamic those NGOs whose mission, vision and activities are inspired and guided by the teaching of Islam, including any sub-sect of Islamic teachings. However, among the faith-based organizations, as Clarke argues, there are many different types of organizations, including faith-based representative organizations or apex bodies, faith-based charitable or development organizations, faith-based missionary organizations, and faith-based radical, illegal or terrorist organizations.[5] This chapter aims to explore the role of Islamic NGOs in changing gender relations in rural Bangladesh through a focus on the practices of everyday religion. After introducing the issue and research methods, the chapter begins with an examination of women and gender in NGO-led development discourse in Bangladesh to explore the issue of empowerment and disempowerment. The next section of the chapter discusses the change and resistance in gender relations to see how Islamic NGOs are influencing the personal and public sphere of rural women, which is then followed by an analysis of the Islamic way of empowerment. The last section of the chapter focuses on the problems and contradictions in women's empowerment of the Islamic NGO, followed by some concluding remarks.

Methodology

I conducted fieldwork in rural Bangladesh during the period of July 2010 to February 2011. Qualitative interviews, Focus Group Discussions, observation and participation were the methods used to study Islamic NGOs, mainly in the Bagerhat, Satkhira and Manikganj districts, which were the main ones to receive aid from Islamic NGOs after disasters and also the only regions to have model villages (e.g. Bagerhat and Manikganj). However, interviews were also conducted with NGO officials at their head offices located in Dhaka, the capital of Bangladesh. A total of 104 interviews and eight FGDs (Focus Group Discussions) were conducted during the fieldwork out of which 51 interviews were conducted with Islamic NGO beneficiaries, and the rest of the interviews were conducted with NGO officials (including Islamic and Non-Islamic NGOs), local key informants and the beneficiaries of non-Islamic NGOs and non-beneficiaries of NGOs. Beneficiaries of NGOs were selected randomly from the list provided by the local offices of the NGOs.

---

[4] G. Clarke and M. Jennings, 'Introduction', in *Development, Civil Society and Faith-Based Organizations: Bridging the Sacred and the Secular*, ed. G. Clarke and M. Jennings (New York: Palgrave Macmillan, 2008).

[5] Clarke, G. 'Faith-Based Organizations and International Development', in *Development, Civil Society and Faith-Based Organizations: Bridging the Sacred and the Secular*, ed. G. Clarke and M. Jennings (New York: Palgrave Macmillan, 2008).

At Bagerhat, data were collected in the 'Shajalal Model Village' of Muslim Aid located at Rayenda Union Parishad[6] under the Sharankhola Upazila.[7] At Sharankhola, I observed and interviewed beneficiaries and non-beneficiaries of the shari'a-based microfinance programme of Muslim Aid, and the Islamic Bank Foundation (hereafter IBF). The Islamic and moral education programme under these shari'a-based microfinance programmes, including *Fael Khair*,[8] was one of particular interest; I participated in many of the meetings relating to this project. Another site for my fieldwork was Satkhira District, which included the three villages in Bazargram of Kaliganj, Nildomor of Shyamnagar and Ataroy of Tala Upazilas where I mainly conducted my interviews with the beneficiaries of Muslim Aid and IBF. In Mankiganj, my fieldwork was mainly limited to the Chandirchar village under Jagir Union of Sadar Upazila, where I explored the *Hasana/Parshi*,[9] a *zakat* (Islamic alms giving) based integrated development programme of MACCA (Masjid Council for Community Advancement). All the programmes of the Islamic NGOs in the study fall under the broad category of 'model' village programmes. Therefore, my investigation into the five different villages corresponds with an attempt to observe any differences in the modus operandi and outcomes of such programmes.

NGO-Led Development Discourses in Bangladesh: Gender Empowerment and Disempowerment

Bangladesh, as an independent state, entered the global economy in 1971 when globalization and neoliberalism were dismantling the traditional welfare state in the West, and women-centric aid policies had become the norm for western aid agencies. After the war in 1971, the already fragile infrastructure of Bangladesh was in chaos.[10] It was in this scenario that developmental NGOs stepped in as rural service providers. NGOs began their work of war reconstruction and rehabilitation

---

6 Union Parishad is the lowest tier of local government of Bangladesh.

7 The *upazilas* are the second lowest tier of regional administration in Bangladesh which is comprised of several Union Parishad.

8 The *Fael Khair* programme was established by the Islamic Development Bank (IDB) in Bangladesh to help the cyclone SIDR victims in coastal areas of Bangladesh. The funding of this programme came from an anonymous Saudi Arabian philanthropist who donated $130 million.

9 *Hasana* or *Parshi* is a *Zakat* (Islamic alms giving, which is one of the five pillars of Islam) based integrated development programme run by MACCA at Manikganj. For more detail on *Parshi*, see T. Mesbahuddin, 'Religion in Development: An Islamic Model Emerging in Bangladesh', *Journal of South Asian Development* 5, no. 2 (2010): 221–41.

10 Richard Sisson and Leo E. Rose, *War and Secession: Pakistan, India and the Creation of Bangladesh* (Berkeley, CA: University of California Press, 1991); Badruddin Umar, *The Emergence of Bangladesh: Class Struggles in East Pakistan (1947–1958)* (New York: Oxford University Press, 2004).

of refugees, occupying an infrastructure vacuum in the newly independent state. The developmental NGO sector soon capitalized on the women-in-development (WID) paradigm of the United Nations and western aid organizations. Hence, the main objectives of the development practices of NGOs emphasized the issue of empowerment of rural poor women in Bangladesh. Even the Bangladeshi state, under military leadership, also capitalized on the WID paradigm to gain development dollars and legitimacy from western democracies. Thus, gender empowerment turned into a prime focus of development in Bangladesh.

Empowerment of women, as conceptualized in the NGO-led development discourse in Bangladesh, has produced debate and contradiction.[11] Using eight different indicators of women's empowerment (e.g., mobility, the ability of women to make purchases, the ownership of productive assets, decision making power, freedom from family domination, political and legal awareness and participation in public protest and political campaigning), Hashemi et al. found that Bangladeshi rural women's participation in NGOs microcredit programmes was a tool for empowerment. For them, one of the important non-economic aspects of women's empowerment is that those women now had made a network outside of their family and 'learned to talk' in public.[12] Access to credit, for them, was found to be associated with the reduction of incidences of violence against women. They cited one of the beneficiaries:

> In the past my father-in-law would never stop my husband from beating me. But after I joined Grameen Bank he said to my husband, 'You had better stop beating and scolding your wife. Now she has contact with many people in society. She brings you loans from Grameen Bank. If you want to you can start a business with the money she brings![13]

In the same way, Amin et al. argue that 'by providing women with control over material resources, microcredit programs may increase women's domestic prestige and their importance in the eyes of their husband'.[14] Other research findings also

---

[11] N. Kabeer, 'Conflicts Over Credit: Re-Evaluating the Empowerment Potential of Loans to Women in Rural Bangladesh', *World Development* 29, no. 1 (2001): 63–84; S. Mahmud, 'Actually How Empowering is Microcredit', *Development and Change* 34, no. 4 (2003): 577–605; E. Selinger, 'Does Microcredit "Empower"? Reflections on the Grameen Bank Debate', *Human Studies* 31, no. 1 (2008): 27–41; A. Parmar, 'Micro-Credit, Empowerment, and Agency: Re-evaluating the Discourse', *Canadian Journal of Development Studies/Revue canadienne d'études du développement* 24, no. 3 (2003): 461–76.

[12] S.M. Hashemi, S.R. Schuler, and A.P. Riley, 'Rural Credit Programs and Women's Empowerment in Bangladesh', *World Development* 24, no. 4 (1996): 635–53.

[13] Ibid., 648–9.

[14] R. Amin, S. Becker, and A. Bayes, 'NGO-Promoted Microcredit Programs and Women's Empowerment in Rural Bangladesh: Quantitative and Qualitative Evidence', *The Journal of Developing Areas* (1998): 225.

suggest that women's access to microcredit has made substantial changes in the empowerment process. Pitt and Khandker, for example, argued that women's preferences carried greater weight in determining decision-making outcomes in households where they received a loan compared to households either where men received loans, or where no loans had been received.[15] Similarly, Mahmud emphasizes the notion of women's choice and active agency in the attainment of greater well-being. She argues that access to microcredit has strongly increased women's ability to exercise agency in intra-household processes, and hence increases women's welfare and reduces male bias in welfare outcomes.[16]

However, contrary to the positive accounts, a large number of (influential) studies argue that access to microcredit reinforces patriarchal norms of women's subordination and both worsens gender relations and disempowers women in rural Bangladesh.[17]

One of the most important works on microcredit is the ethnographic study on Grameen Bank beneficiaries by Rahman, who critically examines the narratives of NGO-led empowerment programmes for women in rural Bangladeshi villages. Using Scott's notion of 'hidden' and 'public' transcripts,[18] Rahman reveals the ideological justification[19] that hides the true reasons behind why Grameen Bank almost exclusively provides loans to women. He argues that women are accepted into credit programmes due to their 'positional vulnerability'[20] in rural society;

---

[15] M. Pitt and S. Khandker, 'Household and Intrahousehold Impacts of the Grameen Bank and Similar Targeted Credit Programmes in Bangladesh', in *Credit Programmes for the Poor: Household and Intrahousehold Impacts and Programme Sustainability* (Dhaka: Bangladesh World Bank and Bangladesh Institute of Development Studies, 1995).

[16] Mahmud, 'Actually How Empowering is Microcredit'.

[17] Aminur Rahman, 'Micro-Credit Initiatives for Equitable and Sustainable Development: Who Pays?', *World Development* 27, no. 1 (1999): 67–82; A.M. Goetz and R.S. Gupta, 'Who Takes the Credit? Gender, Power, and Control Over Loan Use in Rural Credit Programs in Bangladesh', *World Development* 24, no. 1 (1996): 45–63; Parmar, 'Micro-Credit, Empowerment, and Agency: Re-evaluating the Discourse'; Lamia Karim, 'Demystifying Micro-Credit: The Grameen Bank, NGOs, and Neoliberalism in Bangladesh ' *Cultural Dynamics* 20, no. 1 (2008): 5–29; R. Montgomery, D. Bhattacharya, and D. Hulme, 'Credit for the Poor in Bangladesh', in *Finance against Poverty*, ed. D. Hulme and P. Mosley (London: Routledge, 1996).

[18] J. Scott, *Domination and the Arts of Resistance: Hidden Transcripts* (USA: Yale University Press, 1990).

[19] In his ethnographic work entitled 'Women and Microcredit in Rural Bangladesh' he provides both the NGO workers' and the borrowers' testimony in this regard. See Aminur Rahman, *Women and Microcredit in Rural Bangladesh: Anthropological Study of the Rhetoric and Realities of Grameen Bank Lending* (Boulder, CO.: Westview Press, 1999).

[20] Positional vulnerability is understood in relation to culturally and religiously patterned behaviour of women that is associated with limited physical mobility, 'submissiveness', 'modesty', 'purity', 'respectability', 'shyness' and *purdah*. Rahman, 'Micro-Credit Initiatives for Equitable and Sustainable Development: Who Pays?', 73–5.

that women are targeted by NGOs, such as Grameen Bank, since they are an easily manipulated population. For example, one of Rahman's respondents (a Grameen Bank worker) stated that 'women in the village are easily traceable. They regularly attend more group meetings than men. Women are reliable and more disciplined (passive/submissive) than men. Working with women is easier for us than working with men'.[21] Alongside this, Rahman also argues that women are not the primary beneficiary:

> [M]ost of the women borrowers are not the direct benefactors of the credit extended to them. Instead, these women appear to be mediators between their male household members and the Bank. Thus the lending institution invests loans in the village to generate profit, but it uses the prevailing patriarchal norms of the village society and the positional vulnerability of women (immobile, shy, passive) for timely repayment and distribution of new loans.[22]

Whatever the reasons for targeting women in microcredit programmes, the tremendous growth in the number of women as beneficiaries must have some positive economic impacts. However, it is important to ask, as Goetz and Gupta suggest, 'How far have women been able to convert access to credit, and membership of credit organizations, into a process of "empowerment"; in what way does women's access to credit affect gender relations?' To measure empowerment, these authors assess the degree to which women actually control loans once they have gained access to credit institutions. From their research it is evident that about 63 per cent of women fall into three categories, e.g. partial, very limited or no control over credit. Only 17.8 per cent of women have full control over the credit they receive from NGOs. It is the man who controls the credit. Hence, they conclude that the women who receive loans from NGOs have no control over their loans.[23] However, it not just about control over the credit, but rather that credit imposes a burden on the women. This burden is two dimensional: the woman's husband pressures her to get credit from the NGOs on the one hand, and on the other, the NGO pressures her to repay the loan every week. Although the woman has no control over the credit, she is the one who has to face all the hurdles in repaying the loan, whether it is from the bank or from her peers. As one of Rahman's informants put it:

> When a woman fails to make her instalment on time, she experiences humiliation through verbal aggression from fellow members and bank workers

---

[21] Ibid., 69.

[22] Rahman, *Women and Microcredit in Rural Bangladesh: Anthropological Study of the Rhetoric and Realities of Grameen Bank Lending,* 23.

[23] Goetz and Gupta, 'Who takes the Credit? Gender, Power, and Control Over Loan Use in Rural Credit Programs in Bangladesh', 47.

> in the loan centre … In an extreme case peers may take the defaulter to the Bank office.[24]

Moreover, although women are considered to be an important part of the NGO-led participatory development discourse of empowerment, research shows that they are often excluded from this process, because when NGO workers 'take the empowerment of women into their own hands, women's struggle to end sexist oppression is hijacked'.[25] In the context of Bangladesh NGO-led programmes, whether it is microcredit, health or something else, a prescribed version of social change is imposed on the women, which is not grounded in the women's own experiences. On this issue, with regard to microcredit programmes, Fernando has argued:

> … the beneficiaries of credit programs do not participate in the planning, implementation, or evaluation connected with the micro-enterprises in any meaningful or systematic way. These policies are decided by highly centralized administrations primarily accountable to respective donors of NGOs.[26]

Although women's empowerment has become one of the most important goals and programme agendas in the development practice of NGOs, they failed to incorporate the local traditional and religious dynamics of the particular country, and instead prescribed a western model of emancipation for women, which in Bangladesh has led to a confrontation between the NGOs and the rural religious elite on their activities, particularly over gender roles.

Religion, Secular NGOs and Women: The Conflicting Schema

Bangladesh, as many authors suggest, is 'more modern' on the one hand and 'more Islamic' on the other, representing the increased visibility of religion (Islam) with globalized modernity and capitalism.[27] White articulated the paradox of 'more modern' and 'more Islamic' in the context of Bangladesh and shows how religion or moral order is governing the everyday life of rural women.[28] Naher also

---

[24] Rahman, 'Micro-Credit Initiatives fFor Equitable and Sustainable Development: Who Pays?', 70.

[25] Parmar, 'Micro-Credit, Empowerment, and Agency: Re-Evaluating the Discourse', 446.

[26] J.L. Fernando, 'Nongovernmental Organizations, Micro-Credit, and Empowerment of Women', *The ANNALS of the American Academy of Political and Social Science* 554, no. 1 (1997), 164.

[27] Sarah C. White, 'Beyond the Paradox: Religion, Family and Modernity in Contemporary Bangladesh', *Religions and Development Working Paper 32* (Centre for Development Studies University of Bath, 2009).

[28] Ibid.

analysed gender, religion and its relation to the development practices of NGOs in rural Bangladesh and found the activities and programmes of mainstream secular NGOs have unconsciously or wilfully avoided including Islam and cultural values particularly related to gender and women's empowerment in their programmes, a fact, which in turn, led to a backlash against them.[29] Given such findings, Tomalin's view that development discourse marginalizes people in the global South on account of its rights-based development approaches failing to consider the ways in which religious values shape social ethics, is not misplaced.[30]

There are many explanations for such conflict between secular NGOs and religious elites over gender issues. In interpreting the backlash, NGOs were accused by the mullas of doing anti-Islamic work by charging interest (which is strictly prohibited in Islam) on microcredit, by bringing women outside their homes and making them shameless, which violates the norms of *purdha* (veil/seclusion), and breaking up the traditional family system of the village.[31] Conversely, pro-secular, pro-modernist, or the liberal intelligentsia and the NGOs have treated the religious right, which comprises the Islamists and their allies, as 'backward', 'traditional' and 'reactionary' and the main impediment to development[32] and hence have produced the backlash. Yet, Karim argues that NGOs with neo-liberal and modernist agendas have ignored the role of religion, manipulated rural women's beliefs, and exploited women's constructions of shyness, and *purdha*[33] which is better explained as an 'economy of shame'.[34] Thus, both NGOs and the religious elites, or the mullas in the rural areas, were in conflict with each other with regard to their capacity to establish their authority over gender roles in rural Bangladesh. In this context, the emergence of Islamic NGOs as new service providers for women needs critical analysis to examine the efforts on empowerment and gender issues.

---

29 Ainoon Naher, 'Gender, Religion and Development in Rural Bangladesh', (PhD Thesis, Heidelberg University, 2005).

30 E. Tomalin, 'Religion and a Rights-Based Approach to Development', *Progress in Development Studies* 6, no. 2 (2006): 93–108.

31 Naher, 'Gender, Religion and Development in Rural Bangladesh'.

32 Elora Shehabuddin, 'Contesting the Illicit: Gender and the Politics of Fatwas in Bangladesh', *Signs* 24, no. 4 (1999): 1011–44; Geoffrey D. Wood, 'Clashing values in Bangladesh: NGOs, Secularism and the Ummah', in *Recreating the Commons? NGOs in Bangladesh* ed. F. C. Khan, A. Ahmad, and M. Quddus (Dhaka: The University Press Limited, 2009).

33 Translation of the Bengali word *purdha* into English is 'veil' or 'seclusion'. However, in the everyday practice of religion in Bangladesh *purdha* has a greater implication. Not only does it include social control, it also pertains to women's honour, status, and conditions in society. For further detail, see Shelley Feldman and Florence E. McCarthy, 'Purdah and Changing Patterns of Social Control Among Rural Women in Bangladesh', *Journal of Marriage and the Family* (1983): 949–59.

34 Karim, 'Demystifying Micro-Credit The Grameen Bank, NGOs, and Neoliberalism in Bangladesh', 7.

Change and Resistance in Gender Relations: Do Islamic NGOs make a Difference?

A number of scholars have explored religious or faith-based NGOs in Bangladesh to demonstrate their role in development, yet the literature is incomplete.[35] However, some recent works have advocated an 'emerging Islamic model of development' to explore the intricate relationship between religion and development through the effort of Islamic NGOs.[36]

The Islamic NGOs included in the study, as stated in their mission statements, are designed and run using the teachings of Islam. All three Islamic NGOs, particularly in their shari'a-based microfinance programme, targeted women. Although Islamic NGOs consider empowerment as one of their main objectives, they emphasize family empowerment. Therefore women's participation in the programme of Islamic NGOs is considered as a source of empowerment of Muslim women which would ultimately empower their family. The programmes of these NGOs reflect the core values of Islam, as understood by the NGO, and reflect upon their way and commitment towards gender issues. The uniqueness of the shari'a-based microfinance programme, or *Hasana* programme, is that they do not charge any interest, which is considered *haram* (prohibited) in Islam, though they charge a minimum service charge in some cases.[37] Along with the microfinance programme of these NGOs, they also offer religious and moral education to the members of the *samity*.[38] Moreover, when I attended some weekly *samity* meetings, I noticed the observance of Islamic rituals at the beginning of the meeting. Usually the meeting starts with the recitation from the Holy Qur'an followed by a predesigned discussion on moral and religious issues, for example, how to recite the Qur'an

---

[35] M.M. Ahmad, 'For God's Sake: The Religious Non-Governmental Organizations in Bangladesh', in *Recreating the Commons? NGOs in Bangladesh* ed. Farida Chowdhury Khan, Ahrar Ahmad, and Munir Quddus (Dhaka: The University Press Limited 2009); B. D'Costa, 'Faith, NGOs and the politics of development in Bangladesh', in *Civil Society, Religion and Global Governance: Paradigms of Power and Persuasion*, ed. Helen James (New York: Routledge, 2007).

[36] Mesbahuddin, 'Religion in Development: An Islamic Model Emerging in Bangladesh'.

[37] Muslim Aid, 'Fael Khair Program for Victims of SIDR Cyclone in Bangladesh: Annual Progress Report (May–December 2009)', (Dhaka Muslim Aid 2010); Masjid Council for Community Advancement, 'Annual Report 2007', (Dhaka Masjid Council for Community Advancement n.d.); Islami Bank Foundation, 'Quarterly Progress Report April – Jun, 2011 ', (n.d.), http://fkprogram.org/wp-content/uploads/2011.06-IBF-Quterly-report-April-June.pdf. (accessed 5 March, 2012).

[38] As per the guidelines of credit disbursement, all NGO beneficiaries are grouped around certain *samitys* ('association' in English). Every *samity* has around 30 to 40 members who are divided into groups with five or six members to ensure maximum accountability and loan repayment. A *samity* is located usually in any of the beneficiaries' houses/premises known as a centre. In every *samity* there is a centre leader and deputy leader.

properly, instructions on how to offer prayer, how to be happy in conjugal life, how to maintain *purdha* etc. After collecting the weekly instalments, the meeting ends with the *monajat*.[39] Therefore, women's participation in the weekly meeting of these *Islami samity* forms a critical locus of my analysis in the section below on the personal and public spheres of women.

From Personal Life/Private Sphere to Social Life/Public Sphere of Women; From Symbolic Opposition to Engagement

With modernity and increased urbanization, changes are also occurring at the rural level and in community life in Bangladesh. However, in contrast to the modernist identification of religion with a distinct area of life, for most of my respondents in all the three study areas, religion is embedded in their everyday understanding of life, livelihood, death and survival. Moreover, some everyday activities that go beyond formal religious rituals, what Ammerman calls 'everyday religion',[40] have a profound impact on women's lives. Therefore, it is imperative to explore the use of religious references of Islamic NGOs to see how they structure and change women's everyday life, in both personal and social realms, in a way that informs women's symbolic opposition to 'secular NGOs' and their engagement with Islamic NGOs.

Several studies found that one of the most significant accusations against NGOs (for example, Grameen Bank, BRAC) was that they sought to break up the traditional family order by targeting women through the provision of microfinance.[41] In this sense, these programmes would have limited effects on women's empowerment. The perceptions of women I interviewed in rural areas about secular NGOs confirmed these previous findings. In my study areas women beneficiaries of Islamic NGOs repeated popular chants to me about secular NGOs: *Sahmir Kotha Shunbona / Shusilon charbona* ('We won't listen to what our husbands say /we won't leave the Shusilon[42]), *Shami boro na 'Sir'*[43] *boro,*

---

[39] *Monajat* is an Islamic tradition to ask for mercy and forgiveness from God.

[40] Nancy T. Ammerman, *Everyday Religion: Observing Modern Religious Lives* (New York: Oxford University Press, 2007).

[41] Naher, 'Gender, Religion and Development in Rural Bangladesh'; 'Defending Islam and Women's Honour Against NGOs in Bangladesh', *Women's Studies International Forum* 33, no. 4 (2010): 316–24; White, 'Beyond the Paradox: Religion, Family and Modernity in Contemporary Bangladesh'.

[42] Shusilon is a national NGO working with biodiversity conservation, gender issues, and alternative dispute resolution (ADR). This and other chants are also related to other, larger NGOs, e.g. BRAC, Grameen Bank. See Naher, 'Gender, Religion and Development in Rural Bangladesh'; White, 'Beyond the Paradox: Religion, Family and Modernity in Contemporary Bangladesh'.

[43] The NGO officials who collect the weekly instalment and hold the meeting are known as 'Sir' and the manager of an NGO branch office is known as 'boro' (greater) Sir'.

'Sir' boro 'Sir' boro ('Is the husband greater, or is the 'sir' greater, 'sir' is greater, 'sir' is greater). These represent, White argues, not women's empowerment but rather the replacement of 'domestic patriarchy by development patriarchy – or the local by the global; or the (Islamic) universal by the (western? modern? secular?) particular'.[44] During my fieldwork with Islamic NGO beneficiaries, I found that many of them had never joined the mainstream or secular NGOs. Among the reasons stated by the women for refusing to participate in the programmes of these NGOs were the recipients' fears that women would be urged to behave immodestly in the public sphere. As one of my respondents from Manikganj replied:

> I can't be shameless, un-veiled for money. Those who joined Grameen Bank do Physical Training (PT) and parade in front of the strangers, un-veiled their head and tied the sari that once covered their head and into their hip. Now you tell me, should a woman behave like this?

I found the same sentiment at Shyamnar when I interviewed Shafiqul Islam, a beneficiary of Islami Bank Foundation, who stated:

> I try my best to feed and maintain my wife in such a way so that I can keep myself accountable to Allah. I can't send my wife on the street outside of my home just for the sake of money, that she would earn 500 Taka if she goes outside.

When my respondents claimed they can't go outside to meet the strangers (secular NGO workers), I said to Zerin (my respondent at Manikganj), you still appear before the non-kin male strangers (workers) of Islamic NGOs. She simply replied, 'Yes, I go, but not without the veil. And the people from our NGOs ask us to maintain the veil as well as proper manners'. As the discussion proceeded she referred to Ayesha, one of the wives of Prophet Muhammad, who took part in fighting against non-Muslims. She said: 'If *bibi* (wife) Ayesha (of the Prophet) can leave the house and fight alongside the Prophet, why can't we? We are fighting for our development and to maintain *taqwa*.[45] But we are fighting to maintain our religious belief (*iman*) and practice (*amol*)'. This is the way women are redefining their identity in the public sphere, which corresponds to the reconstruction of *purdah* by some Islamic NGOs, as these NGOs maintained 'women can go outside but have to maintain *purdha*'. Therefore, Islamic NGO beneficiaries also hold the same stance on the reconstruction of the norms of *purdha*. One of my respondents claims:

---

[44] White, 'Beyond the Paradox: Religion, Family and Modernity in Contemporary Bangladesh'.

[45] *Taqwa* comes from the word 'waqiya', which means to protect. It is the protection from the Anger of Allah and His punishment. This is why *Taqwa* is used to describe the performing of actions which please Allah and abstaining from all actions that displease Him.

> We are Muslim; we have more or less knowledge of shari'a. What our government says, we are bound to follow this, but our mentality does not allow us to follow this. We also want women's development. [I asked him how and he replies:] Leaving them at home, you still can develop. You buy a sewing machine, chickens or you can buy two goats for her.

Therefore, the efforts of secular NGOs to empower rural women go against their norms of everyday practices of religion, as many respondents claim. Whenever I asked beneficiaries of Islamic NGOs about their perceptions of the activities of non-Islamic NGOs (e.g. BRAC, Shushilan, Grameen Bank), for example, issues related to their mobility (e.g., joining an NGO rally or procession) some of the respondents at Bazargram at Tala of Satkhira replied: 'they [other NGOs] are ill-mannered and the devil'. However, when I asked these women why they considered these NGOs as the devil, the women replied: 'other NGOs bring women to the procession on the street, and make them not follow *purdha*'. Moreover, interest is prohibited in Islam, and all the beneficiaries of Muslim Aid and IBF expressed that they don't want to 'commit the sin'[46] of getting involved in interest on their loans, citing the reason that they have to die one day and have to be accountable to Allah. Therefore, their commitment towards Islamic practices, as they argue, is not hampered if they are with Islamic NGOs. Rather their opportunity to become pious has been increased, and helped them to be regarded as a 'pure Muslim'. In short, Islamic NGOs have an obvious impact on women's piety, which subsequently influences women in both the private and public sphere.

This opposition to the secular NGOs represents rural women's 'desire' to be guided by the norms for *purdah.* Shajia, an IBF beneficiary at Tala, when asked how she feels when she sees other women going out freely and without the veil replied, 'We feel rather bad when we see other woman not maintaining *purdha*'. Therefore, the existing public mood on veiling and traditional boundaries (e.g. staying at home) are rightly appropriated by the Islamic NGOs and thus reflect the feelings and desires of rural women throughout their activities and programmes.

Islamic NGOs or *Islami Samity*[47] have succeeded in influencing the personal behaviour or private sphere of women by mobilizing them to participate in NGO programmes, such as Islamic microfinance and Islamic/moral education, which inform the code of conduct for women in the public sphere. As one of the female beneficiaries of IBF, at 'Shajalal Model Village' at Shrankhola of Bagerhat puts it: 'According to religion, a woman has to obey her husband, take care of her children and follow the rules of seclusion. Then there will be peace in the family and society will treat me as a "good woman".' Yet, this reading of

[46] Some beneficiaries perceive involvement in a loan with interest as being equivalent to committing incest with one's own mother.

[47] It is important to note that for all Islamic NGOs in the study, beneficiaries and even non-beneficiaries refer to them as *Islami Samity*, without knowing the real name of these NGOs.

religion is nothing much different from the views held by the men. Although the notion of the 'good woman' might be debated, in the everyday practices of rural Bangladeshis it corresponds to piety, modesty in dress code (maintaining *purdha*) and behaviour.[48]

Most of the women beneficiaries explained that their participation in the weekly *samity* meeting has helped them to reduce conjugal fighting which led to a happy conjugal life. Zhinu, a 30-year-old woman, who has been a member of MACCA for the last five years, explained how MACCA has changed her conjugal life:

> When I was with other *samity*, I used to have continuous fights with my husband … especially if we couldn't manage our weekly credit instalment. Now it is better than before. There is no fighting. We follow the methods they (MACCA) showed us. We observe and listen to them and therefore offer prayer every day. Look, though we cannot manage time to pray five times a day due to our work load, we must pray the *Jumma* (Friday prayer) now. We have learnt how to be patient (*sabur*), what are the rights of husband and wife, and we try to follow them. We live happily.

Moreover, their participation, as women suggest, has encouraged women to be pious in their private lives, which in turn means that they are represented as 'good women' in the public sphere. The idea of *khate Musulman* (pure Muslim) and 'good women' are linked with each other and depend on the performance of religious activities or piety. 'Good Women', as the beneficiaries of these Islamic NGOs suggest, are those who exhibit modesty in their behaviour and dress code and take good care of their children and husband or family. This also reflects the traditions of the rural society. What is new in this context is the emphasis on piety or performance of certain Islamic activities, e.g., regular prayer, fasting and reciting the Qur'an. Almost all of the respondents agreed that they offer prayer more often than before their participation in Islamic NGOs and are now able to use *surah* (Qur'anic verses) correctly. Afia, 42 years old and the wife of a truck driver at Bazargram, goes further to explain how it also affects other members of the family:

> We don't know when Allah will assign our death. Not everyone is the same here. I am talking about myself. For the last two years I have performed prayer and fasting more than before. My eldest son offers prayer five times a day. I taught him by employing a *Hojur* (Islamic teacher) at home. My younger daughter can read the Qur'an. I am teaching her to lead a life like *Ma* (Mother) Fathima (daughter of the prophet).

---

[48] For a good discussion of the issue of Muslim women, the veil, and empowerment in Bangladesh that details the notion of the 'good woman' see Santi Rozario, 'The New Burqa in Bangladesh: Empowerment or Violation of Women's Rights?' (paper presented at the Women's Studies International Forum, 2006), 368–80.

Another important factor around the construction of the notion of the 'good woman' lies in the naming of every *Islami samity* (in the case of IBF) after the Prophet Mohammad's family members and his companions, e.g. *hazrat* Fathima (daughter of the Prophet) or Ayesha (wife of the prophet). For example, IBF centre no. 33 at Sharankhola is named '*Ma Fathima*',[49] which uses the image of a pious woman as a model for women to follow. The extent to which this is successful is evidenced by the 'desire' of rural women to lead a pious life.

However, this is also evident in the rhetoric in the mission of Islamic NGOs. As one IBF mission statement puts it: 'our program aims not only to empower economically but to make people pure Muslims'.[50] At the same time, the operation manual of the IBF Fael Khair Program[51] explains the duties and responsibilities of the project Program Officer and states, 'Alongside investment, (program officer) will have to teach religious education to live as pure Muslim and inspire them to perform'. Although it would be an issue of debate whether we should and how we could define someone as a 'pure' or 'impure' Muslim, Islamic NGOs endeavour to make 'good women' and 'pure Muslim' men.

During an interview one of the respondents, who led an Islamic NGO programme, related a story from one of his clients that portrays their efforts to construct 'good women':

> My husband did not like me at all. He did not want to look at me at all. Repeatedly he used to behave badly with me. It was such a situation that he used to tell me, 'you leave my house', 'don't come in front of my eyes'. Now, my parents are poor, do they want me to go back to them? But I could not understand why he does not like me, why he is always angry with me. I used to think what my fault is. When I wanted to be a member of Fael Khair, he did not want to allow me. However, when he saw my neighbours are becoming members and getting money from Fael Khair, he allowed me. After joining here, I came to know the duties of wives to their husbands. There were many discussions in our meetings on different topics. In such a discussion, I heard that debating with a husband, quarrelling with a husband, always searching for his faults, annoying him, criticizing him and demanding something beyond his ability or embracing him by always asking for this or that is not right. Our sirs say 'when your husband is back from work, he is tired, sweaty, and already agitated by

[49] *Ma* in Bengali means mother. The use of the examples of Fathima as daughter of the Prophet Muhammad is widely evident in everyday life of Muslim women in Bangladesh.

[50] During my interview with one of the high officials of IBF, he provided me with some documents that stated their mission, modus operandi, though official published material was not available at the time of my visit.

[51] *Fael Khair Prokolpo Manual* (in Bengali) was collected during my interviews with the Director of the Rural Development Scheme of IBF at the Dhaka office. This manual provides a concise guide for the people involved in the project. This specifically mentioned 28 duties and responsibilities of a programme officer.

> working under the sun, so your responsibility is to receive him wearing nice clothes, fan him, present food in front of him, attend him during the meal and see if he needs something'. They (sirs) taught us to look at these issues and follow these instructions. They told us to wear good clothes and be always fresh by avoiding dirty clothes that spread the smells of sweat. Then he (husband) will not look at other women. If he (husband) is not satisfied inside the home he would say, oh hell! I am not satisfied with the wife at home, women outside are very beautiful. I wish my wife is such a beauty! In this way his (husband) *iman*[52] is getting affected. They (sirs) said 'you (beneficiary) may be very good, but you are not well decorated, so he (husband) would see you are disastrous and might think other women are more attractive. Therefore, you need to take care of these issues and you have to try to make them (husband) satisfied. According to Islam you have to please your husband … ' After listening to these things, I found myself I was not doing these. When I started to practise these, I saw my husband had started becoming gentle towards me and my relation with my husband became good …

These practices, my respondents claim, would ultimately let them enter easily into *jannat* (heaven). Therefore, the motivation behind the participation in Islamic NGOs, as my respondents stated, was not just to get an 'interest-free loan', but was also a way to manifest their desire to 'gain the eternal life'. Yet the prescription to be pretty and present themselves to their husband, as well as serve their husband (*shami-seba*), is a very rural, traditional and patriarchal interpretation of the responsibilities of women, which ultimately depicts her as a good and devoted wife. Therefore, the issue of women's empowerment is still a grey area with regard to Islamic NGOs, and requires a more detailed analysis.

The Islamic Way of Women's Empowerment: Muslim Women's Agency in Rural Bangladesh

In order to analyse Muslim women's agency, it is imperative to decide whether agency needs to be understood as the capacity to resist domination[53] or if it is embedded in a particular historic, cultural, social and economic context.[54] My understanding of Muslim agency stems from Saba Mahmood's conceptualization

52 In Islam, *iman* refers to a believer's faith in the metaphysical aspects of Islam, i.e. the belief in the six articles of faith which must be accompanied by righteous deeds. If a Muslim does not believe in any one of the six pillars of *iman* then they are not a true Muslim.

53 J. Butler, *Bodies that Matter: On the Discursive Limits of 'Sex'* (New York: Routledge, 1993).

54 S. Mahmood, 'Feminist Theory, Embodiment, and the Docile Agent: Some Reflections on the Egyptian Islamic Revival', *Cultural Anthropology* 16, no. 2 (2001): 202–36.

of agency as 'a capacity for action'[55] which actively shapes women's desire through embodied practices linked to piety under Islam.[56] Therefore, women who are rural, mostly with little or no education and within the context of an unequal, patriarchal social system, are able to attain and engage their capacities (as Islamic NGO beneficiaries and 'good women'), inhibit the 'development patriarchy' of the mainstream secular NGOs as well as challenge 'traditional patriarchy'. Women's involvement with Islamic NGOs therefore represents a resistance towards secular NGOs that become a financial burden and an obstacle to piety. All the respondents who were formerly members of secular NGOs are now unable to bear the financial burden imposed upon them because of the high rates of interest charged by secular NGOs. Therefore, women's participation in Islamic NGOs should not be portrayed as the victimization of women by 'development patriarchy'. Rather, it represents women's desire for liberation and freedom within the setting of a society where *dharma* is still important.

I have already discussed earlier in this chapter how many women do not join NGOs due to the perception that these organizations encourage women to go outside of the home, which goes against the norms and everyday practice of *dharma*; thus these women join Islamic NGOs instead. Joining Islamic NGOs, as the women beneficiaries suggest, does not go against the norms of *purdha* and their practice of *dharma.* Rather, it encourages Islamic practices. As one of the respondents at the 'Hasana' Programme at Manikganj put it: 'I used to wear my sari with a single swathe,[57] but I now understand that after joining the *Islami samity*, I did not do the right thing'. Therefore, Muslim women's bodies here represent a site for contestation and for exercising their agency to decide what to wear and not wear, which was reinforced through their participation in Islamic NGOs in making an explicit distinction between '*halal*' (approved) and '*haram*' (prohibited) deeds. Through this ordinary and everyday 'embodied practice' as McGuire suggests, people, individually and collectively, literally live their religions and serve to express and support their efforts for social change.[58]

In terms of assessing the effectiveness of women's empowerment programmes, it is imperative to discern the changes that occur in women's lives when they participate. Participation in the Islamic NGOs did bring some economic improvement[59] to their

---

55 Ibid.; S. Mahmood, *Politics of Piety: The Islamic Revival and the Feminist Subject* (Princeton, New Jersey: Princeton University Press, 2005).

56 A.C. Korteweg, 'The Sharia Debate in Ontario: Gender, Islam, and Representations of Muslim Women's Agency', *Gender & Society* 22, no. 4 (2008): 434–54.

57 Women in rural Bangladesh used to wear a *sari* in many cases with a single twist that sometimes exposed the shoulder.

58 M.B. McGuire, *Lived Religion: Faith and Practice in Everyday Life* (Oxford University Press, USA, 2008).

59 Evidence of their economic development was visible during visits to their home, which revealed some of their assets including cows, fishing equipment and agricultural inputs. However, this chapter does not emphasize the economic aspects of Islamic NGOs' intervention.

families. To understand these economic changes I asked my respondents to tell me about some measurable indicators of the changes. The most common answers were the increase in their monthly income (almost doubled), increase in number and amount of assets (e.g. cattle, grocery shops, land), increase in consumption (food and non-food items) and children's education. For example, an Islamic NGO official at Sharonkhola explained to me the changes he observed among his beneficiaries after participation in their programme, when I asked him to give me some concrete indicators of changes:

> I know a member from South Kadomtola who doubled her income with the loan from us. Initially we gave her ten thousand Taka and training by the government official. With the money she has bought an ox and fattens it. Within one year she sold this ox for 24,000 Taka. With this money she bought a cow again and used some portion of her money for her family. The smile I saw in her face tells me how happy she is now. Now she is making money from cultivating betel leaf. Therefore, within two years we gave her a loan four times, and had a very good harvest from her agriculture.

For Muslim Aid the most prominent indicators of self-reliance achieved by their beneficiaries include:

- Family income has at least doubled
- The income is sustainable
- Children are going to school regularly
- Family members use sanitary latrines
- Family members drink safe drinking water
- The family does not borrow from money lenders or other MFIs (microfinance institutions)
- Women take part in the family decision-making process
- They have knowledge of family planning.[60]

Yet, it is imperative to mention that control and use of the money, in some cases, is still in the hands of male members of the family. However, in many other cases, as women respondents explained to me, they control the money and made their husbands listen to their decisions. For example, one of my respondents from Tala told me if her husband wants to expand his grocery shop he needs to consult his wife first to get the necessary financial help.

As empowerment is about self-esteem and increased dignity,[61] Islamic NGO beneficiaries see their involvement with these NGOs as enhancing their

[60] Muslim Aid, 'Annual Report 2009: Microfinance and SME Programme', (Dhaka Muslim Aid, 2010).

[61] J. Rowlands, *Questioning Empowerment: Working with Women in Honduras* (Oxfam Publications, 1997).

dignity. When I asked how it has helped to increase their dignity, they refer to the reduction or absence of conjugal fighting and domestic violence as a measure of dignity. For they are bringing money to the family, maintaining a peaceful life following Islamic principles and helping their husband to consider them worthy and respect them. As my respondents claimed, they know what are the rights and duties of a man toward his wife. When they return from the *samity* meeting, many of them inform their husband what they have learnt, e.g. a husband has to return *mohorana* (bride money) to his wife otherwise he will have to be accountable to Allah after his death. At the same time, they are now more aware of their Islamic rights. However, as Bokul, an IBF member said, 'those (husbands) who are educated realize this quickly, but it's hard for those husbands who are obstinate. They (husband) say you went to understand this, so just you understand this. Don't try to teach me!'

In addition to dignity and the economic implications of participation, e.g., increased access and ownership of assets, women's participation in the weekly *samity* meeting provided opportunities for women to discuss, share, learn and teach each other about Islamic *dharma*. In some cases some of the respondents refer to the *samity* meeting as if they are attending a *Talim*.[62] This illustrates the increased opportunities available to women who were once out of the NGO web and subject to the patriarchal norms of society. As part of these opportunities, the *samity* meeting helps them to make decisions regarding important financial transactions e.g. which business is profitable and which is not, and how to use the money efficiently. One of my respondents at Sharonkhola who is the centre leader of IBF explained to me how participation in the NGOs even strengthens their knowledge of agriculture, since they provide practical training on agricultural activities.

Moreover, during my participation in several *samity* meetings at different locations, I noticed that some women who were not members of the NGO attended the weekly meeting. I asked them why they came to the meeting if they were not members of the NGO. They explained that they had come to listen to the *boyan* (speech) from the *hojur*.[63] This gave women who had never been in contact with NGOs the opportunity to meet with other women, as well as with *hojurs*. Therefore, participation in the Islamic NGOs provides increased visibility of women in the public sphere, particularly for those women who were left out of the secular NGO web.

However, it is important to note that participation in the *samity* meeting is not only a vehicle for religious and moral education, but also makes a space for

---

[62] *Talim* is commonly used to mean a congregation of Muslim women in certain places where a woman preacher (sometime called *Amma Hojur*) makes a speech on Qur'an and Hadith-related topics. It's becoming very common among the urban and educated women, yet it is not uncommon in rural areas.

[63] Usually means a religious speaker or Mulla, in this case the fieldworkers of the Islamic NGOs who collect the weekly instalments and also have a background in religious education.

mutual assistance, sharing pains and pleasure, and figuring out solutions, and hence forms a source of social capital for them. Therefore, unlike the secular NGO-led group approach, the Islamic-NGO-led group approach facilitated strong bonding among the members to respond to any misfortune or crisis collectively, while secular NGOs produce negative social capital. Sabera, an IBF centre leader at Shajalal Model village explained why the bonding is stronger within their organization:

> You will see in my centre, there is no repayment related strife. Even if anyone can't repay, we together would pay. But, *Alhamdulillah* (Praise to God), within the last two years I haven't seen any such trouble.

In the case of MACCA's IDEAL village programme, this bonding is even stronger. Since this is an integrated approach ranging from credit, medication, and all aspects of social life, members are dependent on each other and well integrated. For example, if they themselves or their cattle get sick, their first point of contact is either the group leader, or *Hasana* leader, who arranges any necessary treatment or help. Though it seems to me over-stated, MACCA beneficiaries claimed that they are so connected with each other they never had any strife within the group.

It is imperative here to mention women's voices with regard to the issue of dowry and child marriage. All the Islamic NGOs, like their secular counterparts, take this seriously and consider both as symbols of oppression and indignity. What separates the Islamic NGOs from the secular NGOs is their emphasis on how Islam treats dowry and child marriage, as well as emphasis on the engagement of the Imam to eliminate such practices. For example, MACCA claims:

> With a view to promoting the culture of cooperation and respectfulness in the family MACCA propagates [the idea of] 'Marriages without Dowry'. While marriage is blessed by the Almighty, dowry is prohibited by Islam and thus in the name of dowry any kind of repression on women is strongly condemned. MACCA supports to organize marriage functions of the poor women and also provide some financial support in kind to make a way out for livelihood for the new couples. So far it organized approximately 70 marriages without dowry. MACCA follows up the couples and assists them in various occasions especially during flood and other natural calamities … It also plans to sit with women organizations and activists to share their concerns and to advocate subsequently mainstreaming the issue of the women in the light of Islamic interpretation for translation in policy environment.

By explaining it in this way, I am not claiming that Islamic NGOs are unique in development practice, rather I am simply explaining the discourse. Thus, I can also focus on the contradiction regarding the empowerment of women by Islamic NGOs.

Contested Gender Relations and Islamic NGO Discourse

Although Islamic NGOs in Bangladesh work mainly with women, their agendas on women's empowerment is not always clear, and the notion of women's empowerment among Islamic NGO officials differs from that of secular NGOs. As one Islamic NGO staff member put it: 'we also support women's empowerment, but in a different way. They can be empowered while they are in *purdha*, maintaining *purdha* does not mean to be confined at home, but they can move around while in *purdha*'.[64] While secular NGOs have become a strong advocate for women's empowerment, Islamic NGOs, for example, link the idea of empowerment with family or household empowerment. Moreover, the inclusion of the issue of women's empowerment and gender relations in the programme, mission and objectives of Islamic NGOs varies from one to another. For example, the web page and official document[65] of Islami Bank Foundation did not include the issue of women's empowerment. Other NGOs like Islamic Relief aim to 'root out gender-based discrimination by striving for society in which women and men are able to live equally fulfilling lives' following Islamic principles as outlined in the Qur'an and sunna.[66] For MACCA 'gender equity and women empowerment is one of the priority areas of MACCA. The programme primarily focuses on the issues that stand as hindrances to women's empowerment'.[67]

However, Hussain argues that 'when the mainstream NGOs campaign for women's empowerment, Islamic NGOs reconstruct their gender discourse, as according to them women can work outside under the veil and can be empowered as long as they remain *subordinate to men*' (emphasis mine).[68] Moreover, as my field data suggest, in some contexts, some of the officials from Islamic NGOs personally believe in a man's superiority and women's subordination.[69] This, as Karim notes, has created a positive ground for minimizing 'the resentment of the clergy who were refused before by the Western donor funded NGOs to be included in their system of patronage'.[70] This is also true in my cases. For example, during my fieldwork I met with Rahim Miah, a 55-year old Imam of a local mosque at

64 Interview with one of the high officials of an Islamic NGO held at Dhaka on December 19, 2010.

65 During my interview with one of the high officials of the *Fael Khair* IBF programme he handed me a short resume of the foundation.

66 Islamic Relief, 'Islamic Relief Worldwide', (Dhaka: Islamic Relief-Bangladesh, 2008)

67 Masjid Council for Community Advancement, 'Annual Report 2008', ed. Shah Abdul Baten (Dhaka: Masjid Council for Community Advancement, n.d.).

68 Naseem Akhter Hussain, 'Religion and Modernity: Gender and Identity Politics in Bangladesh'. *Women's Studies International Forum* 33, no. 4 (2010): 325–33.

69 Though some of the officials expressed their personal opinion regarding gender relations, this did not necessarily represent the organization they belonged to.

70 Lamia Karim, 'Democratizing Bangladesh State, NGOs, and Militant Islam', *Cultural Dynamics* 16, no. 2–3 (2004): 300.

Chandirchar. When I asked him how he was selected as the president of *Hasana* he replied:

> For the effective management of their programme, Masjid Council needed an Imam. I am the Imam of this area. So they (MACCA) selected me as the president, and the members of MACCA also supported me. I help members to refrain from paying interest, I push them towards prayer.

Another example of such engagement is also evident in Muslim Aid, as I found in Shronkhola, where the person in charge of the Rainbow Family Program is a local *Madrasa* (Islamic school) teacher. Moreover, the founder of MACCA clearly illustrated the importance of engaging the faith leaders, e.g. Imams, for a better development outcome. He argued:

> We wanted to make the faith leaders the ambassadors and champions of development for the poor people of the country, overcoming the traditional perception that faith leaders often create hindrances to development activities.[71]

Therefore, engagement of the local clergy in the development practice of Islamic NGOs would minimize the resentment of the clergy and resulting backlash.

Conclusion

This chapter did not aim to present a binary opposition towards Islamic and other NGOs; rather it focuses on the primacy of religious references that the Islamic NGOs have used in their programme of shari'a-based microfinance to attain equitable development in rural Bangladesh. Yet, it is worth mentioning that it is the women themselves who resist the hegemony of secular development discourse through joining the Islamic NGOs and rejecting the secular ones. Since Islam and religion in general is the integral part of the social and political fabric and represents the everyday practices of the people of Bangladesh, there is a need to engage Islam and religion in the development practices of NGOs. However, the progress of Islamic NGOs in engaging religion in development practice and the subsequent impacts on gender ideology need to be critically understood to identify further potential implications in society. Though some may contest the extent of the influence of Islamic NGOs on the lives of rural women in Bangladesh, my research findings suggest that integrating religion in development practices and careful engagement of Islamic NGOs (keeping them accountable) will produce better development outcomes for women in Muslim-majority countries like Bangladesh.

[71] Opening speech of *Moulana* Abul Kalam Azad, Chairman of MACCA, in Annual report 2009–2010.

References

Ahmad, M.M. 'For God's Sake: The Religious Non-Governmental Organizations in Bangladesh'. In *Recreating the Commons? NGOs in Bangladesh*, edited by Farida Chowdhury Khan, Ahrar Ahmad and Munir Quddus. 183–206. Dhaka: The University Press Limited 2009.

Amin, R., S. Becker, and A. Bayes. 'NGO-Promoted Microcredit Programs and Women's Empowerment in Rural Bangladesh: Quantitative and Qualitative Evidence'. *The Journal of Developing Areas* (1998): 221–36.

Ammerman, Nancy T. *Everyday Religion: Observing Modern Religious Lives*. New York: Oxford University Press, 2007.

Butler, J. *Bodies That Matter: On the Discursive Limits of 'Sex'*. New York: Routledge, 1993.

Clarke, G. 'Faith-Based Organizations and International Development'. In *Development, Civil Society and Faith-Based Organizations: Bridging the Sacred and the Secular*, edited by G. Clarke and M. Jennings. New York: Palgrave Macmillan, 2008.

Clarke, G., and M. Jennings. 'Introduction'. In *Development, Civil Society and Faith-Based Organizations: Bridging the Sacred and the Secular*, edited by G. Clarke and M. Jennings. New York: Palgrave Macmillan, 2008.

D'Costa, B. 'Faith, NGOs and the Politics of Development in Bangladesh'. In *Civil Society, Religion and Global Governance: Paradigms of Power and Persuasion*, edited by Helen James. New York: Routledge, 2007.

Feldman, Shelley, and Florence E. McCarthy. 'Purdah and Changing Patterns of Social Control among Rural Women in Bangladesh'. *Journal of Marriage and the Family* (1983): 949–59.

Fernando, J.L. 'Nongovernmental Organizations, Micro-Credit, and Empowerment of Women'. *The ANNALS of the American Academy of Political and Social Science* 554, no. 1 (1997): 150–77.

Ghodsee, Kristen. 'Religious Freedoms Versus Gender Equality: Faith-Based Organizations, Muslim Minorities, and Islamic Headscarves in the New Europe'. *Social Politics: International Studies in Gender, State & Society* 14, no. 4 (2007): 526–61.

Goetz, A.M., and R.S. Gupta. 'Who Takes the Credit? Gender, Power, and Control over Loan Use in Rural Credit Programs in Bangladesh'. *World Development* 24, no. 1 (1996): 45–63.

Hashemi, S.M., S.R. Schuler, and A.P. Riley. 'Rural Credit Programs and Women's Empowerment in Bangladesh'. *World Development* 24, no. 4 (1996): 635–53.

Hussain, Naseem Akhter. 'Religion and Modernity: Gender and Identity Politics in Bangladesh'. *Women's Studies International Forum* 33, no. 4 (2010): 325–33.

Islami Bank Foundation. 'Quarterly Progress Report April – Jun, 2011', (n.d.). http://fkprogram.org/wp-content/uploads/2011.06-IBF-Quterly-report-April-June.pdf.

Islamic Relief, 'Islamic Relief Worldwide'. Dhaka: Islamic Relief-Bangladesh, 2008.

Kabeer, N. 'Conflicts over Credit: Re-Evaluating the Empowerment Potential of Loans to Women in Rural Bangladesh'. *World Development* 29, no. 1 (2001): 63–84.

Karim, Lamia. 'Democratizing Bangladesh State, NGOs, and Militant Islam'. *Cultural Dynamics* 16, no. 2–3 (2004): 291–318.

———. 'Demystifying Micro-Credit: The Grameen Bank, NGOs, and Neoliberalism in Bangladesh'. *Cultural Dynamics* 20, no. 1 (2008): 5–29.

Kirmani, Nida, and Isabel Phillips. 'Engaging with Islam to Promote Women's Rights'. *Progress in Development Studies* 11, no. 2 (2011): 87–99.

Korteweg, A.C. 'The Sharia Debate in Ontario: Gender, Islam, and Representations of Muslim Women's Agency'. *Gender & Society* 22, no. 4 (2008): 434–54.

Mahmood, S. 'Feminist Theory, Embodiment, and the Docile Agent: Some Reflections on the Egyptian Islamic Revival'. *Cultural Anthropology* 16, no. 2 (2001): 202–36.

———. *Politics of Piety: The Islamic Revival and the Feminist Subject*. Princeton, New Jersey: Princeton University Press, 2005.

Mahmud, S. 'Actually How Empowering Is Microcredit'. *Development and Change* 34, no. 4 (2003): 577–605.

Masjid Council for Community Advancement. 'Annual Report 2007', 32. Dhaka: Masjid Council for Community Advancement, n.d.

———. 'Annual Report 2008', edited by Shah Abdul Baten, 30. Dhaka: Masjid Council for Community Advancement, n.d.

McGuire, M.B. *Lived Religion: Faith and Practice in Everyday Life*. Oxford University Press, USA, 2008.

Mesbahuddin, T. 'Religion in Development: An Islamic Model Emerging in Bangladesh'. *Journal of South Asian Development* 5, no. 2 (2010): 221–41.

Montgomery, R., D. Bhattacharya, and D. Hulme. 'Credit for the Poor in Bangladesh'. In *Finance against Poverty*, edited by D. Hulme and P. Mosley. London: Routledge, 1996.

Muslim Aid. 'Annual Report 2009: Microfinance and SME Programme', 48. Dhaka: Muslim Aid, 2010.

———. 'Fael Khair Program for Victims of SIDR Cyclone in Bangladesh: Annual Progress Report (May–December 2009)', 32. Dhaka: Muslim Aid 2010.

Naher, Ainoon. 'Defending Islam and Women's Honour against NGOs in Bangladesh'. *Women's Studies International Forum* 33, no. 4 (2010): 316–24.

———. 'Gender, Religion and Development in Rural Bangladesh'. PhD Thesis, Heidelberg University, 2005.

Parmar, A. 'Micro-Credit, Empowerment, and Agency: Re-Evaluating the Discourse'. *Canadian Journal of Development Studies/Revue canadienne d'études du développement* 24, no. 3 (2003): 461–76.

Pitt, M., and S. Khandker. 'Household and Intrahousehold Impacts of the Grameen Bank and Similar Targeted Credit Programmes in Bangladesh'. In

Credit Programmes for the Poor: Household and Intrahousehold Impacts and Programme Sustainability. Dhaka: Bangladesh World Bank and Bangladesh Institute of Development Studies, 1995.

Rahman, Aminur. 'Micro-Credit Initiatives for Equitable and Sustainable Development: Who Pays?'. *World Development* 27, no. 1 (1999): 67–82.

———. *Women and Microcredit in Rural Bangladesh: Anthropological Study of the Rhetoric and Realities of Grameen Bank Lending*. Boulder, CO.: Westview Press, 1999.

Rowlands, J. *Questioning Empowerment: Working with Women in Honduras*. Oxfam Publications, 1997.

Rozario, Santi. 'The New Burqa in Bangladesh: Empowerment or Violation of Women's Rights?' Paper presented at the Women's Studies International Forum, 2006.

Scott, J. *Domination and the Arts of Resistance: Hidden Transcripts*. New Haven, USA: Yale University Press, 1990.

Selinger, E. 'Does Microcredit 'Empower'? Reflections on the Grameen Bank Debate'. *Human Studies* 31, no. 1 (2008): 27–41.

Shehabuddin, Elora. 'Contesting the Illicit: Gender and the Politics of Fatwas in Bangladesh'. *Signs* 24, no. 4 (1999): 1011–44.

Sisson, Richard, and Leo E. Rose. *War and Secession: Pakistan, India and the Creation of Bangladesh*. Berkeley, CA: University of California Press, 1991.

Tomalin, E. 'Religion and a Rights-Based Approach to Development'. *Progress in Development Studies* 6, no. 2 (2006): 93–108.

Umar, Badruddin. *The Emergence of Bangladesh: Class Struggles in East Pakistan (1947–1958)*. New York: Oxford University Press, 2004.

White, Sarah C. 'Beyond the Paradox: Religion, Family and Modernity in Contemporary Bangladesh'. *Religions and Development Working Paper 32*. Centre for Development Studies University of Bath, 2009.

Wood, Geoffrey D. 'Clashing Values in Bangladesh: NGOs, Secularism and the Ummah'. In *Recreating the Commons? NGOs in Bangladesh*, edited by F.C. Khan, A. Ahmad and M. Quddus. Dhaka: The University Press Limited, 2009.

Conclusion
Invisible Aid: Islam, Muslim NGOs and Development

Matthew Clarke, Gerhard Hoffstaedter and David Tittensor

The purpose of this volume has been to lift the veil on Islamic aid, Muslim non-governmental organizations, and practices of Islamic finance that seek to benefit the poor. The history of aid and associated development activities of non-Muslim countries and NGOs has been well documented and is widely accepted as the standard developmental model. The modern history of western NGOs dates back to the turn of the last century with the formation of the Federation of the Red Cross and Red Crescent Societies and the British and Foreign Anti-Slavery Society. More recently, nation-to-nation aid flows date its history to the end of the Second World War. Islamic aid presents a more complex picture as it combines practices that are as old as the religion itself with modern aid practices. Indeed, as the various chapters in this volume demonstrate there exists a more contemporary history of 'Islamic aid' that nonetheless is deeply steeped in Qur'anic and other textual bases that has a much longer history. As such, Islamic aid remains poorly understood in its history, form and quantity. This, in part, explains its relative invisibility in the dominant aid discourses and academic literature.

The invisibility of Islamic aid though must also be understood in terms of the wider tension between the non-Muslim world and Muslim world. It has not been the purpose of this volume to make the case for this standing tension – that can be found in other places – but rather, the purpose has been to move beyond the associated rhetoric and examine in closer detail how Islamic aid is conceived and practised. It is also important to note that it has not been the purpose of this volume to prosecute the case that Islamic aid is superior to Western aid (or indeed vice versa). Rather, again, the purpose has been to highlight in an appropriate manner the value of Islamic aid and to showcase examples of where Islamic religious principles can positively impact upon development outcomes, and where Islamic-inspired development activities can be effective in improving the lives of the poor – particularly the poor from the Muslim world.

It is perhaps this second point that might be considered this volume's most contentious contribution. Whilst a long-held principle of 'development' has been the need to contextualize responses to the specific circumstances of the communities to whom the interventions are targeted, it does remain true that orthodox development thinking largely excludes religious beliefs and practices of communities in the contextualizing of responses. Although considering gender, environment, history, class (or caste), and so forth is now de rigueur for development organizations seeking to be most effective and efficient in their interventions, explicit consideration of communities' religion and spirituality remain taboo.[1]

Whilst this is clearly a sweeping generalization, it is based on an observable truth. The religious beliefs and practices of communities are not widely incorporated into development interventions aimed at increasing their well-being. The common understandings of the interplay between religion and development have not changed significantly over the past few decades.[2] According to these stereotypes, religion is either 1) an instrumental tool that can be used to further the aims of development interventions; 2) part of a society's culture that is often considered an impediment to development; 3) a private pursuit that can assist in furthering development – but only in certain forms (those linked to Protestantism); and finally 4) a factor that is included in vague non-economic considerations of 'culture'. Not one of these understandings is particularly positive, or cause enough to challenge the long-standing hegemony of religious exclusion from development studies.[3] This taboo is common to all religions – though arguably this could be even more so the case of Islam whose 'otherness' is overlaid with recent (and historical) political and social conflict with the West (Buddhism and Hinduism may be equally poorly understood in the West, but they are generally viewed with more benevolence compared to the malevolence with which Islam is viewed). Indeed, if Islam is raised as an issue for development it is usually done so within the spectre of terrorism.[4]

Again, the purpose of this book has been to provide an opportunity to explore how Islamic religious principles are being successfully used to motivate, fund, support and justify interventions which are improving the well-being of the poor. This book contains both reflections on Islamic religious principles that support the 'development' goal, as well as a number of case studies that are illustrative of these successes. It is evident though that both the involvement of Islamic religious principles to further development interventions and the use of Islamic aid flows

---

[1] Kurt Alan Ver Beek, 'Spirituality: A Development Taboo', *Development in Practice* 10, no. 1 (2000): 31–43.

[2] These stereotypes have not differed significantly over time. See works by Wilber and Jameson and by Selinger that both explore similar thinking. Charles K. Wilber and Kenneth P. Jameson, 'Religious Values and Social Limits to Development', *World Development* 8 (1980): 467–79; Leah Selinger, 'The Forgotten Factor: The Uneasy Relationship between Religion and Development', *Social Compass* 51, no. 4 (2004): 523–43.

[3] Tomalin makes a persuasive argument that when engagement with religion has been made, it is largely limited to Christianity, which itself is the dominant religion in the West. Tomalin discusses the hegemony of universal human rights and the 'rights-based approach' to development within the current discourse and how they are based on Western (Christian) views of rights and ignore non-Christian values. See Emma Tomalin, 'Religion and a Rights-Based Approach to Development', *Progress in Development Studies* 6, no. 2 (2006): 93–108.

[4] Benthall, 'The Overreaction against Islamic Charities', *ISIM Review* 20, no. 1 (2007): pp. 6–7.

and activities of Muslim-inspired NGOs occur predominantly within the Muslim-majority world.[5] While the chapter by Riddell does discuss how Christian and Muslim engagement might occur, it does so from the perspective of Christian NGOs operating in a Muslim-majority context more so than Muslim-inspired NGOs operating in non-Muslim countries. This 'location bias' of Islamic aid on Muslim-majority countries is not, in and of itself a negative, nor is it an argument against Islamic aid. Rather, it is simply a reflection of contemporary practices and, as such, can be considered an artefact of the current circumstances. What it does do though is further entrench the invisibility of Islamic aid in a Western dominated aid discourse.

As Islamic aid largely 'serves' Muslim people, such aid remains largely hidden from the non-Muslim world. Suspicions that already exist concerning the motivations and usage of this aid are exacerbated by lack of implementation in non-Muslim majority countries that might be more easily understood and experienced by the wider development sector. While non-Muslim aid and NGOs (DAC donors, secular as well as (primarily) Christian NGOs) do operate in Muslim-majority worlds, they do not do so generally in very integrated ways, and often struggle to align their own values to the values and cultures of those with whom they are working. Muslim-inspired NGOs, such as Islamic Relief and Muslim Aid, on the other hand, state they do not discriminate against non-Muslims in their operations. However, they do have a more significant presence in Muslim-majority countries than they do in non-Muslim majority countries.

These NGOs, Islamic charities and Muslim majority governments are best understood as occupying varying positions in a continuum, stretching from a fully integrated and embedded Islamic vision to a light Muslim orientation. All too often these poles are conflated to increase the lack of knowledge about and experience of Islamic aid and therefore increase its invisibility.

There is very little doubt that Islamic aid and Muslim-motivated development activities will continue to increase in coming decades. With charitable giving a religious expectation for Muslims and Muslim-majority countries becoming increasingly wealthy, domestic and international aid flows can be expected to rise. While this volume has focused on better understanding the current trends and practices in Islamic aid, more work is required in the future, both at the theoretical and empirical level, not only to improve the visibility of Islamic aid, but also to better understand how Islamic aid and non-Muslim aid can work more effectively together. In the first instance, this will require non-Muslim aid providers to increase their religious literacy and have a more sophisticated understanding of and engagement with the Muslim beliefs and practices of their targeted communities in Muslim-majority worlds. This would also presumably see an improvement in

[5] It must be noted that ethnicity, UN voting behaviour and support for Israel can also play an important role and religious affiliation may be a corollary rather than a determinant in aid flows, especially from Arab Gulf states. See Eric Neumayer, 'What Factors Determine the Allocation of Aid by Arab Countries and Multilateral Agencies?', *The Journal of Development Studies* 39, no. 4 (2003): 134–47.

the incorporation of other religions and religious practices as well, which in turn would increase the visibility of all religions within the development sector.

Without doubt, focusing on the important and intrinsic nexus between all religions and development is well overdue. Whether it be Islam, Christianity, Hinduism, Buddhism or any other religion, religious belief is both private and social in its expression and, as such, affects society through both informal behaviours and formal social institutions. For many hundreds of millions of people across the globe, religious belief has been a very personal concern with beliefs in different gods, sacred texts and religious teaching informing and affecting personal actions. Within the largest survey of poor people around the world undertaken by the World Bank, it was evident that worldviews were often based on religious terms: 'When asked why there are rich and poor, they answered, "Destiny", "That's the way God created the earth", and "The rich are of the devil and the poor of God"'.[6] Regardless of religious faith or geographical location, a commonly held view was that overcoming poverty required faith and prayer. Moreover, organizations that are affiliated with religious belief systems have a central role in communities and their influence transects the local, national and international sphere. It is also not uncommon to label nation states in religious terms. There are so-called Christian countries (i.e. the United States of America, the United Kingdom, Australia, the Philippines), Islamic countries (i.e. Iraq, Egypt, Afghanistan), Buddhist countries (i.e. Thailand, Myanmar), Hindu countries (i.e. India) and a Jewish state (i.e. Israel). Not only do these labels reflect the majority religious belief held by the population, but they also speak to the religious underpinning of political, social and economic structures within these countries. A better understanding of religious traditions and their impact on the structures underlying societies will better inform and help to target development interventions.

While the world's major belief systems have historically exerted great influence across traditional nation state boundaries, this influence seems again to be on the rise (if not in different forms) within a newly globalized world.[7] The role of religion is being increasingly discussed in other aspects of public life. For example, the Index of Religiosity, which measures the importance of religion to respondents, is increasing globally, suggesting a retreat of secularization and a return of religion to public life.[8] Religion is garnering greater interest for

---

6 Deepa Narayan et al., *Voices of the Poor: Can Anyone Hear Us?* (New York: Published by Oxford University Press for the World Bank, 2000), p. 229.

7 Stephen Ellis and Gerrie ter Haar, *Worlds of Power: Religious Thought and Political Practice in Africa* (London: Hurst, 2004).

8 C. Rakodi, 'Religions and Development Research Programme: Emerging Findings' (paper presented at the Religion Shaping Development: Inspirational, Inhibiting, Institutionalised? 21–23 July University of Birmingham, 2010); O. Wodon, 'Faith and Development at the World Bank: Building the Empirical Evidence' (paper presented at the Religion Shaping Development: Inspirational, Inhibiting, Institutionalized? 21–23 July, University of Birmingham, 2010).

those interested in politics (both domestic and international), with the 'clash' of religions (more often described as the 'clash of culture') between Christianity and Islam becoming almost a cliché since 11 September 2001. The obvious relevance of this to the closely aligned interest of development has yet to flow over from the field of politics to development studies in any significant way. The relevance is based upon a number of issues. Firstly, there has been an increase in the role that religious groups and religion, as such, have assumed in social movements. For example, the global Jubilee 2000 and the subsequent Make Poverty History campaigns had religious geneses. Secondly, religion has become increasingly significant in terms of civic culture. Religious groups are becoming increasingly important in providing 'identities' for people and communities. Thirdly, the process of globalization has enhanced the reach of religion and religious groups. Religious groups are able to connect across the globe in ways that were not possible until quite recently, resulting in stronger sense of identity and wielding a greater sense of influence. Finally, participation in religion and commitment to religious values is seen as a rational choice with many religious groups actively seeking to 'grow' their congregations.[9] Politics and religion continue to be closely intertwined in many environments (both North and South). While development actors are largely secular, this secularism causes tensions when dealing with constituents or communities (both in the North and South) that are linked to religious groups.

Given this 'rise' of religion (or decline of secularism), the visibility of religion within development must continue to increase to achieve better and more effective improvements in the lives of the poor. While this volume has focused on seeking to reduce the invisibility of Islamic aid, the clarion call for breaking the long-held taboo of all religions remains current within orthodox development practices and principles. The chapters contained within this volume have provided clear evidence that Islamic aid and Muslim-inspired aid activities have been largely effective in improving the lives of the poor and warrant further investigation and interest. This is not to say that Islamic aid and Muslim-inspired aid activities have greater value or 'do development better' – rather the argument is that remaining blind to religion (and in the instance of this book – Islam) limits opportunities to eradicate poverty.

The chapters in this volume have highlighted a number of important issues that do have the potential to increase the efficiency and effectiveness of Islamic aid. By taking into account these lessons, Islamic aid can not only have a greater impact on improving the lives of the poor, but non-Muslim development activities might also be able to more authentically engage with Muslim communities for more positive change.

---

[9] Helen Rose Ebaugh, 'Presidential Address 2001: Return of the Sacred: Reintegrating Religion in the Social Sciences', *Journal for the Scientific Study of Religion* 41, no. 3 (2002): 385–95.

- Charitable giving is inherent within Islamic traditions and the generation of these charitable funds can support significant local and international community development activities. Since the birth of this religion, the practice of charity has been held to be as important as prayer. A good Muslim is a Muslim who seeks to help the poorest and most vulnerable. But not only are Muslims exhorted to offer such assistance, there are very explicit teachings related to the financial type and amount of charity that must be provided. Such a resource can be leveraged far more than is currently the case. The issue of charity must also be explored in more detail to test its applicability and find the most useful framework for development applications. Most studies focus on Islamic theological roots of charity and aid, not necessarily the contemporary practices, many of which include the state as an arbiter between Muslims and their obligations (in the form of zakat payments that can in some cases be tax deductible). As Jan Ali in this volume points out, zakat may be a religious obligation, but remains inefficient as a poverty reduction tool. Thus a huge data gap remains in terms of zakat management and the effectiveness of zakat aid. Perhaps equally interesting from a development perspective is the development of sadaqa, often translated as charity, or the voluntary beneficent giving that is recommended to Muslims. Sadaqa is the manifestation of the process that transforms the 'ancient morality of the gift' into the 'principle of justice'.[10]
- It is important to purposely unravel distinct activities funded through or by Islamic agencies. Following more than a millennium of conflict between Muslims and the non-Muslim world, the past decade has seen a rapid escalation of the suspicion of Islam throughout the non-Muslim world (and vice versa) and a lack of ability to separate actions by Muslims has resulted in the default response to Muslim-inspired activities to be one of negativity and suspicion.[11] Development activities or mission activities are viewed with great nervousness and apprehension by non-Muslims based on a lack of understanding and what might be labelled Islamophobia, in which anything Muslim is tainted and seen as threatening. This makes it almost impossible for co-operation and collaboration between Muslim and non-Muslim aid agencies, or other aid actors seeking to leverage their resources and have greater impact across poor communities.
- Whilst Islamic aid flows (from Muslim-majority countries and private donations) are not well documented, it is evident from existing data that they are of sufficient volume (and likely to grow) to warrant greater scrutiny. While the DAC guidelines are clearly written for the historical context of the traditional OECD donors, similar principles and reporting structures should

10 Amy Singer, *Charity in Islamic Societies* (Cambridge: Cambridge University Press, 2008).

11 Jonathan Benthall and Jerome Bellion-Jourdan, *The Charitable Crescent: Politics of Aid in the Muslim World* (London: I. B. Tauris, 2003).

be developed and adhered to for Islamic aid to ensure greater transparency and the ability to develop and apply world best practice in this area. Greater scrutiny of aid is in the best interests of both donors and aid recipients, irrespective of whether it is Islamic aid or aid from traditional donors. Both need to be held to account and subjected to further analysis.

- There are many opportunities where faith-based aid organizations – particularly both Muslim and Christian – can work together to achieve greater improvements in the lives of the poor. Typically, Christian agencies have greater resources available to them but they can have difficulty in effectively accessing Muslim communities. It must be noted that cultural proximity for Muslim organizations or aid programmes cannot be taken for granted, i.e. Muslim aid organizations do not automatically have greater access to Muslim populations.[12] Indeed, differences within Islam and its many traditions, divergent practices and cultural inflections mean that Muslims may share some cultural and religious proximity with some populations and some other faith-based organizations, but this cannot be generalized. Effective intra- and inter-faith dialogue and understanding will provide opportunities to have a stronger impact within these Muslim communities, but co-operation would be especially helpful for development interventions in mixed communities. Further education and initiatives that demonstrate mutual respect and understanding between faith-based organizations would enhance this space for co-operation. Also more determination from both sides is required to allow better outcomes.
- The world view of Muslims should not be ignored or excluded from consideration. Islamic religious beliefs affect how many Muslims understand the world and their place within it. For most Muslims reference to the Qur'an, the Prophet Muhammad's life (as described in the hadith and sunna) is integral to their everyday life, as it provides meaning and a worldview though which events and life itself can be interpreted. Thus, when advocating and implementing change, development agencies (both Muslim and non-Muslim) need to integrate and engage these beliefs productively. If, based on the example of typical responses to the Indian Ocean tsunami by the Muslim Acehnese, it is believed that the disaster was Allah's will, then the response to this disaster will be enhanced if it can also be couched and framed within this paradigm. This is especially crucial in post-disaster or post-conflict encounters where resilience is vital, as is a continued effort to expand psychological well-being. Religions, as Tittensor and others in this volume point out, provide adherents with community, solidarity, faith and purpose, which all lend themselves to a social and psychological well-being that is not achieved simply through improved material and financial means. Thus, while much of the Western

[12] Victoria Palmer, 'Analysing Cultural Proximity: Islamic Relief Worldwide and Rohingya Refugees in Bangladesh', *Development in Practice* 21, no. 1 (2011): 96–108.

secular aid interventions focus on poverty and the poor in largely financial terms, many Muslim aid organizations and foundations are focused on the poverty of thought, in particular religious teachings, with a focus on building mosques and funding (religious) schools. This is sometimes contentious, but human development, it is argued throughout this volume, is more than dollar/day incomes and economic indicators and this is where religion, whether Islam or Christianity or any other, has a role to play.

- Gender and sexuality must be truthfully and honestly addressed as both a development and Islamic issue. Again though, despite the non-Muslim stereotypes widely accepted within the non-Muslim majority world, gender inequality is not necessarily a consequence of Islamic religious faith. What is evident though is that there may be multiple interpretations of positive gender outcomes that do consider the religious practices and beliefs within different communities. An openness and willingness to engage with these multiple understandings is vital to ensure full participation of women within development activities.
- Islamic banking principles provide innovative opportunities not only to fund development activities, but also to shape certain development tools, such as microfinance. By fashioning microfinance, or micro-entrepreneurship, to be aligned with these Islamic principles, not only is there substantial funding (often locally generated) available to support it, but also a greater likelihood of acceptance by local Muslim communities.

Running throughout all these lessons and chapters of this volume is the singular call for greater understanding of the Islamic faith and its practices. Like other religions, Islam is poorly understood in terms of the role it plays within the development process. A willingness of donors and aid agencies to accept that Islam (like other religions) affects development outcomes and an authentic attempt to engage with this faith will result in more positive impacts for poor communities.

Undoubtedly these chapters predominantly display an appreciative inclination towards the strengths and possibilities presented by Islam. Given the trend of negativity normally associated with Islam, such an appreciative viewpoint is understandable, as some effort is required to re-balance the public debate. Although written by both Muslims and non-Muslims, these chapters do not accept all Islamic principles and practice uncritically. While they do focus on opportunities rather than constraints, the contributions to this volume do present criticisms of Islamic development practices where appropriate. However, Islamic aid has a positive story to share and has much to contribute to the wider development sector. There is no doubt that Muslim-inspired aid activities could also be improved and strengthened through greater exposure to non-Muslim aid practices and knowledge. There is nevertheless much that Islamic aid can offer the non-Muslim development sector. Hopefully this volume will give many development theorists and practitioners pause for thought and prod them to see more clearly what may have once been invisible.

References

Benthall, Jonathan. 'The Overreaction Against Islamic Charities', *ISIM Review* 20, no. 1 (2007): 6–7.

Benthall, Jonathan, and Jerome Bellion-Jourdan. *The Charitable Crescent: Politics of Aid in the Muslim World*. London: I. B. Tauris, 2003.

Ebaugh, Helen Rose. 'Presidential Address 2001: Return of the Sacred: Reintegrating Religion in the Social Sciences'. *Journal for the Scientific Study of Religion* 41, no. 3 (2002): 385–95.

Ellis, Stephen, and Gerrie ter Haar. *Worlds of Power: Religious Thought and Political Practice in Africa*. London: Hurst, 2004.

Narayan, Deepa, Raj Patel, Kai Schafft, Anne Rademacher, and Sarah Koch-Schulte. *Voices of the Poor: Can Anyone Hear Us?* New York: Published by Oxford University Press for the World Bank, 2000.

Neumayer, Eric. 'What Factors Determine the Allocation of Aid by Arab Countries and Multilateral Agencies?'. *The Journal of Development Studies* 39, no. 4 (2003): 134–47.

Palmer, Victoria. 'Analysing Cultural Proximity: Islamic Relief Worldwide and Rohingya Refugees in Bangladesh'. *Development in Practice* 21, no. 1 (2011/02/01 2011): 96–108.

Rakodi, C. 'Religions and Development Research Programme: Emerging Findings'. Paper presented at the Religion Shaping Development: Inspirational, Inhibiting, Institutionalised? 21–23 July University of Birmingham, 2010.

Selinger, Leah. 'The Forgotten Factor: The Uneasy Relationship between Religion and Development'. *Social Compass* 51, no. 4 (2004): 523–43.

Singer, Amy. *Charity in Islamic Societies*. Cambridge: Cambridge University Press, 2008.

Tomalin, Emma. 'Religion and a Rights-Based Approach to Development'. *Progress in Development Studies* 6, no. 2 (2006): 93–108.

Ver Beek, Kurt Alan. 'Spirituality: A Development Taboo'. *Development in Practice* 10, no. 1 (2000): 31–43.

Wilber, Charles K., and Kenneth P. Jameson. 'Religious Values and Social Limits to Development'. *World Development* 8 (1980): 467–79.

Wodon, O. 'Faith and Development at the World Bank: Building the Empirical Evidence'. Paper presented at the Religion Shaping Development: Inspirational, Inhibiting, Institutionalized? 21–23 July, University of Birmingham, 2010.

Index

Bold page numbers indicate figures, *italic* numbers indicate tables.